Learning Activity and Development

Learning Activity
and Development

Edited by Mariane Hedegaard
and Joachim Lompscher

AARHUS UNIVERSITY PRESS

Published with financial support from the
Danish Research Council for the Humanities

AARHUS UNIVERSITY PRESS
Langelandsgade 177,
DK-8200 Aarhus N
Fax (+ 45) 8942 5380

73 Lime Walk
Headington, Oxford OX3 7AD
Fax (+ 44) 1865 750 079

Box 511
Oakville, CT 06779
Fax (+ 1) 860 945 9468

Foreword

Vasily Vasilivich Davydov was an outstanding researcher within the cultural-historical tradition following Vygotsky's theory and research. He graduated from Moscow University in 1956 with a degree in both philosophy and psychology. He started his career as an editor in the publishing house of the USSR Academy of Pedagogical Sciences. In 1959 he was invited to the Institute of General and Educational Psychology and together with Daniel B. Elkonin he formed the Laboratory for Psychology of Younger School Children and the experimental program for the famous school No. 91. From 1973-1983 he was director of the Institute of General and Educational Psychology in the USSR Academy of Pedagogical Sciences. Because of political circumstances he was removed from leadership positions until 1988, when he was elected Vice-President of the Academy of Pedagogical Sciences; a position he held until his untimely death. In his different positions with many administrative obligations he never stopped working theoretically and empirically in the field of developmental teaching. Over the last years he was active in implementing his theory of learning activity and developmental teaching in school practice in several states of the Russian Federation.

The title of this book — *Learning Activity and Development* — indicate central concepts in Davydov's theoretical and empirical research. Davydov's conception of theoretical knowledge and his theory of learning activity and developmental teaching have been important contributions to psychological and pedagogical research. His research method was the formative method of experimental teaching in which he combined research about thinking, knowledge and learning with intervention into social practice.

Many researchers within and outside Russia have been inspired by Davydov's theory and research. The authors in this book all continue his line of research, therefore we dedicate this book to the memory of Vasily Vasilivich Davydov.

September 1999

Joachim Lompscher
Mariane Hedegaard

Contents

Social Interaction and Development of Motivation

Play and Spontaneous Learning

List of Figures and Tables

Contributors

Elena L. Berezhzhkovskaya, Vygotsky Institute of Psychology, Russian State University of Humanities, Moscow

María J. Cala-Carrillo, Department of Social Work and Social Science, University of Pablo de Olavide, Sevilla, Spain

Felice Carugati, Department of Education, Faculty of Psychology, University of Bologna, Italy

Seth Chaiklin, Department of Psychology, University of Aarhus, Denmark

† Vasily V. Davydov, Psychological Institute, Russian Academy of Education, Moscow

Bernd Fichtner, Faculty of Pedagogy, University of Siegen, Germany

Mariane Hedegaard, Department of Psychology, University of Aarhus, Denmark

Elena E. Kravtsova, Vygotsky Institute of Psychology, Russian State University of Humanities, Moscow

Gennady Kravtsov, Vygotsky Institute of Psychology, Russian State University of Humanities, Moscow

Joachim Lompscher, emeritus professor, University of Potsdam, Berlin, Germany

Tatyana A. Matiss, Psychological Institute, The Russian Academy of Education, Moscow

Bert van Oers, Faculty of Psychology and Pedagogy, Free University Amsterdam, The Netherlands

Yuri A. Poluyanov, Psychological Institute, The Russian Academy of Education, Moscow

Juan Daniel Ramírez-Garrido, Department of Experimental Psychology, University of Sevilla, Spain

Georg Rückriem, Department of General Pedagogy, Berlin University of the Arts, Germany

José A. Sánchez-Medina, Department of Experimental Psychology, University of Sevilla, Spain

Nina F. Talyzina, Laboratory of Learning Psychology and Centre for Training of Teachers, Moscow State University, Russia

Galina A. Zuckerman, Psychological Institute, The Russian Academy of Education, Moscow

1   Introduction

Joachim Lompscher and Mariane Hedegaard

In many countries the discussion related to problems of schooling, learning, and teaching has accelerated and broadened during recent years. This has not come about by chance, and the reasons do not — or better, *do not only* — lie in that domain itself. Economic, political, ecological, cultural and other changes and contradictions of present-day societies call for some fundamental new approaches and solutions. As the Club of Rome (1991) stated some years ago, these problems will be resolved only if learning is given a substantially changed, central position in societal life. There is a huge amount of scientific knowledge from different disciplines which could be a solid basis for the necessary changes in learning both *in* and *out of* school, on different educational levels, and under different institutional conditions — public as well as private. The sciences connected with learning, teaching, and related phenomena, cannot create the societal conditions for such changes, but without the knowledge and immediate contribution of science these changes will not be put into practice. The joint effort of scientists to create a synthesis of relevant insights and results gained from different theoretical and methodological scientific views is a prerequisite for the greater influence of educational science in substantially raising the level and changing the character and results of learning and its role in society, and to implement complex and far-reaching solutions.

The authors of this volume put forward their proposals from a cultural-historical point of view and invite colleagues from other traditions and disciplines to take part in a joint discussion and elaboration of the principal theoretical and practical problems associated with issues of learning, both current and future.

Cultural-Historical Theory

Cultural-historical theory has its roots in the work of Vygotsky and his scholars. During recent years and decades (especially in connection with Vygotsky's centenary in 1996), a growing number of Western psychologists, educationists, and other scientists and practitioners (e.g., Martin, Nelson &

Tobach 1995; Moll 1990; Newman & Holzman 1993; Säljö 1991; Tharp & Gallimore 1988; Tryphon & Voneche 1996; van der Veer & Valsiner 1993; Wertsch, 1985; Wertsch, del Río & Álvarez 1995) have become interested in and acquainted with this theoretical approach. It could be observed that cultural-historical ideas, concepts and findings inspired many colleagues with different theoretical backgrounds to look at their findings and problems in a new way, to integrate them into a larger context and to use them for creating new approaches and research programs, proposals, and problem solutions. We interpret these observations as trends in the direction of a synthesis in the above-mentioned sense.

One of the central topics in cultural-historical theory is the relationship between psychic development and learning, the causes, conditions, laws and regularities of development of higher (human) psychic functions, and the role and potentials of learning and schooling in these processes. In this context, learning is considered as a special activity. This means that learning is a particular form of world-man-interaction between conscious subjects (on a certain developmental level) actively acting upon segments or objects of the world and coping with its resistances and influences, interacting in these processes under concrete societal, institutional and social conditions, participating in societal life and culture, and appropriating parts and aspects of it, thus becoming more and more able to contribute to further societal development.

In general, activity is a substantial concept in the framework of cultural-historical theory and a special activity theory was elaborated in this context (Davydov 1991; Engeström 1990, 1991; Lektorsky 1990; Leontiev 1978; Lompscher 1996; Yaroshevsky 1993). The contributions of this book show different aspects and potentials of the approach of activity theory to learning. Concerning a recent understanding of learning, there is, on the one hand, much in common between the approach of activity theory and today's cognitive psychology orienting towards the active learner (performing not only cognitive operations) and his cultural context, and, on the other hand, anthropological and ethnographic approaches to cultural and historical phenomena and conditions of learning.

Learning Activity and School Teaching

Schooling, especially teaching, plays a principal role in children's development as shown by Luria (1976), Scribner & Cole (1981) and many others. First of all, a new kind of activity is formed — learning activity

(Davydov 1988a, 1988b, 1988c, 1990, 1996; Davydov & Rubtsov 1995). With regard to learning activity we stress a special aspect. Learning is a complex of different processes of acquisition of experiences leading to qualitative and quantitative changes in psychic (and physical as well) structures and features of an individual. These processes are necessarily going on in the framework of activity, that is in interaction with the world. The kind of activity may be different (e.g., play, everyday communication, work). Learning activity is one particular kind of activity historically coming into being in the process of development of labor and labor division, whereas in ontogenesis learning activity emerges out of play and everyday communication — not automatically, but depending on a principal change in the lives of children: becoming school children. Their activity is now — not suddenly, but as a process — characterized by fundamentally new norms, demands, conditions and most important by new objects or content — historically developed special systems of knowledge and skills — to be acquired. Learning now occurs not (only) as a function of more or less accidental, immediate situations and events, but based on systems and logic of learning material representing different domains of societal experience and activity. How learning activity develops and how it influences psychic development — if at all — depends, first of all, on the content and character of teaching.

   In short, we may define learning activity as follows: It is a special kind of activity directed towards the acquisition of societal knowledge and skills through their individual re-production by means of special learning actions upon learning objects (subject matter methods and knowledge). Confronted with a certain subject matter area, learners can acquire skill and knowledge within a subject matter area only by actively acting with the material according to its substance and structure (content and methods). The learners have to actively reproduce what society has produced in the historical process. But this reproduction is a very productive performance of individual learners with qualitatively new demands on their activity in psychic and physical respects. Though learning occurs in individuals and changes their cognitive, motivational, and other psychic qualities, learners are always acting in social interrelations that are embedded in social structures and conditions — immediate as well mediated ones. The coordination, communication and cooperation between learners, and with other people, is one of the most essential features of learning activity. The formation and quality of that aspect determines the concrete learning results to a great extent. The study of interrelations between individual and cooperative learning is one of the tasks not yet sufficiently accomplished by researchers of learning and instruction, despite the interesting work already done (e.g., Blumenfeld, Marx, Soloway & Krajcik 1996; Rubtsov 1987; Slavin 1996; Webb & Palincsar 1996; Zuckerman 1993).

Learning Activity and Development

As learning activity develops, learners become more and more independent and responsible subjects of their own activity, setting goals and evaluating their implementation, reflecting on their strategies and social interrelations, developing attitudes and values concerning learning materials, goals, partners, etc. Learning activity is the leading activity of personality development during school years, especially in elementary school (Elkonin 1989; Leontiev 1981).

Differing from other kinds of activity, learning activity is directed towards the self-modification and self-improvement of the learner with regard to the acquisition of new knowledge, understanding of new phenomena and relationships, coping with new tasks, etc. His/her actions with learning materials serve as a means of reaching that very goal, the latter developing from a very global and naive form at the beginning to more or less differentiated and conscious forms. While acquiring literacy, the basics of mathematics and other types of societal knowledge and skills, children develop a mediated relationship with the natural and social world — mediated in the sense of applying several means or tools in order to go beyond the phenomena given and to understand the world in its different relationships. This is the prerequisite and basis for the development of new psychic qualities, first of all, of elementary theoretical thinking and cognitive motivation as constituting a 'zone of proximal development' (Vygotsky 1987) of elementary school children.

Elementary theoretical thinking means the development of deep structural strategies, the children's growing understanding of basic features and relationships lying not at the surface of the learning material, but demanding abstraction from the phenomena and penetrating into the substance. This level or quality of thinking processes has its prerequisites in and is connected with empirical thinking, dealing with immediately given features and relationships, but it differs principally from that level in having other cognitive goals and results. If teaching succeeds in promoting the development of learning activity and — as one of its essential features — elementary theoretical thinking, it should be possible to form, for instance, real scientific concepts and to overcome everyday concepts in the framework of special learning domains (Davydov 1988a, 1988b, 1988c, 1996; Engeström 1987; Hedegaard 1996; Hedegaard, Hakkarainen & Engeström 1984; Lompscher 1989; Vygotsky 1987).

This kind of cognition demands a special kind of motivation and, at the same time, contributes to its development. Such a motivation is not satisfied by isolated facts and new phenomena and their description, but is a driving force for going beyond the phenomenon given. The learner, in this case, is interested in uncovering the internal connections and causes and thus in finding explanations for facts and phenomena. This is the real motivational basis for learning activity in the sense elaborated here. It is clear that learning activity cannot be based on and promoted by constraints and demands from outside — as a subject's activity, it needs its own inner, motivational basis. The cognitive aspect of learning activity, and theoretical thinking and cognitive motivation are not the only new psychic qualities developing in the course of learning activity. They are closely connected with social motivation and evaluation.

Content and Structure of the Book

The content and structure of knowledge is one of the conditions for how learning proceeds. The first section of this book, 'Societal Forms of Thinking and Knowledge', discusses, on the one hand, the interdependence between the societal traditions of production, science, art and public life, and, on the other, personal thinking modes and knowledge.

In the cultural-historical approach, knowledge is understood as being epistemologically anchored in social reality and transcending into personal psychological reality.

In the first chapter 'The Influence of Societal Knowledge Traditions on Children's Thinking and Conceptual Development', Mariane Hedegaard describes different forms of societal thinking modes and knowledge forms. She then discusses the relation between subject matter teaching and school children's concept formation and development of thinking strategies. This theme is illustrated by following the change of a child's development of thinking and motives in fourth grade history teaching.

Juan Daniel Ramirez-Garrido, Maria Cala-Carillo and José Sanchez-Medina demonstrate in their chapter 'Speech Genres and Rhetoric: the Development of Ways of Argumentation in a Program of Adult Literacy', how learning activity is connected with the institutional aspect of schooling and not with the age of the students. Their study focuses on how the adult person's acquisition of literacy influences their skills of argumentation and thereby their development of thinking procedures. But also that literacy is developed through argumentation about themes which matter to the person who is becoming literate. The students were all adult illiterate women from the rural districts of Andalusia in Southern Spain and the theme they worked with in the literacy classes was the role of women in society.

In the cultural-historical approach, knowledge is conceptualized as derived from and dependent on change in social practice. Bernd Fichtner's chapter contributes to an analysis of, and argumentation for, this conceptualization in relation to the change in society that the computer has started. In his chapter 'Activity Theory as Methodology — the Epistemological Revolution of the Computer and the Problem of its Societal Appropriation', he argues that qualitative changes in forms of knowledge are connected to societal inventions in knowledge transmission. He discusses two major inventions: the printing press and the computer. He then discusses the need for development of new societal activities as a consequence of the computer becoming a universal device in Western society. But these activities cannot just be invented, according to Fichtner's argumentation, they develop from the contradictions, oppositions and conflicts within the cultural practice in society. He points to the development of modern art as a place to find inspiration for working out new forms of activities for the societal appropriation of the computer.

Georg Rückriem in his chapter 'The Crisis of Knowledge', digs further into the relation between knowledge forms and societal practice and discusses knowledge from two perspectives. A practical perspective that concerns the growth of violence in school and a methodological perspective that concerns the invention of new forms of subject matter knowledge in instruction. Rückriem points out that violence is not only a problem of upbringing but is also a consequence of the epistemological tradition of school. Aspects discussed are the problems created by 'modern reason viewed as master of the universe' and repression of the emotional and bodily aspect of knowledge. Rückriem argues that violence through this approach has become an inherent characteristic of the knowledge form of Western society today. From the methodological perspective Rückriem discusses the need for development of a new approach to subject matter knowledge in school instruction.

The second section, 'Teaching/Learning Activity in Theory and Practice', contributes to an understanding of the relation between content of knowledge, teaching and learning activity. The congruence between knowledge mediated in school and the structure of teaching are vital conditions for a person's learning activity to proceed and contribute to his/her development of thinking, motivation and competencies. The theoretical considerations and the empirical work that lie behind the formulation of a theory of the relation between learning activity and 'developmental teaching' is presented by the pioneers within this area: Vasily Davidov, Joachim Lompscher and Nina Talyzina. Talyzina's work is very close to the tradition of Piotr Galperin, who has been one of the inspirational sources for developing new forms of teaching practice in both the Moscow and Berlin experimental schools, guided respectively by Davydov and Lompscher.

Vasily Davydov has been a very central person in questioning the kind of knowledge mediated through school teaching, which he calls empirical knowledge, and has argued for the importance of teaching children theoretical knowledge and thinking. The relation between kinds of knowledge, thinking and societal traditions has been discussed in Hedegaard's chapter. Davydov deepens the characteristic of theoretical knowledge and thinking in his chapter on 'What is Real Learning Activity'. Here he presents his theory about how children in school can appropriate theoretical knowledge and thinking. Learning activity is the key to children's development of theoretical thinking and can only be promoted if teaching activity is organized to meet this goal. In his chapter Davydov presents the principles by which such an 'organization' can proceed within different subject matters.

In his chapter, 'Learning Activity, and its Formation: Ascending from the Abstract to the Concrete', Joachim Lompscher concentrates on three central topics within the cultural-historical approach to teaching and learning. First, he analyzes what learning activity is as a background for discussing the characteristics of teaching strategies that can contribute to the formation of students' learning activity. Second, he discusses the main principle for formation of learning activity — ascending from the abstract to the concrete. Finally, he introduces the concept of learning strategies into this tradition and analyzes how differences in students' learning strategies contribute to the diversity in formation of their own learning activity. To illustrate this, Lompscher gives examples from his recent research.

Nina Talyzina's chapter 'Psychological Mechanism of Generalization' contains a presentation of an empirical study of problems of generalization of knowledge. The experiments which involved the solving of geometrical problems, were conducted with normal intellectually developed 5-6 year old children, and children who had been diagnosed as having intellectual delays. The experiments illustrated how the training of children's orientation to different aspects of objects to be categorized influenced their generalization capacity and concept formation.

In the third section 'Social Interaction, Development of Motives and Self-Evaluation', the focus is on three core aspects of learning activity. The theme of the four articles is how social interaction, self, and motivation are dialectically related within learning activity. This theme is discussed both from a theoretical perspective and by the presentation of empirical research.

In the chapter, 'Developmental Teaching in Upper-Secondary School', Seth Chaiklin introduces explicitly the analysis of subject matter content as the basis for formulating core-concepts and a germ-cell model within a subject matter area. He discusses the problem of finding basic concepts within a subject matter area and exemplifies this within physics. Furthermore he discusses how one can conceptualize change in students' motivation from elementary school to high school. The necessity of combining analyses of students' motivation with subject matter analyses as a guiding principle for learning activity is illustrated from physics teaching in Danish upper-secondary schools.

Felice Carugati discusses in his chapter, 'From Piaget and Vygotsky to Learning Activities: A Long Journey and an Inescaple Issue', Piaget and Vygotsky's contribution to our understanding of the social construction of cognition. He then points to two lines which need to be developed in the cultural-historical approach to cognition: The concept of self as mediating between mind and society and the theoretical articulation of society into small groups of significant others — into peer groups and peer culture. Carugati's project focuses on the last part, and to this end he discusses the European social psychology's contribution as well as ethnographic contributions. His focus is on how interaction between peers, and peers and teachers, construct the object of learning activity.

Galina Zuckerman's chapter, 'Diagnosing Learning Initiatives', can be seen as an empirical contribution to the problems of social interaction discussed in Carugati's article. Zuckerman's study focuses on learning cooperation among students, and between student and teacher. She specifies a particular kind of interaction, that is, when children are confronted with a new problem in class. In this situation Zuckerman finds that it is important to be able to diagnose what kind of problem the child has. Studying a child's learning initiative is the foundation for finding out what kind of activity the child is engaged in — be it a game or a learning activity. Setting a learning goal is strong proof that the child is the subject of a specific learning activity. Different models of elementary school instruction are compared to define the educational and interactional factors that most effectively develop learning initiative in seven to ten year old students.

Yuri Polyanov and Tatyana Matiss discuss evaluation as an important aspect of developmental teaching in their chapter 'Development of Evaluation at the Initial Stages of Learning Activities'. They point to the problematic function of evaluation in traditional schools where the objectives of the instruments and criteria of evaluation have mostly been obscure and hidden for the students. Through a conducted teaching experiment based on the formative experimental method in painting and picture creation, they demonstrated how evaluation can be transformed into an instrument that the students themselves can use to guide their creative work and learning activity. The core characteristic of this process was distribution and sharing of evaluation between the students and students and teacher.

In section four 'Play, Spontaneous Learning, and Teaching' the focus is the transition from pre-school to school and transformation of activities as preconditions for children's learning activity in school. In all three studies the focus is on integrating the early schoolchild's playful, creative and artistic activity with his/her learning activity.

Van Oers discusses in the chapter 'Teaching Opportunities in Play' the possibilities of developmental teaching for young children. He argues that teaching within the context of play supports the transition from play to learning. Semiotic activity which reflects the mutual relationship between sign and meaning is analyzed as one of the important psychological qualities in learning activity that emerges from play activity. Based on case studies in several different schools van Oers formulates basic requirements for promotion of semiotic activity. The meaningful embeddedness of the semiotic activity in the play activity, as well as shared participation, turned out to be necessary conditions for children's engagement and development of semiotic activity.

Elena Kravtsova focuses in her chapter 'Preconditions for Developmental Learning Activity at Pre-School Age' on preconditions for young children's readiness for school education. Her exploration of these preconditions is based on a series of experiments she has done with pre-school children. She found that development of communication between children and between children and adults, and the change in young children's ability to evaluate themselves, is of central importance to this readiness. She argues that seven is the crucial age for change in pre-school children's communication and their development of self-evaluation skills into context-free skills.

Gennady Kravtsov and Elena Bereshzkovskaya in their chapter 'The Education of Pre-School Children' discuss a teaching method that follows the child's spontaneous activities combined with the logic of a subject area, and name it spontaneous teaching. This method is especially developed for teaching pre-school children in nursery school or kindergarten. Through an observational study of 3-7 year old's painting activity in nursery school, three different stages of spontaneous teaching are formulated: immersion and creative manipulation, the appropriation of methods, and the formation of new ways as methods in personal creative activity.

References

Blumenfeld, P.C., Marx, R.W., Soloway, E. & Krajcik, J. (1996). Learning with peers: From small group cooperation to collaborative communities. *Educational Researcher* 25(8), 37-40.

Club of Rome (1991). *Die Globale Revolution* [The global revolution]. Hamburg: Spiegel-Verlag.

Davydov, V.V. (1988a). Problems of developmental teaching. *Soviet Education* 30 (8), 15-97.

Davydov, V.V. (1988b). Problems of developmental teaching. *Soviet Education* 30 (9), 3-83.

Davydov, V.V. (1988c). Problems of developmental teaching. *Soviet Education* 30 (10), 3-77.

Davydov, V.V. (1990). *Psichiceskoe razvitie mladsich skol'nikov* [Psychic development of elementary school children]. Moscow: Pedagogika.

Davydov, V.V. (1991). The content and unsolved problems of activity theory. *Multidisciplinary Newsletter for Activity Theory* 7/8, 30-35.

Davydov, V.V. (1996). *Teorija razvivajuscego obucenija* [Theory of developmental teaching]. Moscow: Intor.

Davydov, V.V. & Rubtsov, V.V. (1995). *Razvitie osnov refleksivnogo myslenija skol'nikov v processe ucebnoj deatel'nosti* [Development of students' reflexive thinking in the process of learning activity]. Novosibirsk: Psychological Institute, the Russian Academy of Education.

Elkonin, D.B. (1989). *Izbrannye psichologiceskie trudy* [Selected psychological works]. Moscow: Pedagogika.

Engeström, Y. (1987). *Learning by expanding*. Helsinki: Orienta Konsultit.

Engeström, Y. (1990). *Learning, working and imagining*. Helsinki: Orienta Konsultit.

Engeström, Y. (1991). Activity theory and individual and social transformation. *Multidisciplinary Newsletter for Activity Theory 7/8*, 6-17.

Hedegaard, M. (1996). How instruction influences children's concepts of evolution. *Mind, Culture, and Activity* 3(1), 11-24.

Hedegaard, M., Hakkarainen, P. & Engeström, Y. (eds.), (1984). *Learning and teaching on a scientific basis*. Aarhus: University of Aarhus, Institute of Psychology.

Lektorsky, V.A. (ed.), (1990) *Activity: Theories, methodology and problems*. Orlando: Deutsch Press.

Leontiev, A.N. (1978). *Activity, consciousness and personality*. Englewood Cliffs: Prentice-Hall.

Leontiev, A.N. (1981). *Problems of the development of the mind*. Moscow: Progress.

Lompscher, J. (1989). Formation of learning activity in pupils. In H. Mandl, E. de Corte, N. Bennett & H.F. Friedrich (eds.), *Learning and instruction, European Research in an international context*, vol. 2.2, 47-66. Oxford: Pergamon Press.

Lompscher, J. (ed.), (1996). *Entwicklung und Lernen aus kulturhistorischer Sicht* [Development and learning from a cultural-historical point of view]. Marburg: Bund demokratischer Wissenschaftler.

Luria, A.R. (1976). *Cognitive development: Its cultural and social foundations*. Cambridge, Mass.: Harvard University Press.

Martin, L.M.W., Nelson, K. & Tobach, E. (eds.), (1995). *Sociocultural psychology. Theory and practice of doing and knowing*. Cambridge: Cambridge University Press.

Moll, L.C. (ed.), (1990). *Vygotsky and education. Instructional implications and applications of sociohistorical psychology*. Cambridge: Cambridge University Press.

Newman, F. & Holzman, L. (1993). *Lev Vygotsky: Revolutionary scientist*. London: Routledge.

Rubtsov, V.V. (1987). *Organizacija i razvitie sovmestnych dejstvij u detej v processe obucenija* [Organization and development of joint actions with children in the process of instruction]. Moscow: Pedagogika.

Säljö, R. (ed.), (1991). Culture and learning. *Learning and Instruction* 1(3).

Scribner, S. & Cole, M. (1981). *The psychology of literacy*. Cambridge, Mass.: Harvard University Press.

Slavin, R.E. (1996). Research on cooperative learning and achievement: What we know, what we need to know. *Contemporary Educational Psychology* 21, 43-69.

Tharp, R.G. & Gallimore, R. (1988). *Rousing minds to life: Teaching, learning, and schooling in social context.* Cambridge: Cambridge University Press.

Tryphon, A. & Voneche, J. (eds.), (1996). *Piaget — Vygotsky. The social genesis of thought.* Hove: Psychology Press.

van der Veer, R. & Valsiner, J. (1993). *Understanding Vygotsky: A quest for synthesis.* Oxford: Blackwell.

Vygotsky, L.S. (1987). *Thinking and speech. In The Collected Works of L.S. Vygotsky,* vol. 1. New York: Plenum Press.

Webb, N.M. & Palincsar, A.S. (1996). Group processes in the classroom. In D.C. Berliner & R.C. Calfee (eds.), *Handbook of educational psychology* (841-73). New York: Simon & Schuster.

Wertsch, J.V. (ed.), (1985). *Culture, communication and cognition. Vygotskian perspectives.* Cambridge: Cambridge University Press.

Wertsch, J.V., del Rio, P. & Alvarez, A. (eds.), (1995). *Sociocultural studies of mind.* Cambridge: Cambridge University Press.

Yaroshevsky, M.G. (1993). *L. Vygotsky: V poiskach novoy psichologii* [Seeking the new psychology]. St. Petersburg: Izd. Mezhdunarodnogo fonda istorii nauki (International funds of history of science).

Zuckerman, G.A. (1993). *Vidy obscenija v obucenii* [Kinds of communication in instruction]. Tomsk: Peleng.

2 The Influence of Societal Knowledge Traditions on Children's Thinking and Conceptual Development

Mariane Hedegaard

My interest is how children generate personal knowledge and thinking procedures through school activities. In this paper I will discuss how forms of knowledge and traditions for thinking are connected to procedures for knowledge generation at school and how this relates to children's concept formation and thinking.

School children's thinking and concept formation are characterized by idiographic personal characteristics, while at the same time reflecting the societal and collective traditions of forms of knowledge and methods of inquiry. The aim of this paper is to study and discuss this relation based on theoretical analyses and illustrated by an example of how the activities in a specific teaching experiment influence a particular child's thinking and concept formation.

The theoretical analysis will deal with Vygotsky's theory of psychic development as the foundation for analyses of both the general cultural and the specific idiographic aspects of children's development of thinking and concept formation.

Davydov in his characterization of Vygotsky's cultural-historical theory of psychic development, formulates this dialectic of interaction very clearly between the collective cultural activity and the ideographic personal activity as the basis for development of individual consciousness and thinking:

One pole of his [Vygotsky's] cultural and historical theory is represented by the concept of the historically developing generic, that is, the collective activity of people (and from this it is only one step to the concept of the collective subject and of collective consciousness). A second pole is represented by individual activity, by the concept of the individual subject and the individual consciousness.

For Vygotsky individual consciousness is determined by the activity of the collective subject. For it is just this activity that in the process of interiorization forms individual consciousness. As Vygotsky wrote : 'In the development of the child's behaviour the genetic role of the collective changes. The child's higher functions of thought first appears in the collective life of children in the form of argument and only later lead to the development of reasoning in the child's own behaviour. (1987, vol. 3, 141)'. (Davydov 1995, 15)

Vygotsky's theory (1971/74, 1978, 1982, 1985/87) has influenced my understanding and empirical research of school children's personality development within three areas:

1) development of the personality/psychic as dependent on education and upbringing,
2) the interrelationship between thinking based on daily life activities and formal subject matter teaching at school,
3) the methodology of developmental research based on the 'genetic experiment'.

In the first part of the paper different approaches to thinking will be introduced. In the second part different knowledge traditions in school will be presented. In the third part I will discuss the relation between subject matter teaching and how it influences school children's thinking, concept formation and psychic development, and argue for how the cultural-historical approach to understanding knowledge also gives a possibility to understand individual thinking. In the fourth part I will present categories for interpreting specific children's learning activity with a focus on thinking and concept learning. I will illustrate this by presenting a boy's thinking and concept formation in the subject matter of history in fourth grade.

The boy attended a class which was part of a three-year teaching experiment. The teaching experiment was done within the cultural-historical approach of psychology. This experiment was the last in a series of teaching experiments done in cooperation with different teachers over the last 10 years. I have been involved in four experiments, two in the subject of biology and two in history (Hedegaard 1988, 1990, 1995, 1996, 1997, Hedegaard & Sigersted 1992a, 1992b).

The characteristics of the teaching tradition and the concrete experiment are not the aim of this presentation, but to describe the implication of teaching on a single child's learning activity with focus on thinking and concept formation.

Theories of Thinking

Vygotsky's theory of psychic development has influenced and inspired recent theories of thinking. Cultural and social aspects have become more common in the conceptualization of thinking over the past 10 years. There have been different ways of theorizing about the connection between thinking — culture and social activity. Theories about thinking can be found to vary from a conception of thinking as cognitive processes in persons inside the frame of social activity to a concept of thinking as an integrated part of the social activity between persons. I will distinguish four different approaches:

The *first* tradition can be named the 'cognitive situated approach' with Resnick (Resnick 1987, 1989; Resnick, Levine & Teasley 1991) and Greeno (1989, 1997a, 1997b) as key figures.

The *second* can be named the 'cultural daily life approach' with key persons such as Hutchins (1991, 1993), Lave (1991) Lave and Wenger (1991), and Scribner (1990).

The *third* is the 'socio-cultural communicative approach' with Wertsch (1991) and Billig (1991, 1993) as key persons.

The *fourth* tradition is the 'cultural-historical approach' with Vygotsky (1982), Elkonin (1971), Davydov (1977, 1985), Lompscher (1984, 1985) as key persons, and I will locate myself inside this category.

In the cognitive situated approach, thinking is still seen as an individual function of information manipulation supported by the social context. Collective procedures as a foundation for development of thinking are not introduced into this approach.

In the cultural daily life approach, thinking is located inside the existing practice of daily activities: i.e., manipulating a marine boat, tailoring, and milk delivery. This practice can be characterized by procedures for handling daily life activities. People are, according to this approach, socialized into being participants in procedure-guided activities, but they are not seen as modifying or reflecting on these procedures.

In the socio-cultural communicative approach, Wertsch characterizes thinking as a dialogue with historical roots. The dialogue of thinking takes place between imagined different opinions, characteristic of significant persons in an individual's life. These opinions now appear as part of internal discourses (dialogue). Wertsch is inspired by both Bakhtin and Vygotsky in this characteristic of thinking. In some of his recent work Wertsch connects the discourse in thinking with the narrative form of knowledge in the subject of history. Together with Tulviste (Tulviste & Wertsch 1993) he has analyzed how different historical conceptions about the same event can exist side-by-side at the same time for a person and be part of a personal discourse.

Billig characterizes thinking by the procedure of argumentation with the forms of negotiation, acceptance, rejection, and critique. These forms are found as idealized social practices in the subject area of rhetoric. Billig sees these procedures as anchored in the material world of specific topics or themes of discussion.

Each of these three different approaches to thinking focus on aspects which are important to integrate into a cultural-historical understanding of thinking: the social aspect of thinking and its situated and distributed character being formed by everyday practice as well as the communicative and argumentative character of the thinking process. The integration of these characteristics leads to a characterization of thinking as a process guided by procedures of social practices, either in daily life or in professional life, with dialogue and argumentation as central activities.

There are two other aspects that I find important to mention in qualifying 'thinking', both of which relate the thinking person to the cultural-historical tradition of practice. The first is the content of thinking, in the form of knowledge; the second is the motive for thinking. This has led me to a characterization of thinking as personally acquired procedures of cultural and social activities. There can be qualitative differences between thinking procedures, according to which type of knowledge is available, and even in relation to the same subject area the same person can use different forms of knowledge and procedures dependent on his motivation and the social conditions.

By focusing on content, the procedural aspects of thinking can be related to knowledge traditions, therefore the societal forms of knowledge a child meets in education is important for his development of thinking. The personal aspect of thinking is connected to the problem of how a person's conceived knowledge becomes transformed into active knowledge. This aspect can only be understood if the person's motives are taken into account.

Societal Forms of Knowledge

To understand the relation between the collective and personal aspects of knowledge, a conception about collective knowledge has to be formulated. My theoretical conception is that collective knowledge is generated in daily situations in many different types of institutions by the tasks and problems that characterize these institutions. University is one of the important institutions, although not the only one, but is central in knowledge generation.

Inspired by Juul Jensen (1987), and Knorr-Certina (1981) my hypothesis is that the dominating problems at universities and research centres reflect general societal problems. Knowledge has evolved through the finding of procedures for solving societal important problems in different historical periods. Medicine is a prime example (Juul Jensen 1987). Today we have the information sciences and computer technology as other examples. The procedures for solving problems inside these areas become formalized through scientific methods and become knowledge types that characterize the institutional traditions where they first become formulated. But, gradually, knowledge divorces from the original problem area and through the educational system it becomes a general form of knowledge, no longer connected to the original problem area.

Societal Forms of Knowledge Dominating School Education

If we look at schools in a historical perspective, and use Scandinavia as an example, different forms of knowledge have dominated. Theological, narrative and empirical forms of knowledge can be identified, with empirical knowledge as the dominating form in the school today. When schools became public in Scandinavia in the 19th century, theological knowledge dominated the curriculum. This was because the Scandinavian countries were Protestant countries, with bishops supervising the schools. The Lutheran catechism was used both as a subject matter in itself and as a general reading book.

Theological knowledge and reasoning are not important in form nor content in subject matter teaching in Scandinavian elementary schools today. Neither are other forms of knowledge such as mythical knowledge and medical knowledge and methods.

The form of knowledge found in subject matter teaching in schools today is the empirical/paradigmatic and narrative knowledge with theoretical knowledge providing a new way to conceptualize subject matter knowledge.

Empirical/Paradigmatic Knowledge

Empirical/paradigmatic knowledge and methods have characterized the positivistic traditions in natural science and today characterize the fact-oriented teaching in school.

Empirical knowledge focuses on similarities and differences in the surrounding world and on creating consistency in information by using distinct categories that can be hierarchically organized. Paradigmatic methods according to Bruner (Bruner, Goodnow & Austin 1956; Bruner 1957, 1986) transcend the observable by seeking higher forms of abstractions that can combine observable categories.

This form of knowledge presupposes that the world can be represented correctly, and correct representation gives possibility for accurate measurement. Knowledge in this tradition is conceptualized as mental building-blocks that can be stacked up or conceptualized as puzzle pieces which can be collected. According to this approach, knowledge does not change unless the information is wrong. Just as a building is constructed or a puzzle is assembled, one can construct a whole from elements of knowledge that remains the same. This assumption is reflected in many of the school instructional materials (e.g., in history or biology) where the aim is to *represent* as much of a subject domain ('the whole building') as possible. Another problem in the tradition of teaching empirical knowledge at school is that content of knowledge is not considered as a defining aspect of skills and vice versa, therefore subject matter can be differentiated into skill subjects (reading, writing, mathematics, foreign languages) and content-matter subjects (history, geography, biology). On the one hand, skill in the first subjects can be taught without much attention to the content, and on the other hand the content of the other subjects can be lectured and the child's task is to listen and remember, without caring about the methodological aspects (acquiring methodological skills).

The risk of instruction based on empirical knowledge is that the child ends up with concepts and skills from different subject domains which are difficult to relate to each other. Unfortunately, most school-books present knowledge in a disintegrated way, with a few facts about many different areas within a subject domain and without an easy-to-understand organizing principle that connects the different parts and surpasses the specific facts.

Empirical knowledge influences a great deal of the everyday life of people in Western industrialized societies. The argument is not to dismiss this kind of knowledge but to subordinate it to theoretical knowledge.

Narrative Knowledge

Narrative knowledge and methods can be found in human sciences in literary descriptions as well as 'folk theories'. The key characteristics of narratives are, according to Bruner (1986, 16-25), (a) changeableness in intentions, (b) the possible mutual perspectives and goals which interact, and (c) the involvement of feelings and emotions. The methods of narrative knowledge are connected to the problem of giving meaning to experiences.

Narrative knowledge characterizes the communicative activity of the children's daily life activity at home and among peers but is not so often promoted at school.

The narrative form of knowledge characterized history teaching in Denmark until the 1950s. With a school reform in 1957 this was changed and an empirical approach to history teaching was introduced to the Danish schools. The aim became teaching children objective facts of history (*Historiedidaktik i Norden* 2-3, 1985-1988; Sødring-Jensen 1978; Hedegaard 1998). But the value of the narrative form of teaching history is again promoted by several researchers in history didactics (Depew 1985; *Historiedidaktik i Norden* 3, 1988; Sødring-Jensen 1990) though it may be in another content than in the past. Today the same argument is presented for using the narrative method of history teaching as in the past, i.e., that this kind of knowledge is important for the formation of the children's personality and identity.

Narrative knowledge is a necessary and valid knowledge in subject matter teaching but I will argue that it has to be put inside a frame of theoretical knowledge whereby it is possible to combine situated learning and concrete life situations with theoretical concepts of subject matter knowledge.

Theoretical knowledge

Theoretical knowledge and methods have not been predominant in everyday life nor in the scientific traditions of Western cultures. But one can find this kind of knowledge and strategies for thinking in different professional and scientific areas through the history of social science (i.e., in the work of Marx, Weber, Lewin, Vygotsky and Bourdieu).

Theoretical knowledge of a problem area has evolved through a historical process of experimentation with methods and strategies for solving problems and contradictions central to society.

A method of theoretical knowledge — for acquiring, creating and evaluating knowledge — is Vygotsky's method of genetic experimentation (Bakhurst 1990), in which an object of investigation is changed either concretely or imaginatively, and the effects of these changes are explored in relation to the effects on other objects, thereby the structural connections/or relations of the first object to the explored objects can be characterized.

Another method of theoretical knowledge is characterized by integration of the basic concept relations of a subject domain into models called *germ-cell models*. (Davydov 1977, 1982). The meaning of the concepts in a germ-cell model is dialectically formed through the concepts' relations to each other. For example, in the subject domain of evolution the concepts of species and population define each other.

The epistemological procedures of theoretical knowledge is both to relate concrete instances to general ideas, and to understand generalities in concrete instances (Davydov 1989). Using theoretical knowledge, the specific and unique situations and experiences are related to universal and general concepts. Acquiring universal concepts is not a goal in itself, but a medium that can be used to analyze and understand the complexity in unique situations. The strategies of theoretical knowledge have been characterized as ascending from the abstract to the concrete (Lompscher, 1984), so that more general knowledge is used to find situation-specific solutions.

Theoretical knowledge is a relevant form of knowledge in school teaching, because it opens for possibilities to combine general principles of subject matter studies with the content and cultural practice of the everyday life that children know. The central skills that children have to acquire are to construct models that can guide the research and evaluation of their knowledge of subject matter areas.

In relating empirical knowledge to theoretical knowledge through the use of 'germ-cell models', theoretical knowledge can become a frame for the facts presented in textbooks. Through this relation, the child can get a connected and deeper understanding of the phenomena in the world.

The dialogue characteristic of narrative knowledge is a central method for developing social abilities and an important method for developing democratic institutions in society. However, if one does not have a framework of theoretical concepts for anchoring the dialogue, this method alone promotes relativism. If different persons select different narratives, then the procedures that characterize the production of narrative knowledge do not provide a way to resolve the conflict of what knowledge to rely on. The most fluent or persuasive speaker determines which knowledge is valuable.

By using the frame of theoretical knowledge in instruction it becomes possible to help the school child to organize his experiences and concepts around a conceptual 'germ cell' and thereby to connect empirical knowledge and the narratives of daily life into a system. By helping the child to do this inside the educational activity, the child acquires 'mental tools' that can be used to analyze and understand the complexity of the world around him.

Personal Knowledge and Thinking

One of Vygotsky's (1982) theses is that although formalized subject matter concepts can be learned at school, they do not become meaningful for the child until they become active in the child's life.

Activities in different fields of life — school, home, and work — with their different forms of practice result in different forms of concept formation and thinking. Scribner (1984, 1992; in Toback et al. 1997) and Lave (1988, 1992) have identified different ways of how mathematics is used in the different fields of school and work. The gaps between home, school and work as fields of learning are extended so much that many children have difficulty in combining knowledge of one field with the other. Therefore an issue of school teaching must be to connect the subject matter concepts with everyday concepts in a way that widens and develops children's abilities in these non-school situations.

There can be qualitative differences between thinking procedures according to which type of knowledge is available, and even in relation to the same subject area the same person can use different forms of knowledge and procedures dependent on his motivation and the social conditions. McDermott's (1993) description of 'how a learning disability acquires a child' gives us insight into how social conditions determine a child's capacity to think. He demonstrates how a child, in the relaxed situation of baking a cake, can read and calculate, but in a test situation does not even try to use his capability to read. Theoretical knowledge as conceptualized in the earlier section can combine the life of everyday concepts with the abstract knowledge of different subject matter and thereby help children to overcome this gap between knowledge and thinking within and outside school.

Experiences with children show that most pre-school children have the conditions to develop theoretical thinking, because they can relate matters to each other and can ponder about relations that they cannot experience directly, such as the relation between life and death, the size of the world and where it ends, and many more 'big questions about the world and life'. A Swedish research group has focused especially on pre-school and early school children's conceptions of different domains, i.e., Pramling (1983) has interviewed pre-school children about their conception of learning, Dahlgren & Olsson (1985) have focussed on pre-school children's conceptions of reading. Often children in pre-school age and early school age have developed a connected system of understanding through participating in activities with older children and adults and through their own reflection about phenomena that are important to them.

Vygotsky (1982) characterized the differences between pre-school children and school children's thinking as primarily a difference in systematic methods and amounts of knowledge within the different subject domains.

The problem in teaching is then how can *conceived knowledge* at school be transformed into *active knowledge*. As Vygotsky points out, the formal abstract concepts a child learns at school do not become active until they become functional in the person's daily life. This implies that the aim of teaching must be to teach children concepts and methods that can enrich their understanding and capacity for action in the life they live outside school. As pointed out in the earlier section, theoretical knowledge and thinking procedures open up for this possibility.

Ways to Transform Subject Matter Methods into Personal Thinking Strategies

In a series of teaching experiments conducted from the educational program of the *double move in teaching* (Hedegaard 1988, 1990, 1995, 1996, 1997; Hedegaard & Sigersted 1992a, 1992b), the traditional teaching methods and the methods of cooperation between children changed from learning methods aimed at imprinting the material to methods of research and cooperation around key problems. In these experiments we used a general method of research inspired by Lewin's social science method as well as methods characteristic of the subject matter.

I will draw upon one of the teaching experiments in history (Hedegaard 1995; Hedegaard & Sigersted 1992b) to illustrate the teaching methods, and use the same experiment to illustrate one particular child's concept formation and thinking about historical concepts.

The research procedure was the most dominating method used in this teaching experiment and was characterized by the following steps that were repeated:

> What are we researching?
> What do we know?,
> What do we not know about our research problem?
> How can we model the relation between the important concepts of our research problem?
> Which methods can we use to find out about what we do not know?
> Does the model need to be revised?

We also worked with methods of narrative knowledge: dialogue, argumentation, novel and film interpretation, dramatizing and play-acting.

Through building conceptual models, wholeness and perspective were generated for the single elements of knowledge.

In the history teaching experiment the aim was to build conceptual models. By using these models the children came to use conceptual relations (i.e., the relation between tools and way of living) to analyze historical periods. In fourth grade the teaching was conducted through 36 sessions. Each session lasted 3 hours. In the teaching, different phases can be differentiated: problem formulation, model formulation, model use and extension, formulating of task, evaluation of own capacities model evaluation (see Fig. 2.1).

Individuality in Thinking is Based on Differences in Motives

The individual and personally distinctive character of thinking depends on the child's dominating motive and motive hierarchy. Motives are related to the person's goals and characterizes the person's activities — surpassing the single situation, and can be characterized as longer lasting traits.

For example, a person's motives for learning should be seen as part of the person's motive system (Leontiev 1978), therefore development of the same motive (i.e., a learning motive) does not mean that children become standardized, because this motive interacts with a row of more specific motives for learning. The individual child's motive hierarchy creates the individuality and uniqueness of the person's relation to the world.

According to Elkonin (1971) different periods can be distinguished that characterize children's development. These periods are seen as connected to the institutions that dominate children's life and therefore are the basis for their acquisition of motives. In the industrialized Western societies of the 1950's when Elkonin formulated his theory, the three main institutions dominating children's lives were the family, the school, and work. Being part of the practice characterizing these different institutions the child develops motives. Activities connected to the institutions of family, school and work were, respectively, most important over varying periods. Each of these institutions contributes to the child's development of a corresponding dominating motive.

The pre-school period connects primarily to activities in the family. Two dominant motives develop through the pre-school years, the first acquired through social/emotional connectedness to other persons, and the second through learning everyday activities. So, the dominating motives for family activities are emotional closeness/exploration of the world; for early school activities they are role play and learning connected with literacy; and for late school age they are relatedness to peer groups and the appropriation of work competencies.

Motives develop through common cultural practice. This development takes place in situations where a common motivation can be found characterizing the cooperative interaction of the participants of an activity. To describe development it is necessary to distinguish between motivation and motives. Motivation is related to the practice of the concrete situation. For the person this characterizes the dynamic of her situated activities. Motives are related to the person's goals that transcends different situations, and can be related to imagined activities.

GOALS AND CONCEPTS OF TEACHING	LEARNING ACTIONS
Problem Formulation Exploration of different cultural societies of today and differences in historical periods in Denmark. Focus on types of work, living conditions and division of labor	Picture analyses of different historical periods and different societies of today
The General Research Method Paralleling to researchers' working methods	Construction of a goal-result board based on the children's ideas of how researchers work in general Role play of researcher at work
Model Formulation Modelling the relation between the concepts of nature, form of living, collective tool use and division of labor Introducing a historical dimension	Analyses of the !Kung people's way of living from a film presentation Analyses of the Stone Age people's way of living from reading a text A child's model is discussed and used
Model Extension **1) Collecting Experiences** Model formulation for humans' way of living, focusing on tool production The relation 'nature-human' differs from the relation 'nature-animal' by tool production and by tool-based interaction	Finding analogy between the !Kung people's way of living and the Stone Age people's way of living
2) Formulation of the Relations in the Model Differentiation and change of the relation 'animal-population' to 'ways of living — society'	Two-day excursion to an open-air museum with activities at an Iron Age farm Model making of historical periods The writing and performance of plays showing different ways of living, focusing on differences between tools in the Stone Age, the Iron Age and the Viking Age Solving tasks about the Iron Age with focus on ways of living, tools, division of labor, beliefs and society in the Iron Age

GOALS AND CONCEPTS OF TEACHING	LEARNING ACTIONS
Problem Formulation Again What did we investigate last year? What are we investigating now? What do we plan to investigate?	Cooperation in making posters with models of the evolution of animals; living conditions for humans; the origin of humans'; development of societies
Model Use — Variation — Extension Models of the Stone Age and the Iron Age with focus on tool use Introduction of the concepts beliefs/rules and Models of the Viking Age and the Middle Ages with focus on tool use and beliefs/rules	Cooperation in making posters with models of the Stone Age; the Iron Age; the Viking Age; the Middle Ages. The class library is consulted as source of information
Formulation of Tasks Model use and extension Introduction to division of work as a concept in the model	Formulation of tasks in small groups for the four periods One group works with the Stone Age, the other groups are to solve these tasks, and so on
Evaluation of Own Capacities	Class dialogue about creation of good and bad tasks on the different periods
Model Evaluation	Visiting an exhibition of the Viking Age. The tasks are to create good questions about the Vikings' ways of living, division of labor, beliefs, society and to create a play with focus on these topics

Fig. 2.1. Goals and activities in fourth grade.

It is through participating in the practice of the concrete situations and being motivated through this activity that motives develop. The goal of the different activities can be motivating for the activities and become motives for new activities for a person, so to develop learning motives for different subject matters, the teacher's task is to bring the child into situations where the activities become motivating so that the child acquires a motive to enter into these kinds of activities. Since there are many types of activities with different goals, each child can develop his own motives, but at the same time the tradition for practices in the institutions that characterize different periods of a child's life determinate which kind of activities children enter into, so this creates the common aspects of their motives. Motives, therefore, are not just created individually, but neither are they only collectively determined. The individuality is created through the motive hierarchy each person develops.

Evaluation of Personal Concept Formation, Thinking and Motive Development

The aim has been to formulate a system of interpretation of children's activities in different institutions which catches both the individual person in actual life situations[1] and at the same time building the collective, social and societal aspects into the categories based on the theories of Vygotsky (1982, 1985/87), Elkonin (1971, 1982), Davydov (1982, 1989), and Lompscher (1984, 1985).

The category system varies in relation to the subject area and the aim of the project. The presentation here has been developed for the teaching experiment in history.

An evaluation of the teaching process will not be introduced here (see Hedegaard 1987, 1994) but it is important to see the child's activities and his learning of procedures and knowledge related to the teaching activities. The child's learning is based on his participation in the activities in the teaching.

The categories of learning activity are formulated as a dialectic movement between the interpretation of observation and the conception of the following general categories as central for learning activity: social interaction, intention, thinking procedures and concept formation and problems in conceptual understanding. From these general categories a series of ques-

---

1. An aim I have in common with the phenomenological tradition of Merleau-Ponty (1970) and Shutz (1976).

Social interaction and motivation

How does the child react to the tasks and demands in the instruction?
Is the child, or does the child, become motivated to enter the instructional activities?
What kind of motives and interests does the child have?
What initiates new interests?
Is it the teacher's demands?
Is it demands and engagement from the other students?
Which motives dominate the child's activities?

Thinking and concept formation

What is the child's concept of time and concept of historical periods?
What characterizes the concepts of the child's thinking:

a) Does the child acquire concepts about the themes introduced in the teaching?
b) Can the child work with a model that specifies the relations between nature, ways of living, and society in different historical periods?
c) Does the child's model include an aspect of change?
d) Is the child able to explain differences in ways of living and society in different historical periods?

What kind of methods does the child acquire in his research of the historical problem formulations?
How does the child structure his thinking in relation to the three main activities of the teaching?

a) problem formulation and model formulation
b) use of procedures and models
c) evaluation and change of the model and of own capacity

What kinds of problems characterize the child's concept understanding?
How does the child's thinking develop?

Fig. 2.2. Categories of learning activity in relation to history teaching.

tions have been formulated in relation to both the teaching and learning activity.

In the category system of questions, the social interaction has been the foundation; it is the basis for analyzing the single child and is an integrated part of the main categories.

An example

I will exemplify one particular child's (Lasse) thinking in the *model extension phase* (see Fig. 2.1). Lasse was one of the two pupils who took part in the teaching experiment. A condensed interpretation is presented below of Lasse's learning activity covering a sequence of six sessions (from the 12th to 17th teaching period) in fourth grade teaching in the subject of history. This presentation should illustrate how motivation, thinking and concept formation proceeds as part of the learning activity.

By presenting an interpretation of Lasse's development of motive and thinking in this phase I hope to give an idea of how an analysis of social interaction and motivation, as well as thinking and concept understanding, respectively, can become a foundation for the interpretation of children's development of motives and thinking procedures.

Experimental Teaching of History in the 12th Session in Fourth Grade

To give an idea of how the learning is related to the teaching I will first present a condensed description of the teaching/learning activity in the class in the first session of the model extension phase — the twelfth session. In this session the children are taught to build models to describe historical change. The teacher draws intensively upon the research procedure that has been part of the teaching, also in third grade. The children have now come to a point where they can start to use the research procedure in evaluating their activities.

The children, during the foregoing eleven sessions, have already gone through a sequence of problem formulation, formulation of a general research method and model use (see Fig. 2.1) and they have acquired a first form of the model of the historical change of society. In the twelfth session the children are in the process of starting the second round of problem formulation. The main technique in this specific session is to use the goal-result board which helps the teacher to give an overview of the problems that the children have worked with, and the ones they are going to work with in the future.

The session starts as usual with the teacher writing the plan of the day on the blackboard:

Goal-result board
Text about society
Expanding the model
Pictures from different societies

The agenda helps the children anticipate what is going to happen and gives them an opportunity to reformulate the goals for the day, and provides a reference point for evaluating the days work.

The teaching focused on an overview of what the children have learned in fourth grade until now, (nature, tool-use and living conditions in the Stone age and Iron Age) and what they were supposed to go on with (the concept of society and how it relates to the concept the children have worked with until now). The teacher uses a goal-result board, which has been constructed on a cardboard through the first weeks of teaching. The goal-result board condensed the first relation in the model. This goal-result board helped the children get a connection between what they have done before and what they will be investigating and learning about in the future. In this particular case the children were being oriented toward constructing a model for describing the historical change of society.

The class dialogue began by the teacher's announcement that something was missing on the goal-result board, and that the children knew more than was written and drawn on the board. The children suggested some topics which the teacher wrote down on the blackboard. He wrote:

> What do we know about:
>   The evolution of animals
>   The development of humans
>   The difference between Iron Age and life today
>   Tool use, living quarters and beliefs of the Iron Age people
> What do we not know about:
>   Society
>   Different periods in history

The teacher then gave them the task to work in pairs and write down if they had any more ideas about what should be written on the goal-result board, what they knew about and what they did not know about in history.

The teacher made an outline for new goal-result board in four parts, each with the categories of the research procedure. The children were then given the task of drawing what they did *not* know about. They were told to draw in such a way that even a stranger coming to visit would be able to understand what they were doing.

Several of the children continued with the first task and wrote what they would like to learn about. The teacher intervened and asked them to draw instead. Morten drew the development of humans as an example of what they did *not* know about yet. Lasse drew the development of plants, clothes and tools. After this drawing task the teacher wanted to go on to the next point on the agenda — to read a text about society — but Cecilie redirected the teaching by asking if they could instead show the models they had prepared as homework about the development of society.

The teacher changed the agenda and two children (Morten and Cecilie) drew their models on the blackboard. The teacher then gave the children another drawing task: to draw what they had learned in the fourth grade until now. The teacher read the written suggestions the children made in the first hour of this session, so they could choose from these suggestions what they would like to draw. The children got so engaged in the drawing task that they did not want to stop and go out to play during the break. Instead most children kept on drawing and all finished their drawing in the last hour of the session. The result of their work went into the four posters the teacher had started to prepare. (These posters were finished two sessions later). These posters were formed as four goal-result boards. One showed what they explored last year (in third grade): evolution of animals. A second showed what they had explored the first month in fourth grade: the development of humans. A third showed what they were researching when they made the posters: living conditions in different societies. A fourth showed what they were going to research after Christmas: the historical change of the Danish society.

The last activity on the agenda was for the children to analyze and discuss a series of pictures from the Iron age and the Viking age. These pictures were given as a starting point to introduce a discussion about difference in societies. The children were asked to analyze and discuss with each other in their groups (there were four children in each group) what the pictures can tell about differences between society in the two historical periods. After 10 minutes of group work the teacher tried to start a class dialogue about how people in the Viking Age lived and worked differently from people in the Iron Age, and what significance this had for the formation of their society. There was only a short discussion and the children did not have much to say. Finally the children evaluated the class activity through class dialogue using the agenda on the blackboard. The main critique came from Didrik who meant that the picture-analyzing task was too difficult.

Lasse's Learning Activity in the Model Extension Phase — Social Interaction and Motivation

Lasse's relation to the other children became more active when they started to co-operate on the production of charts concerning what they knew and did not know about their research areas and the relevant models. At the observer's request, Lasse consulted Morten's model and later the two boys cooperated on the production of the goal-result board about the evolution of man. In the 13th session Lasse was aware of the fact that two of the children had not had their drawings put up on the boards and he drew the teacher's attention to this. He was also in enough command of the situation to be able to tease the teacher. During the class discussion concerning development of various matters (techniques, work, etc.) Lasse mentioned the development of the teacher's 'chicken brain'. The teacher ignored his remark, but it showed that Lasse's relation to the teacher was good, though probably characteristic of the traditional teacher-pupil relationship, e.g., the pupil teases and the teacher corrects. When asked by the teacher whether the drawing of models was a difficult task Lasse spontaneously remarked: 'No, it was fun'.

Motive Development

Lasse's engagement grew as the drawing of models came to dominate the teaching. Lasse used the observer for help, consulted the other children for help in solving assignments, and also used books. He cooperated well with Morten in connection with the production of the model for the development of man for the goal-result board. They worked well together and were both interested in and concentrated on producing a good chart. These facts show that Lasse's motive for contacting and co-operating with his classmates had increased in line with his motive for contributing actively to the production of the boards.

Thinking and Concept Formation

In the first session of the model extension phase, Lasse starts to wonder about language in response to Cecilie's tale about the first King of Denmark who was found as a baby on the shore. Lasse asks if people in historical times spoke different languages in different countries. The children end up discussing if there were borders between countries in prehistoric times and if there were countries.

Later on the teacher asks (which is part of the daily procedure) 'What is the theme of research in the class activity?' Lise formulates that they research societies. Lasse corrects her and says that it is the Iron Age they are researching. His commentary shows that he keeps his focus on the historical periods, but at the same time he shows that he has difficulties in combining the historical aspect with the newly introduced aspect of societies.

In the class dialogue during the 14th session, the theme of difference between animals and humans is brought up again (it was brought up just before this phase). Again, Lasse argues against the use of tools as a defining criteria for the difference between man and animal. He gives a counter example: that birds on the Galapagos Islands use sticks; which he probably learned (there has just been a film on television about the Galapagos Islands). Sanne counter-argues that while *all* humans have always used tools, animals have not, and *this* criteria defines being human. Lasse is silent.

In the next task the children are separated into four groups, and each group is given the task of making a goal-result board with research questions and models. The tasks are related to the two themes they researched during the previous school year and the first part of this school year, and the two themes that they will research for the rest of the year. The themes were (a) the evolution of animals, (b) the origin of man, (c) the development of human ways of living, and (d) the historical change of societies.

Lasse's group gets the task to make the goal-result board for 'the development of human ways of living'. There are four children in the group. Two of the children write what they know and what they do not know about this theme. Lasse and Morten decide to draw a model of the central relation of their research.

In their model they have symbolized nature at the top. Just beneath is a symbol of food. Between the symbol of tools and food they have drawn a symbol of a kitchen gadget (a can opener). Society is symbolized in a prehistoric form as well as a modern form. In the class dialogue Morten explains the upper part of their model. Lasse talks quietly as a prompter. When it becomes his turn he continues Morten's explanation and explains that he has drawn a symbol of pollution (he has drawn a bird smeared in oil) between the relation of the symbol of modern society (which is symbolized as a factory) and nature because the factory pollutes. Between the symbol of people and nature he has drawn a signpost to symbolize development of cities (see Fig. 2.3).

The next task in the class is that the children have to draw a model for each of the four different historical periods they have now worked with. Lasse's group has to draw a model of the Stone Age. Each child gets a task of symbolizing a concept of the model. Lasse has to draw symbols of beliefs. Before they start drawing the children discuss what they will draw. Lasse chooses to draw a dead man in his burial chamber surrounded by things put with him in the grave (i.e., a sword and a shield). He also draws on top of the grave a modern gravestone (tombstone) and a vase with flowers and a person kneeling down and crying (see Fig. 2.4).

Development of Thinking and Concepts

In this session Lasse obviously had an understanding of the historical dimension and the time periods with which the children were working. He also joined in the discussion of whether the use of tools is a specific human characteristic. Perhaps he was convinced by Sanne's argument that, contrary to animals, humans always use tools. The fact that he wondered why humans speak different languages, also in the past, made the children discuss society and borders.

Through his characterization of developments in society, he was able to symbolize the historical development of man, although he still regarded society as primarily consisting of buildings and cities.

Lasse displayed insight in the historical dimension, which he did not see necessarily as a positive developmental dimension, as demonstrated by his explanation that factories pollute, and exemplified in his drawing of a bird covered with oil. Lasse's concept of faith and religion was relevantly expressed in his drawings, although he could not quite shake off the modern burial customs with gravestones, etc. He was not yet able to deal explicitly with the concept of 'society'.

Conclusion

I have built on Vygotsky's theory in my research and have argued that personality development is shaped by the social practice of the institution which a child attends.

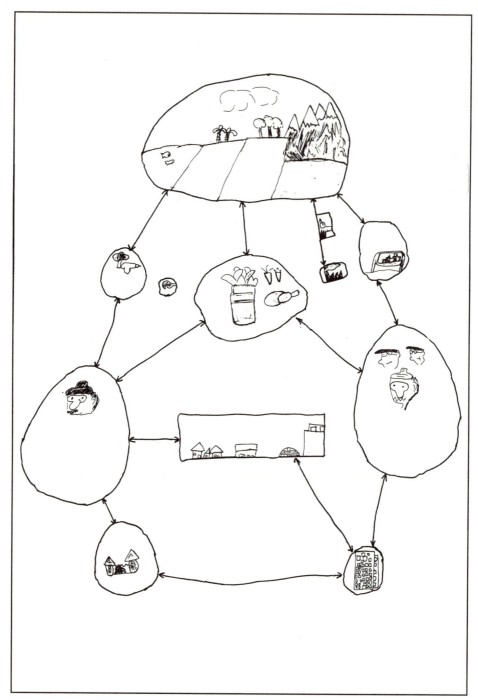

Fig. 2.3. Loke and Morten's drawing of the development of mankind.

Fig. 2.4. Loke's drawing of the beliefs of Stone Age man.

My interest has been to demonstrate how a child generates personal knowledge and thinking procedures through school activities. To demonstrate this I have discussed how forms of knowledge and traditions for thinking are connected to procedures for knowledge generation at school and how this relates to children's concept formation and thinking.

Thinking can be characterized as the personalized procedures of cultural and social practices of both daily life and professional life, with dialogue and argumentation as central activities.

Through participation in the social practice of the school the child conceives the content and methods that characterize the social practice of everyday activities in the classroom as well as subject matter activities. I have argued that the conceived knowledge and methods of school are transformed into individual knowledge and thinking by the child's active use of the formal subject matter content and methods in motivated class activity where children cooperate and communicate with each other.

A child assimilates values of material and spiritual culture in the process of teaching and upbringing through his personal version of procedurally determined activity in collaboration with other people.

A person has multiple thinking procedures available in relation to a subject domain. What is used depends on his conceptualization of the content of the subject domain, and the motives of the person.

References

Bakhurst, D. (1990). *Consciousness and revolution in Soviet philosophy*. Cambridge: Cambridge University Press.

Billig, M. (1991). *Ideology and opinions*. London: Sage.

Billig, M. (1993). Studing the thinking society: Social representations, rhetoric, and attitudes. In G.L. Breakwell & D.V. Canter (eds.), *Empirical approaches to social representations*. Oxford: Clarendon Press.

Bruner, J.S., Goodnow, J.J. & Austin, G.A. (1956). *A study of thinking*. New York: Wiley.

Bruner, J.S. (1957). On going beyond the information given. In *Contemporary approaches to cognition*. Cambridge, Mass.: Harvard University Press.

Bruner, J.S. (1986). *Actual minds possible worlds*. Cambridge, Mass.: Harvard University Press.

Dahlgren, G. & Olsson, L.-E. (1985). Läsning i barnperspektiv [The child's conception of reading]. (*Göteborg Studies in Educational Sciences*, 51). Göteborg: Acta Universitatis Gothoburgensis.

Dansk socialhistorie [Danish social history]. (1979-1980). Copenhagen: Gyldendal.

Davydov, V.V. (1977). *Arten der Verallgemeinerung im Unterricht* [Types of generalization in instruction]. Berlin: Volk und Wissen.

Davydov, V.V. (1982). Ausbildung der Lerntätigkeit [Development of learning activity]. In V.V. Davydov, J. Lompscher & A.K. Markova (eds.), *Ausbildung der Lerntätigkeit bei Schülern*. Berlin: Volk und Wissen.

Davydov, V.V. (1989). *Udviklende undervisning på virksomhedsteoriens grundlag* [Developmental teaching based on activity theory]. Moskva: Sputnik.

Davydov, V.V. (1995). The influence of L.S. Vygotsky on education theory, research, and practice. *Educational Researcher* 24(3), 12-21.

Depew, D.J. (1985). Narrativism, cosmopolitanism, and historical epistemology. *Clio* 14, 357-77.

Elkonin, D.B. (1971). Toward the problem of stages in the mental development of the child. *Soviet Psychology* 10, 538-653.

Elkonin, D.B. (1982). Personlighetsutvecklingen hos förskolebarnet [The pre-school child's personality development]. In L.C. Hydén (ed.), *Sovjetisk barnpsykologi*. Stockholm: Natur & Kultur.

Greeno, J.G. (1989). A perspective on thinking. *American Psychologist* 44, 134-41.

Greeno, J.G. (1997a) Theories and practices of thinking and learning to think. *American Journal of Education* 106(1), 85-126.

Greeno, J.G. (1997b). On claims that answer the wrong questions. *Educational Researcher* 26(1), 5-17.

Hedegaard, M. (1987). Methodology in evaluative research on teaching and learning. In F.J. van Zuuren, F.J. Wertz, and B. Mook (eds.), *Advances in qualitative psychology*. Lisse: Swets & Zeitlinger.

Hedegaard, M. (1988). *Skolebørns personlighedsudvikling, set gennem orienteringsfagene* [The development of school children's personality viewed through the social science subjects]. Aarhus: Aarhus University Press.

Hedegaard, M. (1990). The zone of proximal development as basis for instruction. In L.C. Moll (ed.), *Vygotsky and education*. Cambridge: Cambridge University Press.

Hedegaard, M. (1994). Moving from the concrete to the general. Using participant observation in research on children's learning. *Multidisciplinary Newsletter for Activity Theory* 15/16, 37-44.

Hedegaard, M. (1995). *Tænkning, viden, udvikling* [Thinking, knowledge, development]. Aarhus: Aarhus University Press.

Hedegaard, M. (1996). How instruction influences children's concepts of evolution. *Mind, Culture, and Activity* 3, 11-24.

Hedegaard, M. (1997). Kommunalt projekt med statsløse palæstinensiske børn [Municipal project with stateless Palestinian children]. In M. Hedegaard (ed.), *Praksisformers forandring — personlig udvikling*. Aarhus: Aarhus University Press.

Hedegaard, M. (1998). History education and didactics. In Y. Engeström, R. Miettinen & R.L. Punamäki (eds.), *Perspectives on Activity Theory*. New York: Cambridge University Press.

Hedegaard, M. & Sigersted, G. (1992a). Experimental classroom teaching in history and anthropological geography. *Multidisciplinary Newsletter for Activity Theory* 11/12, 13-23.

Hedegaard, M. & Sigersted, G. (1992b). *Undervisning i samfundshistorie* [Teaching Social Science]. Aarhus: Aarhus University Press.

Historiedidaktik i Norden 2 [History didactics in the Northern countries]. (1985). Copenhagen: The Royal Danish School of Educational Studies.

Historiedidaktik i Norden 3 [History didactics in the Northern countries]. (1988). Malmö, Sweden: Malmö University, School of Teacher Education.

Hutchins, E. (1991). The social organization of distributed cognition. In L.B. Resnick, J.M. Levine & S.D. Teasley (eds.), *Perspectives on socially shared cognition*. Washington, D.C.: American Psychological Association.

Hutchins, E. (1993). Learning to navigate. In S. Chaiklin & J. Lave (eds.), *Understanding practice*. New York: Cambridge University Press.

Juul Jensen, U. (1987). *Practice & Process: A theory of the modern health care system*. Oxford: Blackwell.

Knorr-Certina, K.D. (1981). *The manufacture of knowledge*. New York: Pergamon Press.

Lave, J. & Wenger, E. (1991). *Situated learning: Legitimate peripheral participation*. New York: Cambridge University Press.

Lave, J. (1988). *Cognition in practice: Mind, mathematics, and culture in everyday life*. New York: Cambridge University Press.

Lave, J. (1991). Situated learning in communities of practice. In L.B. Resnick, J.M. Levine & S.D. Teasley (eds.), *Perspectives on socially shared cognition*. Washington, D.C.: American Psychological Association.

Lave, J. (1992). Word problems: A microcosm of theories of learning. In P. Light & G. Butterworth (eds.), *Context and cognition*. Hemel Hempstead: Harvester Wheatsheaf.

Leontiev, A.N. (1978). *Activity, consciousness, and personality*. Englewood Cliffs, N.J.: Prentice-Hall.

Lompscher, J. (1984). Problems and Results of Experimental Research on the Formation of Theoretical Thinking through Instruction. In M. Hedegaard, P. Hakkarainen & Y. Engeström (eds.), *Learning and teaching on a scientific basis*. University of Aarhus: Institute of Psychology.

Lompscher, J. (ed.), (1988). *Persönlichkeitsentwicklung in der Lerntätigkeit* [Personality development through learning activity]. Berlin: Volk und Wissen.

McDermott, R.P. (1993). The acquisition of a child by a learning disability. In S. Chaiklin & J. Lave (eds.), *Understanding practice. Perspectives on activity and context*. New York: Cambridge University Press.

Merleau-Ponty, M. (1970). *Phenomenology of perception*. London: Routledge & Kegan Paul.

Pramling, I. (1983). *The child's conception of learning*. Gothenburg: Acta Universitatis Gothenburgensis.

Resnick, L.B. (1987). *Education and learning to think*. Washington, D.C.: National Academy Press.

Resnick, L.B. (1989). Introduction. In L.B. Resnick (ed.), *Knowing, learning and instruction*: *Essays in honor of Robert Glaser*. Hillsdale, N.J.: Lawrence Erlbaum.

Resnick, L.B., Levine, J.M. & Teasley, S.D. (eds.), (1991). *Perspectives on socially shared cognition*. Washington, D.C.: American Psychological Association.

Scribner, S. (1984). Studying working intelligence. In B. Rogoff & J. Lave (eds.), *Everyday cognition*. Cambridge, Mass.: Harvard University Press.

Scribner, S. (1990). A socio-cultural approach to the study of mind. In G. Greenberg & E. Tobach (eds.), *Theories of the evolution of knowing*. Hillsdale, N.J.: Lawrence Erlbaum.

Scribner, S. (1992). Mind in action: Its functional approach to thinking. *The Quarterly Newsletter of Human Cognition* 14, 103-10.

Shutz, A. (1976). *The phenomenology of the social world*. London: Heinemann Educational Books.

Sødring-Jensen, S. (1978). *Historieundervisningsteori* [History teaching theory]. Copenhagen: Christian Ejlers Forlag.

Sødring-Jensen, S. (1990). *Historie og fiktion: Historiske børneromaner i undervisningen*. [History and fiction: Historic children's novels in teaching]. Copenhagen: The Royal Danish School of Education.

Tobach, E., Falmagne, J., Parlee, M.B., Martin, L.M.W. & Kapelman, A.S. (eds.), (1997). *Mind in Social Practice*. New York: Cambridge University Press.

Tulviste, P. & Wertsch, J. (1994). Official and unofficial histories: The case of Estonia. *Journal of Narrative and Life History*, **vol. ?**, 311-29.

Wertsch, J.V. (1991). *Voices of the mind: A sociocultural approach to mediated action*. Cambridge, Mass.: Harvard University Press.

Vygotsky, L.S. (1971-74). *Tænkning og sprog*. I-II [Thinking and Language]. Copenhagen: Reitzel.

Vygotsky, L.S. (1978). *Mind in society*. Cambridge, Mass.: Harvard University Press.

Vygotsky, L.S. (1982). *Om barnets psykiske udvikling*. [On the child's psychic development]. Copenhagen: Nyt Nordisk Forlag.

Vygotsky, L.S. (1985/87). *Ausgewählte Schriften*. 1 & 2 [Selected writings]. Cologne: Pahl-Rugenstein.

3 Speech Genres and Rhetoric: the Development of Ways of Argumentation in a Program of Adult Literacy

Juan Daniel Ramírez-Garrido, María J. Cala-Carrillo, and José A. Sánchez-Medina

Introduction

The role of literacy in the development of psychological processes is accepted as a central theme in psychology. However, its study has been bound on numerous occasions to literacy in childhood and to its effects on basic psychological processes. In an attempt to enlarge the study of literacy, our contribution focuses on: the literacy of adult people and its influence on skills for argumentation. That is, we try to explore the influence of the participation in a setting of activity (formal school) in the development of cognitive processes (thinking). In previous research projects we found strong influence of literacy in memory and categorization using standard tests. But in this research we use the idea of Billig (1987) to connect rhetoric and thinking; Billig considers that there is a close relationship between the form in which we argue and the way we think. Therefore, we are endeavouring to show that the literacy program influenced the way of thinking of those adults who attended it, and in this regard we shall analyze the way adults argue.

These developments are introduced using an empirical study focusing on the utterances of women attending a schooling program in a debate over women's role in society. The ways of arguing are analyzed by means of Bahktin's concept of speech genres. Our findings show transformations in the use of speech genres in argumentation as the women advance through the schooling program. Especially relevant seems to be the role played by the use of examples and references to daily experience in the construction of rhetorical argument, since this constitutes a discriminate element of different speech genres.

On the Notion of Literacy

The issue of literacy has received a great deal of attention in psychology and other social disciplines, but a certain amount of controversy still exists about what is actually meant by literacy. In addition to this, we find that many of the early studies dealt with literacy in child schooling, ignoring the study of this process in adults. On the other hand, our research program has focused on the changes that literacy promotes in illiterate adults.

First of all, we should clarify what our notion of literacy is. We find many different notions and approaches to the literacy process. While some approaches underline the psycholinguistic processes involved and are mainly concerned with the acquisition of individual skills promoted by the learning of reading-writing, others focus on the way that literacy, as a social practice, transmits patterns and cultural values. Recently, approaches integrating both perspectives have appeared (Cook-Gumperz 1986; Snow and Dickinson 1991). Langer (1987) defends a sociocognitive perspective of literacy going beyond the mere acquisition of reading-writing skills. They incorporate into their definition the notions of social practice, of reading and writing, thereby redefining literacy as a way of thinking and speaking. Literacy is more than a set of skills, it is an activity full of usefulness and social purposes which will adapt to social change, just like particular forms of thinking. At the same time, and as literacy may have different uses, these could promote social and cultural changes in the way in which individuals appropriate them.

Cook-Gumperz (1986) also proposes a social perspective on literacy focusing on the processes in which literacy is built and modified daily on interactive exchanges and discussion of meanings in many different contexts. She emphasizes that literacy, as a socially built phenomenon, consists not only of aptitudes for reading and writing, because through the mastering and use of these abilities, other socially assessed skills, norms, and values are developed.

Scribner and Cole (1981) suggest that it is not the sole acquisition of reading/writing skills which promotes a later cognitive development per se, but that development is more related to the kind of social setting in which those skills are acquired. These scholars argue that formal education activities promote cognitive changes which are traditionally associated to literacy, as a result of the set of skills required by their tasks and the kind of interactions in which they are carried out.

Literacy, Schooling and Language

Almost nobody questions that in modern societies schooling is one of the most important settings that contributes to generating changes in cognitive skills, attitudes, and values, becoming one of the most important contexts of socialization. Although most scholars of the educational process would agree with those assumptions, the problem arises in trying to specify what types of change are produced by schooling and how they are generated. This grey area is mainly due to the limitations in the way in which the educational process is studied, where black-box approaches prevail, missing the connections between socio-cultural input and psychological output (Mehan 1979; Wertsch 1987).

Our interest focuses precisely on this grey area. There is no doubt about the interest of studying changes in ways of thinking, values, attitudes and cognitive functioning. However, to concentrate solely on these points of the educational process could mean leaving out its very own dynamic, abandoning the study of the mechanisms that articulate it and permitting the transition from the social to the individual. Put more concisely, it is not enough to study the product or, if you like, the sediment that schooling leaves in the individual. We need to focus our research on the process which is generating that transformation. This perspective produces even more interest if we adopt the Vygotskyan and socio-cultural assumptions, according to which psychological outputs are determined by the social processes involved in their acquisition (Vygotsky 1977, 1978; Leontiev 1981a, 1981b; Luria 1975; Wertsch 1985). In our study, we are concerned with two principal assumptions of the socio-cultural approach. On the one hand, the idea that the individual psychological processes have a social genesis. That is to say, the basis of higher psychological functions has to be searched for in the interpsychological processes in which they are generated. On the other hand, these interactions are based on a semiotically mediated social reality. In other words, communicative processes, in which individual psychological processes are generated, are themselves mediated by symbolic tools, language being the most important.

The role of language in these communicative exchanges should not be understood in such a limited way, merely as a suitable instrument for interchanging information. More than this, speech endows a particular situation with a structure and, at the same time, it may create a social reality temporarily shared by the speakers. It is just this reality set up through speech, the one which is going to provide the basis of the interaction, creating some minimal intersubjectivity levels or commonly shared knowledge (Rommetveit 1979).

Therefore, the most interesting question for us is not a language's ability to describe the state of things, but its potential to create and highlight perspectives of reality. From this point of view, particular discursive processes generated in formal educational settings have special relevance for our research, because by studying them, we hope to analyze the mechanisms that permit the transition from the social to the individual level. The analysis of students' discourse allows us to study not only the structure of their speech, but also how they analyze their immediate reality, that is to say, it is going to allow us to study their processes of thinking.

When an individual is socialized in a particular discursive activity (such as the case of schooling), he/she is going to take on, master and interiorize its structure in such a way that this is going to be useful as an instrument of regulation and control of his/her own behaviour. It is precisely in this sense that we understand the Vygotskyan idea of the social and semiotically mediated genesis of psychological processes (Vygotsky 1978; Wertsch 1985).

The concept of speech genre developed by Bakhtin (1986) also seems to be especially appropriate for the study of literacy from this perspective. According to Bakhtin:

A speech genre is not a form of language, but a typical form [i.e., a type] of utterance; as such the genre also includes a certain typical kind of expression that inheres in it. In the genre the word acquires a particular typical expression. Genres correspond to typical situations of speech communication, typical themes, and, consequently, also to particular contacts between the meanings of words and actual concrete reality under certain typical circumstances. (Bakhtin 1986, 87)

For Bakhtin, speech only exists in the form of concrete utterances and the speech genre corresponds to 'forms of utterances relatively stable and normative' (Bakhtin 1986, 81). Therefore, in order to distinguish the discursive genres we must start from the utterance which Bakhtin named the 'real unit of communication' (1986, 290).

According to Wertsch (1991), this variety of speech genre corresponds to the mediational means used by individuals to talk about or reflect on reality. These instruments that mediate the human action should not be considered as a whole but as different items that constitute a 'tool-kit'. In relation to verbal thought, Tulviste (1986) proposes that in cultures or individuals, there is not just one unique and homogeneous form of thought. Instead, the different forms of thought are related to different types of activities. Each activity context privileges the use of a specific 'tool-kit', and returning to Bakhtin's notion, particular speech genres. In this sense, there is a lot of research suggesting that school privileges an abstract and decontextualized speech genre, the so-called 'rational discourse' (Wertsch 1987).

According to Wertsch and Minick (1990), the properties of rational discourse at school are related to what they call 'text-based realities'. This term refers to the fact that the realities involved in the classroom are created and maintained through semiotic instruments. One of the characteristics of text-based realities is that they impose limits for operations with semiotic instruments (these limits do not include the subject's daily experience) . Another characteristic is that they involve decontextualization. As Wertsch (1990) points out:

The defining characteristic of the voice of the decontextualized rationality is that it represents objects and events ... in terms of formal, logical, and, if possible, quantifiable categories. The categories used in this form of representation are decontextualized in the sense that their meaning can be derived from their position in abstract theories or systems that exist independently of contexts. (p. 120)

Opposite this type of discourse, we find 'contextualized forms of representation' (Wertsch 1987) in which the objects and events are represented in terms of their concrete particularity.

As stated above, the way school interactions are produced, how the contents are imparted, the treatment given to reality, aim at enabling students to acquire new and varied instruments in order to think, acting on a higher number of settings, enlarging their possibilities of adaptation and understanding of different and very diverse realities. The subjects learn to dominate a 'rational discourse' but, as Wertsch and Minick (1990) pointed out, this implies that not only are they able to use a decontextualized language but they can also recognize and create contexts in which the use of this discourse is appropriate. Again, we insist on the fact that although school privileges are a type of discourse, this does not mean that when the individual is able to dominate this type of decontextualized discourse, he/ she stops using a discourse related to concrete experiences. It does not imply the substitution of one form of discourse for another, but the possibility of using different forms of representing the context and acting on it, depending on the setting in which the individual is acting. Instead, another tool is added to the 'tool-kit'.

The individual mainly uses one form of discourse or another depending on the activity setting where the action develops. But even within a setting that privileges this type of decontextualized discourse and with subjects that dominate it, particular examples are used where the students can include the perspective derived from their own daily experience, making reference to their own (or close) particular situations.

In this sense, Billig's contributions about two opposite processes such as particularization and generalization seems very useful (Billig 1987). This author highlights the importance of argumentation in human thought and he attempts to promote an argumentative rhetoric more than a rhetoric of adornment. This is the context in which he suggests that thinking should be seen as a conflict between this opposing of categorization and particularization.

Instead of building a psychological portrait principally upon the single, and unopposed, process of categorization, the tensions between categorization and particularitazion will be seen as central. Thinking will be viewed in terms of the conflicts between these two processes. (Billig 1987, 120).

Study of Adults' Discourse in a Literacy Program

Research Setting

The literacy program that was introduced in Andalusia (Southern Spain) in the 1980's and early 1990's formed a kind of natural laboratory for studying the process of becoming literate as well as the changes in the sociocognitive skills related to this. The P.E.A. program (Programa de Educación de Adultos de Andalucía — Andalusian Adult Education Program) was inspired by Paulo Freire's pedagogic ideas (Freire 1970). Educational practices must be adapted and generated from the social and cultural reality of the students, reflecting the problems of the community, and, at the same time, the students must be given an active role in the teaching-learning process. The P.E.A. program was mainly directed at adults with no or very little previous schooling. The majority of students attending literacy courses were women between the age of 30 and 60. All the students were from a working-class backgroud, with a low income level and a high unemployment rate in the family. It is important to realize that, although in the beginning most of these women started to attend the program just to acquire or improve their reading and writing skills or to get a diploma, they soon found it a way to extend their social relationships, and the adult school became a public scene where they could talk and be listened to.

Debate: A Promoted Practice

Our interest in studying the discourse processes generated in the interactive dynamic of these literacy practices led us to focus on debate activities. This choice follows the criteria of a diverse nature.

Previous observations and the ethnography study that we carried out both showed the importance of these practices in the activities of a school of adult education, and the importance attached to it by institutions. Regarding this aspect, literacy and adult education programs like the P.E.A. program, inspired by Paulo Freire's ideas, consider dialogue to be the axis that articulates most educational practices. Among the main goals of the P.E.A. program's Curricular Design, we find the 'development of the spirit of tolerance and solidarity' for which it is necessary that '... schools of adult education be places of encounter, coexistence and interpersonal relationships' (Curricular Design of Adult Education, 1988, 20). Later on, describing the first cycle of Initial Literacy, it proposes as an objective 'to work on the acquisition of better mechanisms of oral and written expression, always starting from half-organized dialogue as a fundamental way of exchanging experience and knowledge' (op. cit., 47). The combination of both objectives, the more general one, referring to adult education as a whole, and the more particular one, centred on literacy, gives us an overview of the importance of dialogue in the setting of educational practices. For a better development of oral and written expression, promoting dialogue is recommended. At the same time, dialogue should be the direct consequence of a school intended to provide a place of encounter and coexistence looking towards the development of a spirit of tolerance and solidarity that should characterize a democratic society.

This institutional proposal has been assumed by teachers of adults who consider debates to be one of the main teaching-learning tools which they often promote. They utilize these practices not just to extract new topics and/or to generate words, detect ideas or contradictions, and develop oral expression as a base for written understanding, etc., but they also use them to stimulate the development of moral criteria of tolerance and solidarity and encourage group cohesion. These debates deal with everyday problems facing the students attending the adult school, mainly women, and they provide an ideal context for conversation and expression of opinions for people who do not normally have much access to public settings where they can set out their ideas or problems; they provide a setting for social relationships, as stated above, and in many cases for the account of their own experiences. Common topics in these debates include: unemployment (in many cases affecting their husbands), their children's education, drugs, health education, etc. In this sense, there are many characteristics in common with the El Barrio Popular Education Program developed in New York with Puerto Rican women (Torruellas, Benmayor, Goris, Juarbe 1991; Benmayor 1991) even though it is not the same case because our women do not constitute such a marginal group.

These debates may include a wide range of structures and participation depending on the educational level, the rate of formalization and the activity in which it is set.

Occasionally it occurs spontaneously, although sometimes it is pro-posed by the teacher as a more formalized activity. Once the dialogue has begun, the teacher's level of participation and role varies depending on personal style, although we found one function common to practically all teachers: giving each student a turn to talk, and re-establishing dialogue if, for any reason, it breaks down.

These practices became important in all the sectors (institution, teachers and students) and therefore they became so widely used in the adult school. In our ethnographic study we observed the patterns of these debates at all educational levels (literacy to graduate), in the development of different school tasks (reading, handiwork), in the treatment of very diverse subjects (language or history) or constituting itself in more or less formalized specific activities (debate about problems facing the adult school). Obviously, in each situation and educational level, the conversation had specific characteristics and the performance of the participants was different.

To us, as researchers, the debate has a special psychological significance precisely because of its marked interactive nature. This character makes it an important tool for the learning of school subjects and social and com-municative skills. The debate requires and permits exposition, conflict and negotiation of information and points of view, involving an effort on behalf of the participants to create shared realities. It permits access to new ideas, the search for agreements, the possibility of arguing and counterarguing in order to give one's own opinions, aspects that finally give the individual a new way of understanding her reality, that give her a new way of relating to her physical and social environment. Following Billig, who again takes up the connection that rhetorical theorists had already established between thinking and arguing, we understand that 'the structure of the way we argue reveals the structure of our thought' (1986, 111). In the process of deliberation, we use the same argument that we employ when we try to persuade others. This way, thinking should possess a dialogic character. 'Learning to argue may be a crucial phase in learning to think' (1986, 111).

Since negotiation in an interpsychological plane is explicit, debate facilitates the observation of the process of interiorization or the individual appropriation of ways of argumentation and reflection that are initially found on a social plan. So the debate gives us a setting to study how the acquisition and mastering of new forms of thought and of new speech genres that formal education privileges are produced.

Method

Subjects

The subjects were 16 women in an adult education program: Eight women from the beginner level and the other eight from the advanced level. The women from the beginner level were attending their first year of schooling. They were learning how to read and write. Women from the other level had almost finished their studies which lead up to an elementary school certificate.

Design

The design of the debates was organized taking into account a previous ethnographic study which consisted in the observation and registration on videotape of the educational activities of two adults schools located in Andalusia (in the South of Spain). One of these centres was found in a peripheral neighbourhood of an important city, Seville. The other was a school located in a small town next to this city. The data collection was accomplished using the participating observation technique, the researchers acting as assistants to the teachers. They observed the educational activities (formal as well as informal) during an academic year, three days each week. A selection of the video-recordings was commented on and analyzed jointly by the researchers and teachers. At these meetings the teachers would interpret their own, and the students', behaviour by explaining the motives, objectives and expectations of various school tasks.

The women were divided into two groups. Each group was made up of a teacher and eight students. Both started with a short video recording that presented two different opinions about the topic of discussion. One of them supported a view of equality between women and men, while the other supported inequality between women and men. Debates were focused on two different topics: women's work and children's education, and were both audio and video recorded.

Analysis Categories: Forms of Discourse

With these categories, we intended to translate the notion of the decontextualization of mediational means. The unit of analysis was the utterance. Three categories were used:

1) *General*: Some argument referring to a general case was formulated. No reference was made to a concrete situation nor to a particular indi-vidual. The argument was related to a group of persons (women, mothers, men, etc.) or to a general category. In case it was formulated in terms of a particular situation, this situation did not correspond to any specific person, but was used as an example (hypothetical situations, for instance). In this case, students usually spoke about abstract concepts, like education, responsibilities, etc.

2) *Contextual*: A particular situation is presented. The student speaks about her own case or about the situation of relatives or friends.

3) *Mixed*: Both previous ways of discourse appeared in the same utterance. This kind of utterance might start by presenting a general problem and proceed by presenting some particular situation or vice versa.

Results and Discussion

The analysis carried out on discourse employed in the debates showed that the educational level has a strong influence on the forms of debating (see Table 3.1 and Fig. 3.1) In general terms, we have found two different forms of debating that are associated to the different educational levels studied.

	Beginners		Advanced		X^2	Prob.
	Frq.	Pct.	Frq.	Pct.		
Contextual	183	63.3	92	40.0		
Mixed	29	10.0	34	14.8	25,675	0.0001
General	77	26.6	104	45.2		

Table 3.1. Comparison of the influence of educational level on the form of debating.

In the *beginners'* group, the interventions are marked by their use of narrative structures in order to argue in the debate. For the most part, the argumentation consists of narrating a story, either about oneself or others, some facts are given, and then some sort of judgement, not necessarily explicit, is made. An example of this type of utterance is:

Subject 1: My husband helps me a lot. Now he doesn't help me so much because he is not at home, but my husband, ... the weekends I am not at home..., because I have to go to work, if I have to clean up he helps me.

Subject 2: I have a friend, whose husband works in the post office ..., well, she is not a friend of mine, she is friend of my daughter, but that doesn't matter, and when her husband comes home is when they begin to bathe the boy, and when... and she waits until her husband comes home. They share everything.

As can be seen, these utterances refer to the speaker's everyday existence. The content of this type of utterance is situational rather than abstract. It belongs to the field of the daily experience and where subjects introduce the perspective from which their own experience is derived.

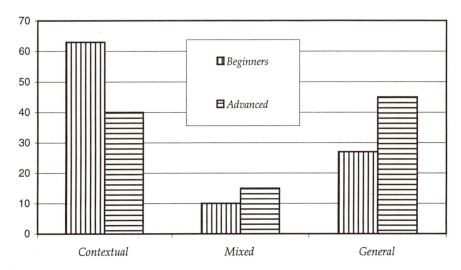

Fig. 3.1. Analysis on Discourse in Debates.

So, this way of argumentation is characterized by the use of contextualized signs that refer to objects or concrete events extracted from the ordinary experience of the speaker. They often concern people and situations that come directly from the daily life of the student who argues — my husband helps me; or to stories that have been told to them where real and recognized people are involved — a friend, whose husband works in the post office ..., well, she is not friend of mine, she is friend of my daughter. As can be observed in the table, this type of utterance constitutes 63.3% of the total utterances used during the debates by the students of this educational level.

A different pattern appears in the debates at the more advanced level. *Advanced* students more frequently use a discourse mediated by decontextualized signs where causal relationships frequently appear between the events or facts that are brought into the rhetorical action. So at this level, the following type of utterances were observed:

Subject 3: I believe that children are educated to be independent from the beginning. Today, you see housewives who have their children doing the washing up, that is they are educated in a way to prepare them for the future.

Subject 4: I think that if a woman feels satisfied with her home and with her children, then that is fine. But I believe that every person should fulfil his/her aims and woman's aims do not just have to involve having children and running the house. Because there are a lot of women who die with an idea in their head and they can't get it. If you are happy and satisfied, then OK, go on! But if not, you should not keep your desires to yourself. It is not right that a man fulfils his desires while the woman has to stay at home taking care of the children.

Here we have utterances where the use of decontextualized signs is predominant. In this case, the strength of the argumentation does not lie, as in the previous examples, in the verisimilitude of the story told, but in the capacity for describing a situation in a generic way — *now you see housewives ...* — and for establishing the chain of acts and circumstances that have generated it. These argumentations are emitted more frequently than in the beginner groups due to the establishment of causal relationships between these decontextualized signs or hypothetical formulations where they meditate on generic situations that may be totally unrelated to the life and daily experiences of the women taking part in the debate. As could be observed in the table, this type of utterance was more frequent in the advanced group and they constituted 45.2% of the total utterances made by these subjects.

Although the data referred to showed clear differences in the way of debating between the two groups of students, two data must be underlined. First, it must be said that these ways of debating were not the only ones used on the two educational levels. The beginner subjects, although less, also used decontextualized utterances (26.6%), although it must be pointed out that on numerous occasions these utterances come as a result of generic statements of an institutional character and clearly socially acceptable — *men and women are equal under the law*. More significant is the fact that the advanced subjects often used particular utterances in order to argue. In fact these types of utterances were almost as frequent as the decontextualized ones (40.0%).

So, we are not trying to state that once they have mastered these new forms of discourse, they abandon the former ones. These data indicate that the school does not substitute one form of discourse for another. Different forms of discourse can coexist and the subject will select them depending on the situation.

The second relevant datum is related to mixed utterances, in other words, with those utterances that combine the use of generic statements based on decontextualized signs with references to the particular experience of the subject who is talking. These utterances, although few in number (12.1%), provide us with data that allow us to look further into previously developed ideas. The interesting aspect of these utterances lies in the fact that they show us forms of stereotyped transition allowing us to tie the particular discourse, typical of the beginner level, to the decontextualized discourse, more characteristic of the subjects from the advanced level.

We found utterances where an attempt at generalization exists, where the subjects go beyond their own specific situation to affirm something that ties in with a group of situations. However, the way of justifying this statement is through their own personal situation. In the following, we give an example of this type of utterance.

Subject 5: I see a woman who gets married, her children are educated better with her than when she is out working. I can see it. Look at my granddaughters ... I can distinguish between my granddaughter who has her mother at home and the other who doesn't, who has been with me. And they are completely different.

In these cases, as in the particular utterances, the strength of argumentative rhetoric lies in the ability to introduce a credible story. If the story is credible and real, the generic part of the utterance acquires a normative value. Otherwise this type of argumentation can be clearly refuted using a story that contradicts the story that supports the rhetorical strength of the utterance.

As we can see, this type of argumentation is not accepted in the school setting. Only on very rare occasions would we consider our students' interventions acceptable if they tried to establish a general statement in science based only on the credible experience of the student — i.e.,

when I am going to buy food I never make a list putting the things that I have to buy into order and I never forget them, so the organization of information is not important in the way memory works.

A radically different case are those utterances that formulate a general norm. They are illustrated or paraphrased through examples extracted from the daily experience of the subject:

Subject 6: I think that men must collaborate at home regardless of whether they are accustomed to it or not. Take me for example, if my husband doesn't help I wouldn't like it, because he has his job, all right, but when he gets home he has finished his work and the woman never finishes. Even at night you have to take care of the children if they are ill. However your husband goes to bed and sleeps very well. So, what I mean is that it is a question of men's conscience.

In this case the particular part of the discourse is not the one which supports the argumentative strength of the utterance. This is only a paraphrase of the part of the utterance formulated in decontextualized terms, that is the one which really supports the rhetorical strength. Unlike the previous case, this type of utterance is totally acceptable at school. Teachers frequently utilize this type of utterance to improve the rhetorical strength of their discourse. The organization of information plays an important role in memory. For example,

when I am going to buy something most times I write down an organized list of the things that I want to buy in order to be sure that I do not forget anything and I think that this is a very good strategy to remember.

The constituent elements of both types of utterances are the same, although we are clearly dealing with different forms of discourse. In the first type, it is the particular and daily experience of the speaker which constitutes the rhetorical axis. In the second type, it is the formulation of a law or norm in decontextualized terms that makes it more difficult to challenge and which constitutes the foundation of the speaker's argumentation.

Due to the scarcity of these utterances we did not carry out a statistical analysis on their frequency of appearance; however a general tendency could be observed. We found that the first type of mixed utterances appeared more frequently in the beginners group, whereas the second type was more frequent in the advanced group.

Analysis of the different kinds of utterances gives us data in the sense that schooling influences the development of the types of discourse used by the student. As we pointed out before, these data seem to support the hypothesis that suggests that schooling promotes the development of speech genres that we can include under the general term of decontextualized rationality. The frequent use of terms like 'men' or 'women' in the utterances of advanced students when referring to individuals contrasts with the use of terms like 'my husband' or 'my granddaughter' in the case of beginner students. The first type of term allows a great variety of objects, events and particular experiences to be included under the same label. They allow the categorizing of the objects and events we referred to, and their use as an abstract entity that possesses the capacity of representing a wide variety of particular situations. The use of these signs is indicative of a way of thinking identified as decontextualized. In the second type of signs this generalization is not produced. They refer to clearly identifiable objects or events within the speaker's particular experience. They are more clearly associated to contextualized thinking.

But our data not only suggest this preference in the use of one sign or another. Even the way of constructing arguments also clearly shows the influence of the school setting. The construction of arguments moves between particularization and categorization. We saw how argumentations constructed with the almost exclusive use of decontextualized signs were frequent in the advanced group. Their statements as well as their justifications moved in the area that we have identified as decontextualized rationality. In the other group, we found a type of utterance in which statements and justifications are built on a particular plane. In both cases the strength of the argument lies in a different dimension. While in the first one the rhetorical strength of the argument is based on the speaker's capacity for establishing connections between the decontextualized signs employed, in the second one this strength resides in the speaker's capacity for constructing a likely story with which the listener could identify.

These ways of arguing only represent the two extreme points in a continuous line linking particularization and categorization. Utterances that have been coded as mixed are placed in intermediate positions. As mentioned above, these utterances are characterized because they encapsulated this tension between particularization and categorization. This tension is settled in different ways depending on the educational level. The mixed utterances used in the advanced group incorporate particular elements as illustrative examples, and allow better apprehension of the generic statements established in them, achieving the justification that is established primarily through the mechanisms of the decontextualized rationality. In the case of the beginners group, the generalization included acquires its value by being directly derived from a particular justification. It is the verisimilitude of this justification that gives the value to the generic statement.

Our data show an evident influence of the process of literacy on the way students debate. These changes seem to be articulated with regard to two types of acquisitions. On the one hand, subjects are able to use more decontextualized signs as they feel more confident in the school setting. On the other hand, this experience promotes changes in the argumentation structure. The conjunction of these elements lies in the change in the modes of thinking associated with the process of becoming literate. This influence is exercised through the student's mastering of new mediational means. However, the fact that some types of signs or arguments are not used at a given educational level does not imply that the schooling process has substituted old ways of thinking for new ones.

Final Remarks

To summarize the main goals of our study, it is important to indicate that it has been situated historically in the frame of a long tradition started by Luria and Vygotsky in the expedition to Uzbekistan (1931-32) and continued by Scribner and Cole in the late seventies in Liberia. If the first one permits us to make inferences about the role of literacy and schooling in the promotion of use of decontextualized signs and the development of advanced cognitive functioning, the second one points out that all those transformations are possible when literacy is connected with formal education. So, when writing is acquired in non-formal contexts — consequently out of schooling — cognitive processes remain at a rudimentary level of functioning.

In this study we try to advance in a socio- or historic-cultural way of research adopting a complementary rhetorical approach. If the first approach, in a very general sense, has considered the relation between signs and higher mental functions, the rhetorical perspective would be oriented in a more pragmatic way of connecting signs and modes of argumentation, a form of reasoning in a social context. So, we attempt to analyze the relation between the complex literacy-education and the development of argumentation framed in the debate, a particular form of dialogue that is a crucial element for the praxis and theory of deliberative rhetoric. The findings of this study led us to infer which school activities of adult education privilege the development of discourse genres oriented towards the categorization, since it must be performed using decontextualized signs. However, the appearance of this kind of genres does not inhibit the use of other genres more contextualized and centred in the particularization. On the contrary, both of these forms of discourse are combined by speakers in the course of debates.

This research makes us conclude that advanced students of the adult education program use decontextualized forms of discourse more frequently than beginners do. The last ones express themselves in a more particular and contextualized way. Finally, we infer that research in Adult Education opens new ways of gaining insight into the cultural transformation promoted by schooling and literacy, and the capability of schooling and literacy to develop new modes of verbal thinking.

References

Bakthin, M.M. (1986). *Speech genres and other late essays*. Austin: University of Texas Press.

Benmayor, R. (1991). Testimony, action research, and empowerment: Puerto Rican women and popular education. In S.B. Gluck & D. Patai (eds.), *Women's words. The feminist practice of oral history*. New York: Routledge.

Billig, M. (1987). *Arguing and thinking. A rhetorical approach to social psychology*. Cambridge: Cambridge University Press.

Cala, M.J. (1990). *El Programa de Educación de Adultos y el papel social de la mujer: un estudio sobre valores, actitudes y modos de pensamiento*. [Adult education program and women's social roles: A study of values, attitudes and ways of thinking]. (Memoria de investigación. Proyecto subvencionado por el Instituto Andaluz de la Mujer, convocatoria 1989).

Cala, M.J., de la Mata, M.L. & Sanchez, J.A. (1994). Attitudes and values in women: An investigation into discourse in adult education. In J.V. Wertsch & J.D. Ramirez (eds.), *Explorations in socio-cultural studies: Vol. 2. Literacy and other forms of mediated actions*. Madrid: Fundación Infancia y Aprendizaje.

Cook-Gumperz, J. (1986). *The social construction of literacy*. Cambridge, Mass.: Cambridge University Press.

Freire, P. (1970). *Pedagogia del oprimido* [The pedagogy of the oppressed. New York: Seabury, 1968]. Madrid: Siglo Veintiuno. (Original work published in 1968).

Laboratorio de Actividad Humana (L.A.H.) (1993). La educación de adultos y el cambio de valores, actitudes y modos de pensamiento en la mujer: Un estudio etnografico del discurso [Adult education and change of women's values, attitudes and ways of thinking: An ethnographic study of discourse]. (Memoria de Investigación. Proyecto subvencionado por el C.I.D.E. — M.E.C. — en el Concurso Nacional de Proyectos de Investigación Educativa). Unpublished manuscript.

Langer, J.A. (1987). A sociocognitive perspective of literacy. In J.A. Langer (ed.), *Language, literacy and culture: Issues of society and schooling*. Norwood, N.J.: Ablex.

Leontiev, A.N. (1981a). *Problems of the development of mind*. Moscow: Moscow State University.

Leontiev, A.N. (1981b). The problem of activity in Psychology. In J.V. Wertsch (ed.), *The concept of activity in Soviet Psychology*. Armonk, N.Y.: Sharpe.

Luria, A.R. (1975). *Cognitive development: Its cultural and social foundations*. Cambridge, Mass.: Harvard University Press.

Mehan, H. (1979). *Learning lessons: Social organization in the classroom*. Cambridge, Mass.: Harvard University Press.

Ramirez, J.D. (1992). Texto y dialogo en el aprendizaje lecto-escritor: Nuevas perspectivas en el estudio de la alfabetización de adultos [Text and dialogue in learning how to read and write: New perspectives in the study of literacy in adults]. *Infancia y Aprendizaje* 59/60, 73-86.

Ramirez, J.D., Sanchez, J.A. & Santamaria, A. (1996). Making literacy: A dialogical perspective on discourse in adult education. In J. Valsiner & H-G. Voss (eds.), *The structure of learning processes*. Norwood, N.J.: Ablex.

Rommetveit, R. (1979). Language games, syntactic structure and hermeneutics: In search of a preface to a conceptual framework for research on language and human communication. In R. Rommetveit & R.M. Blakar (eds.), *Studies of language, thought and verbal communication*. London: Academic Press.

Scribner, S. & Cole, M. (1981). *The Psychology of Literacy*. Cambridge, Mass.: Harvard University Press.

Snow C.E. & Dickinson, D.K. (1991). Skills that aren't basic in a new conception of literacy. In A. Purves & T. Jennings (eds.), *Literate systems and individual lives*. New York: Sunny Press.

Torruellas, R.M., Benmayor, R., Goris, A. & Juarbe, A. (1991). Affirming cultural citizenship in the Puerto Rican community: The El Barrio popular education program. In C.E. Walsh (ed.), *Literacy as Praxis: Culture, language and pedagogy*. Norwood, N.J.: Ablex.

Tulviste, P. (1986). *The cultural-historical development of verbal thinking*. New York: Nova Science Publisher.

Vygotsky, L.S. (1962). *Thought and language*. Cambridge, Mass.: MIT Press.

Vygotsky, L.S. (1978). *Mind in society: The development of higher psychological processes*. M. Cole, V. John-Steiner, S. Scribner & E. Souberman (eds.). Cambridge, Mass.: Harvard University Press.

Wertsch, J.V. (1985). *Vygotsky and the social formation of mind*. Cambridge, Mass.: Harvard University Press.

Wertsch, J.V. (1987). Modes of discourse in the nuclear arms debate. *Current research on peace and violence*, 2-3.

Wertsch, J.V. & Minick, N. (1990). Negotiating sense in the zone of proximal development. In M. Schwebel, C.A. Harer & N.S. Fagley (eds.), *Promoting cognitive growth over the life span*. Hillsdale, N.J.: Erlbaum.

Wertsch, J.V. (1990). The voice of rationality in a sociocultural approach to mind. In L.C. Moll (ed.), *Vygotsky and Education*. Cambridge, Mass.: Harvard University Press.

Wertsch, J.V. (1991). *Voices of the Mind: A Sociocultural Approach to Mediated Action*. Cambridge, Mass.: Harvard University Press.

4   Activity Theory as Methodology: The Epistemological Revolution of the Computer and the Problem of its Societal Appropriation[*]

Bernd Fichtner

Introduction

Beginning in the 1430's Johannes Gutenberg worked on the technical realization of the distribution of written information. Twenty years later the technology had matured and an effective working organization came into practice. The printing press could begin its triumphal procession. Fifty years after its invention, eight million books had already been printed and over 1100 printing shops, where several presses were used, existed in more than two hundred and fifty different locations in Europe. The printing press had developed from a practical means for coming to grips with the great bulk of written material to a very necessary technology without which science, administration, organization of production and commerce would have been as unimaginable as the realization of the cultural ideals and those of the educational policies of that era (cf. Giesecke 1991, 63ff.).

But the printing press was neither a neutral medium nor simply the technological basis for communication and the processing of data. Rather, from the beginning it functioned as a processor of a fundamental transformation of knowledge and its social functions. At the outset this manifests itself in the development of the autonomy of knowledge. The coding, standardizing, and classifying methods brought into existence by typography contribute to the development of knowledge as an independent social reality. Knowledge becomes a text which appears as the autonomous representation of knowledge. But exactly the manifold methods of coding, standardizing, and classifying make possible a formerly unknown development and transformation of knowledge, its *dynamism*. Tables, diagrams,

---

[*]   Translated by Thomas La Presti, University of Siegen.

illustrations, and maps allow the discovery of contradictions, the formulation of relationships, the use of supplementary information and alterations, and the corrections of imprecision or mistakes. Finally, typography allows the role of intellectual devices (instruments of navigators, astronomers, surveyors, etc.) to become more apparent since they can now be presented as a *total system*.

If the printing press has, above all, modified the relationship of man to knowledge and thus the conception of knowledge in society, there is some indication that, at the present time, a similar revolution is taking place in a similarly intrinsically social way as in the 15th and 16th centuries. There is also some indication that we encounter the present social implementation with the same sort of blindness and with similar wishes and fears as did the social communities of the 15th and 16th centuries — an attitude which is a hindrance to an adequate understanding.

This is quite evident from the discussion about the New Technology in educational science. Aside from the arguments of a number of proponents which are often characterized by naive fascination, positions expressing a critique of culture prevail in educational science. The core of this criticism is composed of three arguments: synthetic or potential reality replaces reality; this promotes emotionally direct ways of confronting reality while impeding rational, more reserved ones; finally, it destroys the 'literateness' of classical western education (Raeithel & Volpert 1985). On the other hand, J.-F. Lyotard, one of the protagonists of postmodernism, discusses a perspective related to the transformation of knowledge and to the problematic of the concept of the subject. He argues that knowledge has fundamentally modified its statute since the end of the 1950's, the end of the phase of reconstruction in Europe. Furthermore, he suggests that with the New Technology only that knowledge is processed which is transferable into information quantities and thus leads to a pronounced externalization of knowledge in reference to the person possessing this knowledge as well as to that person's economization. At the same time, according to Lyotard, it becomes apparent that the subject himself is only to be considered as a product of production and not as its producer (Lyotard 1986).

Thus, the relationship of the transformations of knowledge and of the subject concept become the central problem within the discourse of postmodernism: 'The old principle that the acquisition of knowledge is indissociable from the formation (Bildung) of minds, or even of individuals, is becoming obsolete and will become even more so. (...) Knowledge is and will be produced in order to be sold, it is and will be consumed in order to be valorized in a new production: in both cases, the goal is exchange. Knowledge ceases to be an end in itself, it loses its 'use-value'. (Lyotard 1986, 24f.)

Lyotard describes the transformation of knowledge as an inner 'crisis of knowledge', as the deterioration of science as a form of communication, which results in the disintegration of philosophy of history with its concept of progress and in the abandonment of the concept of the subject. Like Lyotard, we are also interested in the transformation of knowledge, but above all as the transformation of its social functions and the transformation of the concept of the subject, not as the abandonment of the latter.

My main argument is as follows: Similar to the printing press, the computer is to be understood as the processor of an extensive thrust in modernization and civilization which, above all, will effect a transformation of knowledge and its social functions and will result in a new notion of the subject.

Regardless of how this thrust in modernization and civilization might be described in detail, it is evident that it has, and will continue to have, profound effects on education as a form of social practice. At present, these transformations are primarily being discussed as a crisis of public instruction and the promotion of personal development. But we wish to consider the possible perspectives of the origin and development of something new which could be involved in this matter.

The Computer as Processor of Knowledge Transformation

The systematic combination of formerly separated communicative techniques (print media, telephone, radio, television, teleprinter) to automatic data processing in electronic computers is usually considered to be the decisive qualitative leap ahead manifested in the New Technology. With this development, formerly unknown possibilities of the establishment of a technical network involving persons and groups have come into existence, as well as fully novel possibilities for the simulation of various aspects of reality. From this viewpoint, the effects of the New Technology are described as a continuous intensification, formalization, and standardization of social and personal communication and are evaluated in a widely divergent manner.

Rather than using this approach, I would like to take up a discussion of the computer as a 'symbol machine' and thus as a means of making new possibilities available to knowledge and various forms of practice. Here, knowledge is not understood as an internal psychological reality, as cognition, but as an epistemological and social reality. In contrast to a psychological one, this discussion proceeds from an *epistemological concep-tion of knowledge* which allows the analysis of problems of the social application of knowledge. The following aspects of this discussion are significant for our treatment of the question:

– Every epoch or culture develops an implicit world view and self-concept which is based upon a particular conception of reality. The reality of knowledge is constituted within this context.
– Knowledge is a result of concrete (i.e., social-historical) human vital activity and exists only within these relationships. Knowledge is itself to be understood as a social relationship and not as some factor *supplementary* to social relationships.
– The entirety of man-made devices is to be comprehended as a system of objectified forms of knowledge detached from man. Subjective forms of knowledge such as perception, emotion, etc. can, on the contrary, not be separated from the persons involved. Both forms of knowledge must be understood in reference to their social character (Fichtner 1996).

I consider a thrust in the theorization of knowledge to be the primary instance of the new possibilities and dimensions which the computer as a symbol machine makes available to knowledge and the various forms of practice (Otte 1985). This means that knowledge is not becoming more and more abstract, but more and more universal. To express this point in a figurative manner: knowledge is becoming less and less a place to linger and more and more like a door one goes through without knowing exactly where it leads.[1]

Common sense presupposes that knowledge results from a quite direct description of the particular scope of reality and experience. Thus, common sense believes in a fixed relation between the form of presentation and meaning. By contrast, theorizing knowledge means that knowledge exists

1. Knowledge can be considered more and more as an open resource to which meaning and content are attributed only within the realm of its social application. If knowledge and theories are considered as means, one can agree with Bateson that 'we are more concerned with the "directions" and "values" inherent in the means than with aiming at a planned goal and thinking that this goal justifies or does not justify manipulative means' (Bateson 1983, 221; my translation).

primarily as a form, as a coherent relationship among formal elements. Considering knowledge more and more as a formal and structural relationship also means that its contents, its meaning, are not immediately apparent; only by the 'application' of this formal aspect in the broadest sense can the contents be developed. Only when mediated by way of this formal aspect can knowledge be related to reality.[2]

With respect to knowledge the computer is, on the one hand, a means of theoretical reflection. It promotes the tendency of the theoretical to become more and more an autonomous reality. On the other hand, the computer is a means of a formerly unknown extension of the scope of application for knowledge. Thus, in addition to the independence of the theoretical, that of the practical, of the applications, of the effective operations also acquires totally new qualities from the computer's possibilities of simulation. M. Otte (1985) suggests that, in a way, the computer can help to overcome the alienation between theory and practice by making the distinctive features of theory and practice vivid and more self-evident.

The Computer: A Universal Machine

Up to this point I have been describing the transformations of knowledge and of its social functions brought about by the computer. Now I would like to discuss the computer as a device and the social forms of the application of this device. The computer is comprehended in an incomplete manner if it is only considered as a means in itself and positive or negative effects are ascribed to it in an objectivist way, whereby the social forms of its application are ignored. The great variety of these forms can only be alluded to here. For production, service, and administration, the computer and its new technology have become an unquestioned and inevitable fundamental. Within the range of social intercourse it is causing continuously increasing intensification, formalization, and standardization of social and personal communication. The systematization of formerly separated communication techniques results in a more and more pronounced technical interconnection of all spheres of life — a phenomenon which is described as 'telematics' (Nora & Minc 1979).

The computer is, however, not only a *constructive* device, but also a particularly *projective* one. It is not only the result of our behaviour and thought, but also modifies these in a fundamental manner. In an ethno-

---

2. The mathematical concepts of fractal geometry and their application in chaos research verify this in a variety of ways. Cf. Mandelbrot 1977.

logical study about the origin of the computer culture, S. Turkle (1984) explains how we are forced to fundamentally modify our conception of ourselves.

The universal machine of our times does not only 'work' in the sphere of production, but also, as mentioned above, in all the spheres of social life. This means that this machine is effecting a comprehensive socialization thrust in which people are becoming more and more dependent on one another. N. Elias calls this intertwining of dependencies 'figuration' and, with this term, means the cooperative social patterns which as a system of social forms in every society constitutes the whole-scale societal mode of communication (Elias 1976, vol. 1, p. LXVII). At the present time, not only production, but also the production of the *coherence* of society, the whole-scale societal mode of communication is being modified by the computer.

I assume that thus our concept of ourselves as a subject will alter fundamentally. Computers as symbol machines allow us to observe our cognition itself or, more exactly, its algorithmic segment, in symbolic processes.[3] In doing so, the symbol machines call our attention to the fact that our understanding of our active cognition is still very inadequate. Every action which can be described by an algorithm can also be carried out by a machine or, to put it another way, every algorithm is a machine (Otte 1984; Raeithel 1985).

New perspectives of the machine-like aspects of man result from this trans-classical concept of a machine which is no longer related to a particular exterior appearance of the machine — primarily perspectives of machine-like aspects in spheres which formerly represented the actual subjective qualities such as consciousness, cognition, language, etc. (Turkle 1984, 333ff.). This already indicates that not the *concept of the subject altogether*, but, rather, the *traditional philosophical subject concept of German idealism*, which is associated with the self-consciousness of an ego and its self-certainty, becomes obsolete (Lektorsky 1985, 119-66).

Thus, it becomes apparent to what extent the computer presently functions as a processor which offers a formerly unknown variety of relationships to reality and at the same time is the clamp which holds this variety together. Making this assertion does not, however, already entail a statement about the profit and loss balance involved.[4] With reference to the various levels and social forms of application the computer can be

3. Mathematically speaking, an algorithm is a procedure by which output data are drawn from input data of a specified area in an exactly prescribed manner (cf. Kondakov 1978, 22ff.).

considered to be the epitome of a *universal machine*. The universality of this machine is constituted by the fact that it is not applied in a specified sphere, as is, e.g., typography, but, rather, functions as a new device horizontally and vertically in all social spheres. In doing so, it connects all of these spheres, permeates them, and unifies them. The consequences of this universalization remain inestimable at the present stage.

The Societal Appropriation of the Computer
— Activity Theory as Methodology

Apparently, the point at which the potential possibilities and particular dangers of the computer as a universal machine, as a functionally controllable device for our social thought, action, and planning, has already been comprehended and actually socially appropriated, is still quite remote. The 'societal appropriation' of this device is one of the pressing key problems of our times. But what is meant by societal appropriation?

By societal appropriation I do not simply mean the organized development of individual abilities to deal with the possibilities of this device in a technically adequate way. Nor does societal appropriation mean dealing with the many-facetted, media-related didactic problems concerning this device which arise at school, in the course of instruction, or under other circumstances.

Societal appropriation of the 'universal machine' means the development of social patterns appropriate to the potential of this machine, the development of habitualizations, standardizations, as well as their preservation, reproduction, and transmission. Societal appropriation means a process by which we learn to consider the new technology as an essential part of ourselves, to integrate it consciously into our daily lives as our culture, and to develop and make use of it as a means of social self-direction.

I will attempt to approach the problem by drawing on the activity theory of the cultural history school as a methodological context. This school of thought is aimed at researching the connection between individual and social developments. In drawing on this context, I will be adopting the main line of inquiry of this school: 'How does that which is objectively socially new in human development originate?' (Engeström 1986, 160). The general answer to this question, which organizes the direction of the search, is: 'That which is new does not originate from the

---

4. So I do not agree with N. Postman's view that the 'power of technologies' is necessarily related to making society dependent once again (Postman 1992).

old, but from the vibrant movement which leads away from the old'
(Engeström 1986, 161).

In order to make these processes available to scientific investigation in
the first place, Engeström employs Vygotsky's concept of the 'zone of the
proximal development' and modifies it in its essential characteristics. For
Vygotsky, the 'zone of the proximal development' characterizes the social
nature of *individual* learning. It designates the direction of development and
describes the particular level of activity that an individual can only achieve
in cooperation with adults. With the aid of Bateson's 'learning levels' (1983,
219-40; 362-99) Engeström relates the concept of the 'zone of the proximal
development' to learning and developing processes of groups and communities and thus makes these processes available to empirical
investigation (Engeström 1987).

For Bateson 'learning level III' encompasses a level of learning and
development which is only rarely achieved by the *individual*. It necessitates
calling into question the context, the prerequisites of one's own structure,
and the premises of self-concept. Thus, the particular subject is exposed to
changes involving a number of conflicts and, in this way, fulfills the
conditions necessary for the formation of something new (1983, 392ff.).

The motivation for putting oneself into a situation promoting insecurity,
a situation that is threatening for the individual as well as for the collective
subject, originates from the intensification of the contradictions which
characterize the usual situation (Bateson 1983, 390ff.). Now, there are
various possibilities to evade these contradictions. Furthermore, contradictory situations do not at all necessarily bring about the development of
something new. That type of development which does produce something
new requires an intuitive or conscious control of the situation. For this to
occur, a transgression of the individual level of action is of the utmost
necessity: 'Human development is a dialectic union of the individual and
the social. It is real production of new social systems of action and not
simply the appropriation of individually new actions perhaps combined
with the individual production of original fragments of behaviour'
(Engeström 1986, 166).

The cultural history school considers activity to be something produced
by society in contrast to individual actions with their orientation to purposes (Leontiev 1982). Thus, the origin of a new social system of activity is
to be considered as the decisive process in the subjective development of
the subject. Here, the 'zone of the proximal development' is something like

the open dimension allowing for the formation of a new social system of activity:

We can now attempt a provisional re-formulation of the concept of the zone of the proximal development. It is the distance between the present daily actions of individuals and the historically new form of social activity, which can be collectively produced as the solution to potential double-bind situations in daily actions. (Engeström 1986, 166)

So, what follows from this discussion for our inquiry into the effects of the new universal device and the attempt of individuals to appropriate this device socially — in the form of 'conscious control of the situation'?

From our point of view, the societal appropriation of the computer as a universal device requires the construction of new social systems of activity. There is no such zone of the proximal development at the level of individual action.

The development of qualitatively new systems of activity can neither simply be derived from an extension of the everyday action of the individuals nor directly from a critique of the existing forms:

The zones of the collective level can be characterized as the distance between current everyday actions of the individuals and the historically new form of their social system of activity which can be produced collectively as a solution to the contradictions inherent in everyday actions. (Engeström & Cole 1991, 46).

Thus, all the suggestions for solutions to the problem which assume that a change in the school system can be derived from the phenomena of altered educational action in daily life seem to be naive. The everyday actions of individuals are contradictory and not very coherent. They do not indicate the direction the resolution of their contradictory nature could take.

One cannot invent new 'social activities'. Nor does it happen that they just occur to someone, and it is equally impossible to establish them in a normative manner, to postulate them or impose them by decree. They are quite literally worked out by society. They develop from the contradictions, oppositions, and conflicts within the cultural practices of a society. They are relevant to change in social relations which involves universal devices such as the written word or the computer.

We owe an informative suggestion to Karl Marx' theses on Feuerbach, a suggestion which was formulated in a more concrete manner in the later 'Grundrisse': Change in social relations, as Marx states here, is always accompanied at first by a consciousness of dissolution and decline, of pessimism and an apocalyptic mood. According to Marx, this stems from the circumstance that the strangeness and independence of the inception of something new still exists in opposition to individuals, even though they have actually created that which is new themselves:

It is equally certain that individuals cannot subordinate themselves to their own social relations before they have created them. But it is absurd to consider that material relation as indigenous, as inseparable from and immanent to the nature of individuality (as opposed to reflected knowledge and will). It is their product, an historical product. It forms a part of a particular phase of their development. The strangeness and independence by which it seems to exist in opposition to them is only proof of the fact that they are still engaged in the creation of the conditions of their social life instead of having begun this life, using these conditions as a starting point. (Marx 1953, 79)

From this perspective one could say that at present the process of appropriation of the computer as a universal device is advancing in a more natural way, i.e., on the level of individual human action. The appropriation of the computer is geared toward a simple, naively technical use of the device and toward its often brutal implementation in daily life without any reflection upon its consequences and effects.

   This implementation is accompanied by individual anxieties about the dissolution of traditional ways of life and the identity they guarantee. It is accompanied by a fear of the destruction of highly regarded elements of traditional culture and of the values associated with them. Former ways of life become fragile, contexts are changed, habits dissolved — all of this is experienced as a crisis and is reflected upon as a crisis.

   The results of current research on the structural transformation of childhood, youth, and schooling in Germany and other countries seem to indicate a fundamental change in the way internal and external coherence of our society is produced in the first place (cf. Bracht & Fichtner 1993). On the whole, an image of many-facetted, differentiated, and somewhat diffuse actions within these realms of practice is depicted, and in the process distinctive contradictions become evident:

1) Parents, educators, and nursery school teachers are all presently engaged in intensive work on the autonomization of individuals as a conscious, reflective self-relationship of the individual, as the development of a conscious self-concept. However, a contradiction arises

between this autonomization and pedagogization as an increasing structuration and control of youth's daily life with pedagogic intentions.

2) At the same time, the autonomization demonstrates the other side of the coin with its privatization and therapeutization in the sense of a concealment of systematic factors such as politics, society, and the external world.

3) It is accompanied by new dependencies such as alienation, mediatization and reification of human and social relationships. This is all contained within a social context that is characterized by sharp contradictions as, e.g., the individualization of life-styles combined, at the same time, with a social normalization, standardization, and conformism of behaviour never before observed.

I consider these contradictions to be an indication of insecure, groping, searching actions in the course of everyday life on the part of individuals and social groups, actions directed toward aligning oneself with some sort of 'compulsory modernization'. At the same time, it seems to me that exactly these contradictions also express something that reveals itself to be a process of the creation of something new.

If the assumption is correct that something new never originates organically or in continuation of, so to speak, as a prolongation of something old, but rather only as a result of a *dynamic*, i.e., always contradictory movement that leads away from that which is already extant, then one could inquire about the current processes in a totally different manner: Are they related to the social acquisition of new activities? Does this acquisition have a particular direction or perspective? If so, in what way is this relevant to developing the potential of our universal device? In the course of that process, how do individuals express themselves as subjects who — to connect the inquiry with Marx' perspective — are engaged in becoming the proprietors of their social relations?

The Societal Appropriation of the Universal Machine: A Perspective

Cultural scientists, semioticians, and cognitive theorists all agree that man can only develop new possibilities for action with symbolic representations (media of presentation, language, writing, formal sign systems of any type). If symbolic representations or signs in the broadest sense are not simply considered to be psychological, internal realities, but rather primarily social realities which exist 'between' persons, then they can be regarded as semiotic tools of the common social consciousness and of the social practice of these persons (cf. Vygotsky 1978). Then, the 'historic self-modification of human activity', as Marx discusses it in his Feuerbach theses, can be pursued consciously only by means of the communicative and collective reflection of these 'signs' as social patterns and structures of actions (cf. Raeithel 1992).

Where might there now be a perspective that, in its appropriation of the universal machine's potential, is directed toward developing new social activity systems? Suggestions for changing the educational and teaching practice at this or that point, for modifying one or the other aspect of schooling, do not seem to contain such a perspective. I suspect that this perspective is contained in the potential of the new device itself.

Among the earliest developments of writing systems we find the erect inscription, which then leaned over to the slanted handwriting on the desk-top and finally put itself into horizontal position in the letter-press. The computer has brought the characters back into vertical position. Users sit in front of 'typeface', of which the characters and their image become more and more similar. Thus, the importance of seeing comes to the fore in a most significant way if one considers seeing to be not simply perception, but rather a 'modeling conceptualization'.

Arne Raithel has directed attention to the fact that computers render procedures, that is, something that is strictly formal, conceivable (1985). On their monitors the 'universal machines' display moving views from formal worlds in process, which in former times were only accessible as ideas to humans engaged in deliberating or discussing something. Computers are devices that objectify formal procedures and that allow one to situate oneself in reference to such procedures, to examine them, and to reflect upon them.

Accordingly, the computer requires a type of seeing that is more than purely sensual perception. It requires a type of seeing as a *modeling* conceptualization (cf. Judin 1978) or, as mathematicians or natural scientists express it, as the representation of something 'qualitative' (e.g., with reference to chess: 'seeing' a good constellation). By means of this type of 'seeing' as a modeling conceptualization, the computer can become an enormously important tool of theoretical reflection (as, for instance, in fractal geometry). By the same token, this type of 'seeing' can allow the computer to become an instrument of a hitherto unknown expansion of the possibilities for the use of knowledge (as, for instance, in the area of computer simulation).

It appears to be a basic characteristic of any sort of human perception that its actualization has to do with something concretely real and at the same time imagined, and this in the sense of the complementariness of, on the one hand, taking and dealing with something directly, *literally*, *rigidly*, *operatively* and, on the other hand, of seeing something as something, taking and dealing with something *metaphorically*.

I would like to conclude by formulating the thesis that with regard to the societal appropriation of the computer an astonishing topicality and actuality will be assigned to art, that in particular avant-garde art provides an arsenal that will become more and more important for the societal appropriation of the universal machine.

One can consider art history to be a history concerned with the presentation of the human ability to see something as something, of the possibilities of seeing as 'modeling conceptualization', of seeing as 'representation of the qualitative'. Works of art are metaphors, concrete models, in which the competence to see something as something is crystallized. I call this competence a metaphorical one. We might say that in art and in works of art the metaphorical comes into its own.

However, this cannot be rendered comprehensible by means of a linguistic concept, but rather by means of an anthropological one like that developed by G. Bateson in his study 'Angels Fear. Toward an Epistemology of the Sacred' (1987). Metaphors are neither abnormal linguistic expressions to be understood in contrast to ordinary language, nor are they figurative meanings in contrast to literal ones. Nor are they illustrations, visualizations, or comparisons.

It is difficult to determine what metaphors are from a purely linguistic perspective because their linguistic form is only one possibility of their realization. Metaphors are not things, but, rather, systems of relationships.

A metaphor does not say: 'This is a tree' (a process of which the final result would be a concept). The metaphor says: 'The tree is a hero.' The metaphor says, 'A is B', which is not to be confused with 'A = B'. The metaphor says: 'This *is* that' and at the same time: 'This is *not* that'. It contends the validity of something and at the same time its invalidity. Gregory Bateson has very neatly worked out an explanation for this, maintaining that a pre-verbal logic is articulated in metaphorical competence — a logic of the type found in the grass metaphor: grass dies — humans die — humans are grass.

The logic of metaphors is amoral, non-temporal, and non-spatial. We find the following metaphor in a novel by the Portuguese writer Saramago: 'The moon, a silk sieve, strews a flour-like whiteness over the exhausted countryside'.[5] This metaphor is neither a comparison nor an illustration, nor does it demonstrate a similarity between the moon and a silk sieve. Here, Saramago calls to mind a variety of associations connected with sieve, silk, and flour. Anyone who attempts to understand this metaphor constructs a new meaning for the moon, dependent upon his own concrete, individual context. Here, the moon is perceived, imagined, or experienced from a certain perspective.

With a metaphor, a phenomenon, a process, or some sphere is perceived and structured along the pattern exhibited by something else. The tension between these spheres is not eliminated, but, rather, put to productive use. Metaphors are strictly complementary; they cultivate oppositions such as those between coherence and difference, cognition and emotion, image and concept, object and subject. Metaphors organize an extensively effective perspective on reality in such a way that it is never dissolved into a direct referential relationship. The development of this perspective is a subject's achievement which is brought about by means of the momentary realization of subjectivity.

Metaphors are an expression of a fundamental human capability to make oneself, human experience, and the world in which people live, understandable. This is achieved by producing relationships and contexts by means of metaphor in the first place. With metaphors, we construct imaginary conceptions as 'new images', as relationships between totally different spheres, phenomena, and processes. These relationships are of a systematic nature.

Metaphors are fundamental to the systematization of our experiences, but also to the alteration and restructuring of such a system. Metaphors can be highly innovative. The limits of a fixed experiential realm can be extended and a stereotype and automated relationship to reality can be broken down by means of metaphors. Metaphors do not alter reality, but they make its alteration possible.

Metaphors are like children. They affect their environment in a unique way. They are points of intersection, new relevant aspects of meaning that are oriented to the future.

---

5. Cf. Saramago, J.: *Das steinerne Floß*. Reinbek 1994, 344.

From a metaphor-related perspective, works of art are specific models, more precisely, models of types of perception, of modes of vision or seeing. In this sense, every work of art is a metaphor: a work of art presents something and at the same time a mode, a type, of its perception. This seemingly simple observation actually involves rather complicated problems. From Cézanne to the present, modern avant-garde art has repeatedly treated these problems as its own major concerns and worked on their exploration.

Around the middle of the last century, the possibility of constructing an eye external to the human body was realized for the first time — a possibility that had been subject to various attempts at realization since the invention of the *camera obscura* (Leonardo) in the Renaissance. As far as the fine arts of the 19th century are concerned, photography initiated an incredible revolution. Suddenly, art was relieved of the task of reproducing the dominant culture — in whatever form this might be done — and transmitting it to succeeding generations. But what task can be assigned to the arts if photography is able to represent any situation, any power relationship, any significant moment that should be preserved for posterity much more quickly and precisely?

The reproducible technical images aim at a 'visual image of the world' that is mediated by 'visual machines' which induce two-dimensional linear vision. But human vision is more diverse, more complicated, and less settling than photography. Human vision is always vision of a complex, non-linear world, a vision that implies approximations. If it is free, it never fails to question, to compare, and to do many similar things. By no means does human vision imply a mechanical reflection of reality, but rather the problem of constructing reality.

This is exactly the problem that is a central theme of Cézanne's work. Cézanne is concerned with the indivisibility of the objective and subjective dimensions of vision, with the indivisibility of the person who sees something and that which is seen. Such vision can never be passive; it is fundamentally a constructive act. Cézanne produces 'impossible pictures'. Similar to human vision, they contain numerous, simultaneously subjective and objective dimensions and perspectives. This implies much more than simply a formal aesthetic problem; it is an existential philosophical problem related to the cultural production of knowledge and, thus, to the historical and social development of mankind.

Practically every work that art historians have written on Cézanne contends that he was a genius. One could agree with this judgement, considering that he succeeded in breaking down the stereotype, canonized models of vision which are developed and established in any culture. In his own epoch, Cézanne's existence was only possible because he himself was an 'expression' of a society in a state of permanent change. His suggestions were accepted because the society had a need for them.

From Cézanne on, the fine arts demonstrate in all their various directions the possibilities of being abstract in a totally fundamental sense, of abstracting from reality and, at the same time, of being subjective. In 'Psychology of Art' (1925) Vygotsky describes this as a domain allowing for generalization, for a synthesis of knowledge about reality that, at the same time, offers the possibility to discuss and reflect upon one's own subjectivity.

At the beginning of the 20th century, the ways prepared by Cézanne very quickly became fixed clichés and trite formulas of such various 'isms' as expressionism, cubism, surrealism, and constructivism — especially when formal and technical problems were the sole considerations.

The work of M. Duchamp provides a response to this dilemma. Duchamp is confronted with a society that is in a particular situation: An industrial society is in the process of consolidating itself into a capitalistic society which, for the first time, develops the structures of a consumer society with its double-bind mechanisms. This society has just experienced the shock of the First World War and is confronted with the October Revolution and its attempt to develop a new society and new men, as well as with totally contradictory social and intellectual trends.[6] In the light of social changes which had never been known before in the entire history of mankind, this epoch forced the arts to reconsider their role in a fundamentally new way. How can art focus on a world so full of contradictions and how can this art refrain from simply providing new opportunities to ossify into stereotypes and formal clichés?

In 1912, Duchamp paints his last figurative picture, *Nude Descending a Staircase*, and in doing so terminates his career as an artist. From now on, he is engaged in a battle against the hitherto prevailing concept of the artist and of the work of art as an object.

His work treats topics ironically, disrupts contexts, ridicules, considers, reflects upon and reacts to the problems of capitalistic society and its form of consumer society with its fetish of objective scientific knowledge as a

6. Eric Hobsbawm has described these contradictions in his book *Age of Extremes. The Short Twentieth Century 1914-1991* (1994). He begins his survey with the role played by the arts and concludes his assessment of the century with the death of the avant-garde.

seemingly solid basis — at the same time, though, a society that is deeply chaotic and torn apart with its false images and appeals, with its pretended securities.

For him, indifference with regard to social and political events is the only form that prevents his being formalized in some movement or becoming absorbed in some 'ism'. He calls himself — in analogy to the term anarchist — an 'an-artist' and he conceives of his works as a revolt against mechanisms and power structures of the art market, against the consecration and mystification of the artist and of the work of art as an object.

Duchamp returns to the crucial questions posed by Cézanne and transforms them. Cézanne treats his central theme of human vision as a diverse unity of the subjective and the objective by dismantling the traditional form of presentation and by clearing the way for new possibilities of materializing or representing ways of seeing. Duchamp destroys all the traditional genres of the fine arts from the picture to the sculpture and replaces them with *thought* in the broadest sense as the basis of any representation of reality, which for him is representation of society.

His works are no longer objects, but rather radical devices that allow reality, as social reality, to be reconsidered. His works demonstrate a world of images that poses questions or is itself to be interrogated. His 'multiples', 'ready-mades', and 'semi-ready-mades' activate the metaphorical dimensions of words, concepts, and of our subjective relationships to objects. The metaphorical basic structure of his work is no longer dependent upon prescribed hierarchic meanings of a certain culture. In a very intensive way his works become devices by means of which reality and the relationships between its phenomena and processes can be imbued anew with meaning.

In the onlooker he provokes curiosity and a metaphorical competence which enables one to treat each work as a metaphor in which something is seen and dealt with as something. At the same time, these devices provoke the onlooker — if he/she allows him/herself to be affected by them — to reflect upon him/herself.

In exemplary fashion Cézanne and Duchamp personify basic tendencies of modern art. A systematic characterization of such tendencies would seem to be in order before I return to the problem of the societal appropriation of the computer as a universal device.

Modern art is neither didactic nor pedagogic, nor is it technical. It is a way of thinking — thinking of something that has thus far gone unsaid. It is something that is at the bottom of what has so far been said. Above all, modern art is ambiguous; it doesn't provide any answers or simple formulas. It doesn't declare what it knows, and is nonetheless a form of knowledge.

Modern art shows us something which is not understandable at first glance. It becomes totally incomprehensible if, in the attempt to understand, we turn not to ourselves but to others, to the experts, the critics, and the art historians. Understanding something new always implies a qualitative change. Understanding something new implies understanding the future, a projection of the present and the past into a time that has not yet been experienced.

Modern art teaches us that works of art are no objects to be mystified or consecrated, but are rather devices. But in contrast to all other devices developed by humans, these devices exhibit a special quality: They *mediate contexts and distance* at the same time. They are empirical, part of our concrete real world, and, at the same time, they are symbolic. They are of this world, yet, at the same time, they relate to us about this world. A work of art is fundamentally different from the reality to which it refers. At the same time, it is a comprehensive way of viewing this reality.

The avant-garde's excessive preoccupation with the forms of presentation teaches us that works of art are materializations of ways of seeing, i.e., that they have a metaphorical structure. This structure is to be found in the presentation or, more precisely, in the system of material forms of presentation.

With their materialization, ways of seeing, ways of perceiving provide possibilities to go beyond currently given conditions. But, at the same time, in every work of art something is taken literally as well as dealt with strictly, rigidly, and operatively. This is its mode of *presentation,* the system of its forms of presentation. The truth of a work of art does not consist in the content presented, but rather in the presentation. Primarily, a work of art is a formal, structural interrelationship; it is not a duplication of reality. Although it is a real object and thus a part of this reality, every work of art is, in principle, different from what we call reality.

The work of art represents a reality and with this presentation lets reality become something with which one is confronted. It is a highly astonishing device for creating a detached standpoint and at the same time establishing an interconnection to reality. It realizes this interrelationship as a model of a comprehensively effective way of seeing a reality. Thus, the work of art realizes interrelationship and detachment at once. In achieving this, the form, the system of forms, the mode of presentation occupies a key position. A work of art presents something and at the same time it demonstrates the way it presents something. This is exactly what is realized by its mode of presentation.

The greatness of a work of art might be seen in how successful it is in organizing and presenting its metaphor, its metaphorical structure. The metaphor is, as noted above, not to be localized within the content represented, but rather within the presentation itself.

Picasso considered his sculptures to be material metaphors. Instead of forming his figures from traditional materials such as clay or plaster of Paris, he made them primarily out of discarded junk like old vases, baskets, bicycle parts, and similar materials. By this means, his sculptures maintain a fascinating double orientation when, for example, instead of modeling the rib-cage of a goat out of clay, Picasso puts a wicker basket in the place where the ribs would be. In that case, this *is* a wicker basket that is to be seen as a rib-cage, and the reverse is also true, if one examines the entire figure of the goat one can see its ribs as a wicker basket. Thus, we find here a metaphor going in two directions. If the ribs were formed of clay, then the vision of the observer would only be guided in one direction: one would see formed clay as the rib-cage of a goat (cf. Aldrich 1983, 144-45). Picasso described this situation in a very appropriate way as follows:

I retrace the path from the basket to the rib-cage, from the metaphor to reality. I make reality visible because I make use of a metaphor. (Gilot & Lake 1964)

My argument has now come full circle. In art, that sovereignty could be found which is required in dealing with the computer, that sovereignty which would make its specific potential accessible. For in art, in the unlimitable variety of its languages, there is that sort of autonomy and independence of the formal which the computer requires and which make it so useful.

Here, art is not being considered as a realm that increases our perception in an aestheticizing and formalistic manner, but rather as a unique synthesis of forms of knowledge. In art we learn something about the reality in which we live and at the same time it is a mirror in which we see our own image. Works of art are metaphors. I understand them as materialized 'modeling conceptualizations'. I find that sovereignty required by the computer in the ways by which these materializations are put into a form or into a system of forms of presentation.

Accordingly, the 'zone of the proximal development' for working out those new social patterns and new forms of activity which correspond to the potential of that universal machine would be found in art. I do not believe that these new social activities can simply be postulated, prescribed, and then developed in an organized manner — for example, by means of new teaching methods for art instruction at public schools or new concepts of museum pedagogy.

New social activities develop — as noted above — from the contradictions and conflicts of the *cultural practices* of a society. My prognosis regarding the topicality and relevance of modern art for the process of a societal appropriation of the universal machine is aimed at regaining the computer's nature as a device and thus at our role as subjects of activity.

References

Aldrich, V. (1983). Visual Metaphor. *Journal of Aesthetic Education* 2, 73-86.

Bateson, G. (1983). *Ökologie des Geistes. Anthropologische, psychologische, biologische und epistemologische Perspektiven.* [Steps to an ecology of mind. Collected essays in anthropology, psychiatry, evolution and epistemology] Frankfurt: Suhrkamp. (Original work published in English 1972).

Bateson G. & Bateson, M.C. (1987). *Angels fear. Towards an epistemology of the sacred.* New York: Macmillan.

Benites, M. & Fichtner, B. (1996). Kunst als Zone der nächsten Entwicklung für ein neues Lernen [Art as zone of proximal development for a new kind of learning]. In J. Lompscher (ed.), *Entwicklung und Lernen aus kulturhistorischer Sicht*, vol. 2. Marburg: Bund demokratischer Wissenschaftler, 417–29.

Bracht, U. & Fichtner, B. (1993). Das Lernen des Lernenlernens oder die epistemologische Revolution der Neuen Technologie [Learning the techniques of learning or the epistemological revolution of the new technology]. *Jahrbuch für Pädagogik*, 229–51.

Bruner, J. (1986). *Actual minds, possible worlds.* Cambridge, Mass.: Harvard University Press.

Elias, N. (1976). *Über den Prozeß der Zivilisation. Soziogenetische und psychogenetische Untersuchungen* [The civilizing process]. Frankfurt: Suhrkamp.

Engeström, Y. & Cole, M. (1991). Auf der Suche nach einer Methodologie: eine kulturhistorische Annäherung an Individualität [In search of a methodology: A cultural-historical approach to individuality]. *Dialektik. Individualisierung in der Gesellschaft* 3, 37-52.

Engeström, Y. (1986). Die Zone der nächsten Entwicklung als die grundlegende Kategorie der Eziehungspsychologie [The zone of proximal development as a basic category of educational psychology]. *Marxistische Persönlichkeits-*

theorie. Frankfurt: Institut für Marxistische Studien und Forschungen, 151-71.

Engeström, Y. (1987). *Learning by expanding. An activity-theoretical approach to developmental research*. Helsinki: Orienta Konsultit.

Fichtner, B (1992). Metaphor and learning activity. *Multidisciplinary Newsletter for Activity Theory* 11/12, 3-8.

Fichtner, B. (1996). *Lernen und Lerntätigkeit. Phylogenetische, ontogenetische und epistemologische Studien* [Learning and learning activity. Phylogenetic, ontogenetic and epistemologic studies]. Marburg: Verlag Bund demokratischer Wissenschaftler.

Giesecke, M. (1991). *Der Buchdruck in der frühen Neuzeit. Eine historische Fallstudie über die Durchsetzung neuer Informations- und Kommunikationstechnologien* [Printing in early modern times. A historical case study about the establishing of innovative information and communicative technologies]. Frankfurt: Suhrkamp.

Gilot, F. & Lake, C. (1965). *Leben mit Picasso* [Life with Picasso]. München: Bertelsmann. (Original work published in English 1965)

Hobsbawm, E. (1994). *Age of extremes. The short twentieth century 1914-1991.* London: Michael Joseph.

Judin, E. (1978). *Systemnyj podchod i princip dejatel'nosti. Metodologiceskie problemy sovremennoi nauki* [German translation by I. Maschke: Systemvorgehen und Tätigkeitsprinzip. Methodologische Probleme der modernen Wissenschaft. IDM, University of Bielefeld]. Moscow: Nauka.

Kondakov, W. I. (1978). *Wörterbuch der Logik* [Dictionary of logic]. Berlin: Volk und Wissen. (Original work published in Russian 1971).

Lektorsky, V.A. (1985). *Subjekt — Objekt — Erkenntnis. Grundlegung einer Theorie des Wissens* [Subject, object, cognition]. Frankfurt: Lang. (Original work published in Russian 1964).

Leontiev, A.N. (1982). *Tätigkeit, Bewußtsein, Persönlichkeit* [Activity, consciousness, personality]. Köln: Pahl-Rugenstein. (Original work published in Russian 1975).

Lyotard, F. (1986). *Das postmoderne Wissen* [The postmodern knowledge]. Wien: Böhlau.

Mandelbrot, B. (1991). *Die fraktale Geometrie der Natur* [The fractal geometry of nature]. Basel: Birkhäuser. (Original work published in English 1977).

Marx, K. (1968). *Das Kapital. Kritik der politischen Ökonomie*, vol. 1. Berlin: Dietz. (Original work published in 1867).

Marx, K. (1953). *Grundrisse der Kritik der politischen Ökonomie* [Grundrisse. Foundation of the critique of political economy]. Berlin: Dietz. (Original work published in 1939).

Nora, S. & Minc, A. (1979). *Die Informatisierung der Gesellschaft* [The computerization of society]. Frankfurt: Campus.

Otte, M. (1985). Computer und menschliches Denken oder die historische Objektivität des Subjektiven [Computer and human thinking or the historical objectivity of the subjective]. *Düsseldorfer Debatte* 6/7.

Otte, M. (1984). Können Maschinen denken? — Die Gottesfurcht vorm Denken der Computer [Can machines think? — The reverence for computer's thinking]. *Düsseldorfer Debatte* 2.

Postman, N. (1992). *Das Technopol. Die Macht der Technologien und die Entmündigung der Gesellschaft.* Frankfurt: Fischer.

Raeithel, A. & Volpert, W. (1985). Aneignung der Computer oder Telematik-Monokultur? [Appropriation of the computer or telematic-monoculture]. *Zeitschrift für Sozialforschung und Erziehungssoziologie* 5(2), 209–35.

Raeithel, A. (1985). Das Lebendige, das Tote und die Symbolmaschinen [The living, the dead and the symbol machine]. *Düsseldorfer Debatte*, 1.

Raeithel, A. (1996). On the Ethnography of cooperative work. In Y. Engeström & D. Middleton (eds.), *Cognition and communication at work.* Cambridge, Mass.: Cambridge University Press.

Turkle, S. (1984). *Die Wunschmaschine. Vom Entstehen der Computerkultur* [The wishing machine. From the beginnings of the computer culture]. Reinbek: Rowohlt.

Saramago, J. (1994). *Das Steinerne Floß* [The stone raft]. Reinbek: Rowohlt. (Original work published in Portuguese 1986).

Vygotsky, L.S. (1976). *Psychologie der Kunst* [Psychology of Art]. Dresden: Verlag der Kunst. (Original work published in Russian 1925).

Vygotsky, L.S. (1977). *Denken und Sprechen.* Frankfurt: Luchterhand. (Original work published in Russian 1934).

Vygotsky, L.S. (1978). *Mind in Society. The development of Higher Psychological Processes.* (Edited by M. Cole, V. John-Steiner, S. Scribner & E. Souberman). Cambridge, Mass.: Harvard University Press. (Original work published in Russian 1960).

Vygotsky, L.S. (1985/1987). *Ausgewählte Schriften* [Selected works], vols. 1-2. (J. Lompscher, editor). Köln: Pahl-Rugenstein.

Winograd, T. & Flores, F. (1986). *Understanding Computers and Cognition.* New York: Ablex Publishing Cooperation.

5   The Crisis of Knowledge*

Georg Rückriem

Introduction

In what follows I want to focus on a category that I regard to be of central importance to the educational sciences. It is, however, one that has been unduly relegated to the background of educational attention. This category is 'knowledge'. I will not be concerned with the social and historical causes of its degradation to second-rate status but with the epistemological causes found in the understanding of knowledge itself, or, more precisely, in the understanding of this category current in the pedagogical sciences. To avoid any possible misunderstandings, however, I am not intending any kind of epistemological treatment of the subject, but rather what Norbert Elias (1988, 230ff) has called a 'process-theoretical' analysis, that is, an analysis that expressly reflects the fact that not only particular knowledge is historical but, using Elias' terminology, so too are the 'means of thinking' that determine the origin and development of individual knowledge. Judin (1984) takes a similar view of the matter, and if I understand him correctly, Tenorth (1981, 152) chooses the same procedure, which, following systems theory, he calls 'temporalizing complexity'.

My hypothesis is that schooling and learning are in the first instance epistemically connected. Only by focusing on this connection can historical and current phenomena be analyzed in a way that can be regarded as pedagogical. I shall clarify first what is meant here by offering some critical remarks on contemporary historical research in education as it has pro-liferated into a wide range of theories and interpretations since the beginning of the 1970s, and then I shall make some brief comments on the term 'epistemic context'.[1] According to Fichtner, all of these widely varying interpretations of historical research in education are characterized by a singular lack of epistemic context. Schools are understood as educational systems or as institutions whose historical connections with economics,

*   I wish to thank Charles Tolman very much for his untiring help in both clearing my thoughts and making my English readable.
1. I base these remarks on work by Fichtner (1996).

politics, and societal structure are the focus of interest. These contexts are as a rule interpreted in terms of societal expectations of the educational system and in terms of their functions such as selection, allocation, qualification, and legitimation. As a consequence, the particular structure of the institution is thought to be adequately characterized as a system of institutionalized societal mechanisms by means of which these expectations are constantly regulated and relatively independently fulfilled. Fichtner rightly notes that in such structural-functional analyses school learning appears 'only marginally' and not 'with the status of an independent object of investigation'. A pedagogical study of history — or, I may add, of the present — that resists reduction to the rank of a 'hyphenated science, dependent on a dominating social science' will have to define its own subject matter, and this lies precisely in the epistemological connection between schooling and learning (Fichtner 1992). In other words, knowledge is a central category of pedagogy.

Concerning the epistemic context, this approach regards the fundamental change of knowledge and its social function as much more important for understanding the origin and formation of formal schooling than the development of production, trade, traffic, administration, technology, or power. (Bracht, Mies, Fichtner & Rückriem 1990; Fichtner 1992; Rückriem 1992) Regarding history (see Bracht et al. 1990), we have to remember that since the Enlightenment knowledge became universal, subjective and — on a societal level — practical, that is: knowledge and attitude towards knowledge became a complementary system of elements which defined one through the other. This specific connection of knowledge and attitude made it a means of self-organization for individuals and societies. In this sense it emerged as the centre of a new knowledge-based 'cultural scheme' and a fundamental prerequisite for developing bourgeois societies. So knowledge acquired a new social function. To foster this function as a requirement for their new self-organization power, and as an advanced organizer for their industrial development, those societies formed a new autonomous communication system which was explicitly meant for generalizing knowledge and attitude towards knowledge: the system of formal schooling. So formal schooling is not primarily a specific social institution realizing social aims and needs but a societal function for mediating the complementary system of knowledge and attitude towards knowledge. It is a relation of knowledge itself, a new knowledge form, which created a new type of knowledge: the subjects,[2] a new form of communication: instruction, a new social space: school, a new science:

pedagogy, and new categories: 'Erziehung und Bildung'.[3] This is why
Fichtner insists on refering to the epistemic context and at the same time
it makes clear the meaning of knowledge as a central category of pedagogy.

As a starting point for consideration of my thesis I shall refer to
Sandkühler's argument for a 'crisis of knowledge' (Sandkühler 1991a,
1991b). As he points out, theories of knowledge are elements of images of
the self and the world and at the same time they are systems which
constitute world-views and universals of meaning. They are the base of
concepts of what is called 'reality' which on the other hand constitute the
reality of knowledge. Thus they serve as theoretical framework for the
choice of ontologies and — what is most frequently forgotten — of philo-
sophies of history and their practical-philosophical consequences. The
actual epistemic revolution — as Sandkühler continues — produces a
specific form of paradox: it expands and extends the knowledge of mankind and diminishes and decreases the knowledge of the individual.
Objective expansion and subjective restriction of knowledge are both
increasing at the same time. Within this process, rational world-views and
their potentiality to integrate the whole knowledge to a totality of knowledge as a whole, are suffocated by the irreversible development of
scattering and diffusion through the chaotic emergence of single knowledge. This leads to the disintegration of cognitive systems, isolation from
everyday life's culture, segmentation of societal experience, resignation to
a meaningless mass of data and alienation from knowledge to a hitherto
unknown degree. Knowledge becomes an abstract possibility without sense
and aim. It loses its quality as subjective ability of human ratio to construct
reality according to human measurement. 'This is the crisis of knowledge'
(Sandkühler 1991, 16).

2. In this specific context here I use the term 'subject' as the translation for 'Unter-
    richtsfach'.
3. The German notions 'Erziehung' and 'Bildung' cannot be translated into English
    without severe loss of meaning. 'Erziehung' is not quite the same as 'education' as it
    might seem to be. But neither is it synonymous with 'rearing', 'training' nor
    'breeding'. 'Erziehung' has to do with behaving oneself or acting rightly. In the
    following I shall use the nearest meaning which is 'upbringing'. 'Bildung' has more
    to do with understanding why certain actions are right and others wrong. Bildung is
    thus more profound than Erziehung and is traditionally seen as the truer aim of
    education. Synonymous with 'Bildung' is 'erudition' or 'culture' more than at least
    'formation' or 'refinement'. Despite all remaining differences I shall use the most
    current term 'education'.

Following this argument soon reveals that it is addressing a categorial context that touches not only current problems of pedagogical practice in schools but also historical and theoretical problems of pedagogy itself. It also has methodological consequences for the future development of research into learning and teaching.

In what follows I will be approaching my idea of the category of knowledge from two different perspectives. The first will be a practical one in which I will focus on a detailed analysis of violence in school. The second will be methodological, in which I will offer some brief reflections on my theoretical framework. Finally, I will examine some methodological consequences for research into teaching and learning.

Usual Models of Explanation of Violence in School

I shall assume that the reader is familiar with the phenomenology of violence in school and that no detailed description is needed.[4] It is interesting that while causal explanations of violence in school are available, they are rarely discussed as such. Some of the most common of these are listed below, with no claims to completeness or validity.

Violence is caused by the media. Children watch too much violence on television. For the 14,000 hours that children spend in school, they spend on average 17,000 hours in front of the television. This cannot fail to have a significant impact.

Violence is part of a developmental phase that children go through. Young people necessarily experiment with social norms as a way of finding their own identities in a changing world.

Violence is mainly a problem in the former East Germany. These people are suffering most from the collapse of hopes and prospects for life that they had linked to Reunification.

Violence is a consequence of a disproportionate increase in the numbers of foreigners and asylum-seekers. This is because there is a forced mixture of cultures with no effort made to make the opposing values and customs of the newcomers understandable and tolerable.

Violence is a medical problem. It comes from widespread minimal cerebral dysfunctions caused by bad diet and an increasing sensitivity among

---

4. For such details, see Pilz, 1990; Rückriem 1993, 1994. The reader should keep in mind that the societal and scientific background of this contribution is Germany, although the conclusions, as I think, have a more general importance.

children to phosphates. It can therefore be treated only by medication (see, e.g., Hafer 1990).

Violence is an implication of the symbolic or structural violence of schools. This latter expresses itself in the form of unfair grading, grinding competition, intolerable learning conditions, authoritarian structures of communication in the pupil-teacher relationship, etc. The upshot is that 'authoritarian teachers produce violent pupils'.

Violence is a result of the spineless liberalism of the teachers. It is the unwanted side-effect of an unoriented laissez-faire pedagogy that sets no limits and invites pupils to fill the vacuum left by the frightened helplessness of the teachers. 'Left-leaning teachers produce right-leaning pupils.'

Violence is the result of one-sided schooling that emphasizes the cognitive and that is thus abstracted from the real lives of the pupils. It is the consequence of government-run formal schooling that has become thoroughly bureaucratized. It ignores the concrete experiences of children and neglects education in values, feelings, and social relations.

Violence is the result of the fact that nearly all social institutions that provide norms and guide conduct have dissolved, leaving only money, consumption, and status as standards. With the loss of this social anchoring, the need also vanishes to be clear about the consequences for others of one's own actions. The result is a lowering of the threshold for violence.

Of course, one also encounters mollifying claims — mostly from politicians — that explanations of this sort are really just panic-mongering because the instances of described violence are exceptions that stand in contrast to the majority of 'good' schools with no violence. Violence, it is claimed, is a marginal problem that in no way justifies such pessimistic generalizations.[5]

With the exception of the medical explanation,[6] it is interesting that all

---

5. See, e.g., Schwind & Baumann 1990, vol. 1, 70, 91.
6. I do not reject the argument that increased aggressivity in single cases under some circumstances may be related to phosphate incompatibility and wrong diet. However, I have severe doubts whether the MCD-concept is really able to deal with learning difficulties and learning deficiencies in an appropriate way. But even more important: regarding the increasing tendency in school and society to medicalize educational problems, it is necessary to make clear that it corresponds to still existing related tendencies in discussions on separation or forced sterilization of mentally handicaped people, on eugenics or even euthanasia. (See, e.g., Lewontin 1974, Rose & Rose 1976, Weingart 1988, Stellmach 1994). The ideology of which medicalizing social problems a political strategy comes from, is a widespread objective knowledge form and to be found in many facets and variants in many different social fields. (See Lewontin, Rose & Kamin 1988).

these proposed causal models are psychological or sociological in nature. Even when the school itself, the mode of instruction, or the teacher is cited as cause, it is cited within a theoretical framework of communication or socialization. This means that acts of violence appear as expressions or results of altered societal or psychical circumstances, which are taken as somehow providing important conditions for learning. Even when analyses of violence deal directly with the school or educational system, they focus on organizational, communicational, or political conditions of instruction. They thus acknowledge the structural-functional context of educational and learning processes, at least in form if not in content. In short — and this is my first point — pedagogical research as such on the problem of violence does not yet exist.

This is an astonishing claim. But even more astonishing, I think, is the fact that educationalists are not disturbed by it. I can imagine only one explanation for this. Pedagogical science is at the moment simply not yet equipped with any appropriate theoretical concepts of its own that are able to grasp the epistemological connection between social change and the purpose of the school as a societal institution. And because of the lack of a genuine educationalist concept it thus capitulates to a view of itself as an applied science of a sociological or psychological type. I hope to make this clearer as I proceed.

The Criterion in Common: Violence as Behavioural Problem

Without exception, all attempts to grasp the specific potential for conflict in the violence problem have been fascinated by the violent patterns of behaviour and concentrate on the forms they take (e.g., scatological language, physical assault, vandalism, and criminal acts like fraud, blackmail, theft, and robbery) or on the type of violence (against property, against teachers, against fellow pupils — whereas violence in the form of everyday sexism directed at girls or female teachers tends to be ignored; see Krausch 1990; Gräning 1993; Kämper 1993).

This one-sided concentration on behavioural forms of violence, as if they were the only aspect that mattered, corresponds strikingly with the descriptions given by teachers when they are asked about the details of their conflicts with pupils. Here they speak of disobedience, unreliability, lack of discipline, failure to be punctual, lack of tidiness, lack of control, and the like. The list reads like a catalogue of negative values, or like the diagnosis of a total collapse of values. Teachers' descriptions are similar when the question is about the morality of children and young people. In this connection they mention loss of sensitivity, loss of empathy, lack of conscience, absence of fairness and solidarity, lack of consideration and responsibility, etc. These are all diagnoses of deficits. Both diagnoses are confirmed in conversations with teachers, who go on to point out that children and young people are rarely at all responsive to the positive values and norms of adults.

Obviously, the problem for the teachers is that pupils distance themselves from the operative adult norms and values of the school. They no longer behave as the teachers are accustomed to expecting. They no longer behave as if they feel the least bit obliged by such norms and values. Teachers interpret expression of violence as a behavioural problem which they are not prepared to deal with.

But there has been a complementary behavioral development among the teachers themselves. This has been noted by the media, parents, and other interested parties, and even by school administrators. These changes are characterized as follows:

– a decreasing commitment and willingness to accept responsibility, coupled with increasing indifference;

– increasing dissolution of teacher identity and loss of the related sense of pedagogical responsibility toward the younger generation;

– increasing ossification and formalization of pedagogical communication in the school;

– increasing tendency toward bureaucratizing and legalizing of pedagogical work altogether.

Reactions of teachers make it clear that they sense themselves as incapable of effective action because the sanctions that they have at their disposal for dealing with pupils' violent behaviour are no longer accepted, either by pupils or their parents. Moreover, many teachers find that they are not supported by their school administrations in cases of serious conflict. Thus the problem appears once again to be one of a contradiction between behavioural competencies and behavioral possibilities, that is, as a behavioural problem, even if seen here in its societal dimension.

In other words — this is my second point — violence in schools is seen exclusively as a problem of behaviour. Insofar as it is treated pedagogically and not merely as a problem of discipline, it appears at best as a problem of appropriate upbringing, not as a problem of education as such.

As a consequence of thinking in these terms, the school develops its function of upbringing in reaction to society's failure to develop it. All disintegrative processes create new tasks of upbringing, such as those relating to multi-ethnicity, war and peace, drugs, media, the environment, etc. Recommendations for procedures like relaxation training and role-play for venting the aggressiveness of hyperactive children, extramural activities for intensifying the relationship between parents and school, specialized advanced training for teachers, increased use of counselors and therapists, special education programs, as well as new forms of cooperation with street workers and the police, etc., all clearly indicate the consequences of adopting this approach. The school is forced into the role of a general repair shop for the breakdowns of societal disintegration. But this means a shift of the primary function of the school from school pedagogics, in which the aim 'is to create in a person the ability to look at the world for himself, to make his own decisions, to say to himself, this is black or this is white, to decide for himself whether there is a God in heaven or not' (James Baldwin), to social pedagogics which insidiously redefine the school as a centre for social therapeutics. Understanding violence exclusively as a behavioural problem, and more precisely as an individual behavioural problem, makes it a problem for psychology and individual therapy. It is completely consistent with this view of things that persons become problems, with the devastating consequences to which German history dramatically testifies — I refer to the way foreigners and the handicapped are treated at present, and to the current discussions around euthanasia. Above all, according to this point of view, violence appears once again only as a negative background problem for teaching, or at best a problem of its form, but never of its content.

Once again, I find it an astonishing fact that — regarding violence — the connection of knowledge and attitude toward knowledge can be torn up so far that knowledge, that is content, is no longer visible, and this in a science which is most usually founded on the mediation of knowledge! But if this connection of knowledge and attitude toward knowledge is indissoluble — and I assume it is, as described above — then we must be able to make it clear, even in the case of violence. What is needed, then, is to understand violence as a behavioural aspect of knowledge.

The Alternative: Violence as a Problem of Knowledge

In fact, knowledge and behaviour (or attitude toward knowledge) are more likely to be treated as independent dimensions or as polar opposites. It is usually said that school mediates knowledge, not attitudes. Its central category then is education, not upbringing. The value pluralism of the open society virtually forces it into a neutral position on questions of attitude. Values and norms are matters of one's philosophy of life and are therefore private. The fact that the necessity to mediate secondary values is propagated again and again doesn't alter the general agreement that knowledge is objective and attitudes are subjective and therefore it is the function of the state to guarantee a balance in the event of conflict. The consensus about this is itself an objective knowledge form that is appropriated by everyone and thus regulates individuals and society in all aspects of life.

Now it is high time to discuss the hypothesis that violence is already contained in this objective knowledge form and that this is evident from both sides of the connection between knowledge and attitude toward knowledge. In other words, violence is not only a problem of behaviour, but also one of knowledge. That means, it is not only a question of upbringing, but also one of education. On the side of attitude it is contained in the particular form in which the relationship between the individual and society is regulated in all developed industrial societies. Privacy is here a societal form that contains so much potential for conflict and violence that the state monopoly on violence has to be built-in as a safety valve for a functional regulation of the relationships between people and between the generations. Developed states are thus also state societies. The violence inherent in this aspect of the knowledge form is evident in so many everyday phenomena as to be hardly controversial.

Less obvious, and thus more difficult to demonstrate, is the thesis that violence is also inherent in the knowledge aspect itself. To make this thesis easier to comprehend, the above mentioned 'temporalization of complexity', that is, the historicity of the forms of knowledge has to be considered. It appears first in the form in which all developed societies since the Enlightenment have sought to re-regulate the relationship between humans and nature. This changed the structure and the forms of knowledge.

What is novel in the new mode of regulation is on the one hand the enthroning of the human being as the autonomous subject of cognition through the installation of Ratio as the new 'operating system of man'

(Schmale & Dodde 1991, 39), and at the same time the degrading of Nature to the status of object of cognition, and the assertion of mastery over Nature as the form of individual self-realization. A similar though less emphatic formulation is that the classical natural sciences develop on the basis of epistemic presuppositions like these:

–   Nature, in the form in which we experience it, is eternal, unchanging, and independent of human beings;

–   Humans are isolated observers of a Nature that proceeds according to immutable and deterministic laws;

–   Whoever wrests from Nature the laws of its functioning can subdue and master it;

–   By making Nature serve us, we humans have proved ourselves the masters, and therefore also the subjects, of Nature, using Ratio as our optimum tool.

Thus human self-realization is achieved through the mastery of Nature. Such progress is linear and infinite. In other words, all ideas of objectivity, causality, precise measurement, rationality, and empirical knowledge are implications of this new understanding of subjectivity. The new understanding, according to Norbert Elias:

was formed as symptom and factor of a specific transformation that — touched at once all three basic coordinates of human life: the shaping and positioning of the individual human being within the societal structure, the structure itself, and the relation of the societal human being to the processes of the non-human universe. (Elias 1988, 137)

This understanding of the world and the human species shaped the new knowledge of the Enlightenment. It formed the 'intellectual infrastructure' in which all parts of society and all individuals are located. 'It carries within itself the perspective of future change, because change is a feature of it. As school knowledge it becomes experimental knowledge. Its full use-value is only reached when the future perspective for change is achieved' (Schmale & Dodde 1991, 40).

In other words, the idea that has dominated the whole of modern history since the Enlightenment, and all philosophy of history, including Marxism, has been that of a linear progress of society as humanization through mastery of both internal and external nature. It is nothing less than the societal aspect of the knowledge concept formulated in the Newtonian world view. Newton's way of looking at the world is at the same time a way of dealing with it. World-views are systems of objective forms of knowledge. They are thus not only forms of classifying knowledge; they are also schemes for the direction of action.

I want, however, to distinguish my understanding from the radical ideology-critical variant that takes the historicization of the subject to be a mere form of knowledge — a view associated with names like Derrida, Lyotard, Baudrillard, and Foucault, for whom the subject is completely dissolved in the conditions and presuppositions of its existence. This makes the subject a mere effect of its history, 'a simple wrinkle in our knowledge that will disappear as soon as our knowledge takes a new form' (Foucault 1981, 14). The forms of knowledge in an epoch are forms of thought and above all practice that are never completely taken in by the necessarily false consciousness of the epoch.

The violence in this form of knowledge is discussed in modern natural philosophy, as well as in historical anthropology (e.g., Kamper 1987; Wulf & Gebauer 1992), as repression of sensibility and alienation of the body, as suppression of the irrational and unconscious, and above all as the 'subjection of Nature in the Feminine and of the Feminine in Nature', and summed up as 'Reason's Other' (H. & G. Böhme 1985; see also H. Böhme 1988). I shall illustrate this with some quotations. From this perspective of reason's other, the formation of modern reason appears:

as the history of a grandiose self-empowerment in which a program of eman-cipation is set in motion simultaneously with a program of repression. The Enlightenment began, through critique, to dissolve the irrationalities of the world — religion and superstition, feudal authorities and inequalities, will-o'-the-wisps and natural forces. The expulsion of these irrationalities constituted reason, but was at the same time a loss of self-evident socio-cultural under-standings and of the connection with nature. It was an estrangement from one's own body and a suppression of valuable experiential resources and kinds of knowledge. Above all, it meant the exile of fantasy, passion, and instinct. By setting itself up as the measure of man, reason defines unreason as abnormal. If the medium is health, then the other is disease. If it is the picture of manly self-control, then the other is the figure of womanly chaos. If it forms itself as culture, then the other forms nature. If it is assured in knowledge, then the other is enraptured in delusion. Power always works in dichotomies like these. (H. & G. Böhme 1985, 187) (My translation).

But the mistaking, forgetting, and repressing of Nature is a mistaking, forgetting, and repressing of humanity itself. Destroyed Nature is an indication of a destroyed relationship of humanity to itself. Absence of freedom in nature means a self-estrangement of the [human] spirit. (H. Böhme 1988, 29)

The Böhmes quote from Horkheimer and Adorno's *Dialectic of the Enlightenment*:

What humanity had to do in order to create the self, the identical, goal-oriented, manly human character now forms the hellish underworld of bourgeois morality. (H. & G. Böhme 1985, 15, 17)

From this perspective, the global destruction of Nature, which is the universal application of the modern form of knowledge, is not a capitalist misuse of knowledge. It is rather the very use of it, its necessary implication. Auschwitz, as a metaphor for all incomprehensible inhumanities of civilized humankind, lies not outside it but inside it. The Enlightenment does not remain incomplete: it is simply unenlightened. It is the historical achievement of Freud to have made the recognition of the historicity of this form of knowledge and its inherent violence into 'an inescapable lesson of the Enlightenment about the Enlightenment' (H. & G. Böhme 1985, 19).

Violence as an Inherent Characteristic of a Historic Knowledge Form

That in the end, all things considered, the behavioural crisis of everyday violence signals a crisis of the form of knowledge upon which our culture is based, appears to me at least to be a plausible hypothesis. One question, however, remains unanswered: What is it that brings this form of knowledge to a stage of crisis? Or, alternatively, what is it that increases the general, everyday acceptance of violence and lowers its threshold such that even eight-year-olds are now capable of previously unimaginable brutality?

Naturally, it is correct to say, that violence has always existed. But this very often used argument overlooks the fact that violence has appeared historically in a very different form and in a very different societal context. So we here also should 'temporalize complexity'. Since an approach is unable to interpret violence as an expression of discrepancies that have existed historically within the cultural patterns that govern relations between individuals and society, violence becomes for it a trans-historical, anthropological constant. In contrast, Foucault describes in detail how the specific form of violence in bourgeois society has changed from an individual behaviour to a structural principle of the societal formation. Violence becomes at once generalized and internalized. What is new in our time is that we can now see what surprises were contained in the epistemic foundations of western culture, the mechanics of European civilization, and the functioning capacity of all developed industrial societies. Violence is global and pervasive. It determines our entire relationship to the world, to nature, to other people, and to ourselves. Violence is generalized to all levels of humanity and expresses itself in conflicts between generations, between the sexes, and between ethnicities. Sexism and xenophobia are thus implications of the violent form of knowledge that underlies the present relationship between people and the world and must be dealt with in this context (Sperling & Tjaden-Steinhauer 1992). But the knowledge problem manifests itself differently in these different contexts, each with its own regularities and dynamic, each with its own special effects and interactions.

In order to understand why we are becoming conscious of this just now, we need only point to experiences common to us all. Start with Chernobyl, the pollution of the Arctic Ocean by Russian nuclear waste, pollution of the Irish Sea by British nuclear processing plants, pollution of the North Sea by French pesticides, pollution of the Persian Gulf by Iranian oil, and so on and so forth. What created the functioning capacity of industrial society now threatens it in incalculable ways. The instruments that people have produced in order to gain mastery over nature have become obvious instruments of the destruction of Nature and the undermining of the human condition. The scientification of societal practice, which was supposed to mobilize knowledge as an instrument of rational control so as to free practice from the whims and tyranny of nature, has become an obvious means-end calculus that takes no account at all of its social consequences. But it has become very clear that this is not a capitalist perversion of knowledge; it cannot be attributed to any misuse of power, patronage, or corruption of this or that political party, but must have other causes. People are beginning to see it as the implication of a type of knowledge that, having made both bourgeois society and its socialist negation possible, is now independent of the political constitution of any particular society.

The crisis of knowledge — the hypothesis under consideration — therefore means not only an obsolescence of particular claims to knowledge or a lack of knowledge in certain areas. What is critical here is the type of knowledge, that is, the general semantics of the Enlightenment and the Newtonian world-view. The epistemic parameters of industrial society — as is made clear not only by Greenpeace — necessarily encourage individualistic solutions and thus fundamentally obscure more general societal solutions. The crisis of knowledge is not just a deficit or limitation in our orientational foundation that can be made up; it is a destruction of that foundation by the new knowledge that cannot therefore be repaired now with the help of that knowledge.

This means that with the crisis of 'all knowledge' the 'whole of knowledge' becomes suspect (Fellsches 1993). But without an adequate concept of the totality of knowledge (Sandkühler 1991b) people can no longer consider themselves to be the producers of a possible rational world, either ecologically or socially. So crisis of knowledge does not just mean a crisis of science; it is a crisis of the practical, social self-governance of the species in the interest of creating a humane and rational world.

But: the end of enlightenment is not 'the end of the possibility to grasp the totality' (Fellsches 1993, 141). The new and increasing tendencies of individualization — as sociologists like Beck (1986a, 1986b) describe actual developments — do not necessarily mean the 'disintegration of society as a whole', as Heitmeyer puts it (Heitmeyer 1992). Crises are transformations, not eclipses. What we see is not the end of knowledge in general but only of a previous, i.e., a historical form of knowledge. Not every but only one specific human 'operating system' became dysfunctional. Only from the perspective of the thing that became anachronistic is the process of change seen as a decline. In the transition from the old to the new not only structures of knowledge and structure-based social behaviour face each other, but human beings who create their subjectivity by appropriating and applicating knowledge. What we are experiencing in the forms of violence behaviour today could therefore be described as an expression of a change of knowledge forms with all its objective and subjective manifestations, as a kind of 'formation theory' of knowledge. Or — as one of the German philosophers sees the transition from 'conventionalist' to 'post-conventionalist forms' of social and individual autonomy — it could be viewed as 'a phylogenetic crisis of adolescence of mankind' (Koppe 1994).

Viewed less abstractly, it must be taken into consideration that in their own experience young people find that the knowledge they are offered is useless for coping with the present, for shaping a worthwhile future, or for developing a harmonious personality. What seems central to me is their experience of the fundamental hypocrisy with which adults confront them. Adults openly and cynically embrace the violent forms inherent in the dominant knowledge form and yet deny and forbid them to young people. That over 25% of all children are abused by adults, that adults profit from the sexual abuse of their own children, that tour operators complain that their business will be hurt by the presence of disabled people, that adults trade in foetuses and body parts, that adults produce pornographic and horror films and then are upset by the effects on their children — all of this, openly discussed, seen, and read in the media and in the street, cannot fail to have an impact on children and young people.

If this diagnosis is right, the readiness for violence on the part of children and young people expresses a much more profound loss of orientation, which helps explain the coincidence of the inability to learn and the inability or unwillingness to socialize. If the analysis is correct — and there is much to suggest it is — then the crisis of knowledge is at the same time a school crisis of the most profound order, for it touches not just school knowledge but the school itself as a knowledge form and thus also the basis of the school's function as a social institution publicly transmitting knowledge so as to regulate the generations in a developed industrial society.

School is the socially institutionalized instrument that governs the relationship between knowledge and attitude toward knowledge, or, in other words, between objective meaning and personal sense, between technical and social progress *in the individual subject.*

School knowledge mediates between scientific and everyday knowledge in both directions and thus gets into the crisis from both ends. As a consequence, the self-assertion of the younger generation is expressed as destructive violence, not only against the school, teaching, and subject matter, but against all representatives of false knowledge, that is, against the adult generation and its social institutions. It is their war against the 'war of adults against children' (Nicklas 1984; see also Tremmel 1996).

The Sum Total

In light of this analysis the sense of school knowledge and of the school itself that children and young people currently have must be upside-down. Knowledge is not just deficient; it is perverse, it is destructive. For them, knowledge is not just impotent; it is disempowering, it robs one of the capacity to act. Thus the lack of motivation and interest on the part of pupils can be seen as a form of distancing themselves from an institution that is characterized by compulsion and which mediates a knowledge that, in fact, is no knowledge at all. It is useless for understanding the new reality of the increasingly global social integration of humanity (Elias 1988). And it is no help in dealing with the new emphasis on the individual. It neither enriches nor strengthens the new ideas of individuality, but rather burdens and weakens individuals, because it ties them to a level of individualization and integration that has long since disappeared. It lends no support to the new possibilities of individualization, but promotes a perception of them that is old-fashioned. And it also fails to support the new forms of integration, but rather reproduces the old forms of relating that are seen by young people as outmoded moral shackles. It obstructs and damages young peoples' chances of gaining the independence to which they are entitled and of realizing a new subjectivity appropriate to current trends in social development. It offers no vantage point from which young people can orientate themselves in the world. Since no social ties exist any more except for money, consumption, and status, all governed by indi-vidualistic and instrumentalist principles (see Beck 1983, 1986a, 1986b; or Heitmeyer 1993a), the only maxim left to the isolated individual is to get one's own way (Heitmeyer 1993b, 1993c). Success without consideration of social costs becomes the criterion and 'being a winner' becomes a requirement for normality. The less the social consequences of one's own actions are taken into account in the social habitus, the more the acceptance of everyday violence rises and the threshold for violence decreases.[7]

My conclusion is thus a negative one. I expect that acts of violence in schools will increase and the difficulties that teachers have in getting along with their pupils will become more general — at least as long as the schools and the contents of instruction are not essentially changed.

Methodological Assumptions

In what follows I will discuss the theoretical framework that I am using to interpret the violence of young people so as to reinforce the plausibility of my hypothesis about the pedagogical significance of the

---

7. Criminal statistics published by the Department of the Interior show that the number of registered criminal acts committed in Germany by pupils had increased by 9.6% p.a. during the last two years. The German Union of CID officers says this is a totally new fact and emphasizes the increasing tendency to use brutal violence 'in a most frightening way'.

category of knowledge. I shall begin by clarifying my understanding of the category of 'knowledge'.

Knowledge as a category designates neither particular finding nor special forms of knowledge, but rather a historical cognitive space. The category of knowledge embraces the forms of thinking and practice of epochs and megatrends, and thus represents a level of abstraction above the developments and changes taking place within epochs. Even the discrepancies and tensions of a societal structure in a particular epoch, notwithstanding all their contradictoriness, mark the space and limits within which they move. A variety of categories has been used to describe the extent and limits of the dimensions of this space, for example: 'world-view' (Groethuysen 1978); 'paradigm' (Kuhn 1978); 'explanatory principle' (Judin 1984); 'cultural scheme' (Sahlins 1986); 'social habitus' (Elias 1988); etc. Compared with these, I prefer the category 'knowledge' for the following reasons:

- It makes it possible to understand ritual, magical thinking, norms, religion, art, and ideology as knowledge forms and as dimensions in a unitary space.

- It avoids the danger of normatively ranking science and world-view one above the other, which itself would be understood as an implication of a particular historical concept of knowledge.

- It overcomes the narrowness of Kuhn's theoretical approach which confined itself, as Mittelstraß (1982, 209) correctly noted, to 'a single research practice as constituting scientific community'. Knowledge expressly includes the practice of technology, production, communication, administration, and politics. It is understood as a unity of the theoretical and practical relations to the world.

- It guarantees the understanding not only of accumulated material experience but also of social habitus, 'the fundamental structure of the social personality' (Elias 1988), as a unity of material and social approaches to the world.

- It makes it possible to investigate and compare not only the overall relationship between individuals and the world, but includes groups, collectives, associations, institutions, societies, and megatrends. In a similar way Sahlin uses the 'culture scheme' as a means of organizing the experiences of individuals, groups, and society at large. He uses this category to describe all fields and domains of social life in terms of unified space (Sahlin 1986). Gurjewitsch (1978, 1986) applies the category of 'cultural unity' in a similar manner to emphasize the characteristics of medieval society that underlay its internal contradictions.

– It interprets the cultural scheme as a unity of objectified forms of knowledge, that is, as a unity of the means that humans themselves produce in order to shape the conditions of their lives. Viewed in this way, the cultural scheme not only demonstrates the fundamental mediatedness of human behaviour, it also emphasizes the social nature of this mediatedness and shows 'what necessarily follows from mediation, namely, that culture is the inner unity and systematic context of the human way of life' (Fichtner 1989, 117) under specific conditions of time and space. 'From a methodological point of view, it reveals the ways in which people produce society and its various aspects, including the specific system character of its culture, as the substantively integrated result of their activity, and, as well, how society produces the activity of its constituent individuals' (Fichtner 1989, 117).

– It argues that culture, as the unity of all objectified knowledge forms, is not so much the result of the conditions of economic production, but can be seen as a relatively independent organizer of all human activities. This avoids all vulgar materialist and reductionist distortions. 'The Tallensi farmers are not in a father-son-relationship by the way they produce, but they produce in that way because they are in a father-son-relationship' (Sahlins 1986, 23).

– It makes it possible to understand that what is a means of thinking in one epoch, is a culture-specific instrument for producing knowledge that in the next epoch can become the historical content of knowledge, and thus constitutes the possibility for a unitary object for historic treatment, a kind of 'formation theory of knowledge'. In my opinion the most comprehensive and sophisticated formulation of the specific methodological function of the category of knowledge has been proposed by Judin (1984). He maintains that an explanatory principle forms the precondition and result of the overall practice of a society at any particular time. This is reflected in the fact that there is unity in all forms of knowledge and thus in the expressions of the collective subject in all aspects of life, and these, in their totality, determine the type of rationality that characterizes a society, an epoch, or an entire social formation.

- It is itself an interdisciplinary category that facilitates relations between sociology, psychology, and epistemology. Thus Leontiev's dialectical theory of the genetic difference between reflection in activity and activity in reflection, as well as his law that the structure of reflection lags behind the structure of activity, find application as a methodological basis for historical research on the origin of knowledge forms. It is interesting that Elias (1987, 281) uses the law about the lag of reflection in his 'process sociological' analysis of the social habitus.

- It is crucial that only in this way can we hope to clarify the indissoluble dialectical relationship between objectified knowledge forms as social systems of meaning and subjective knowledge as personal sense, which forms the theoretical basis of Fichtner's thesis on the relationship between school and learning activity. It also provides a basis for discussing the crisis of knowledge, about which I shall have more to say below.

It is important to see in this context that knowledge is always a subject's knowledge. Contrary to Popper's understanding, I shall regard only a subject's knowledge as real knowledge. Outside its relationship to the subject knowledge does not exist (cf. Leontiev 1979; Lektorsky 1985). Knowledge is the means by which the subject appropriates the world. It is the subject's general capacity to direct and determine himself and thus to develop individuality and personal identity.

Knowledge seen in this way resolves the contradiction between two of its dimensions: its objectivity and its subjectivity. Knowledge is knowledge about something, a means of grasping the world in its amodality (Leontiev). In its independence from me it becomes objective meaning. At the same time knowledge is my knowledge, a means for understanding the world in its meaning for me. It is personal sense. The subjectification of knowledge is part of its becoming both scientific and democratic. Viewed as a process of activity, this is called learning. The universal production of new knowledge in society becomes a permanent activity of every individual, that is, life-long learning as a way of life. The social rendering of all aspects of life into scientific knowledge puts an enormous burden of responsibility onto the subject. Every individual has both the general ability to contribute to the development of new knowledge and the general predisposition toward social legitimation of knowledge practices. How knowledge shall be used socially is no longer automatically decided with its production. The problem of application is shifted as a social problem onto the subject, thus making the formation of personal sense a task of society at large. That knowledge becomes subjective means from this perspective that the social separation of knowledge and activity becomes a problem of its mediation by the subject. The question is how the universal becomes real for the individual. How can learning become a general capacity to learn? How can ways of thinking be produced? Or, to return to our concrete problem, how can this social demand be mediated as personally sensible for young people today?

The cultural scheme of our society understands society as an association regulating itself by means of individuals regulating themselves. The objectified knowledge forms that are produced in this context are taken as adequate for mediating the self-regulation of individuals. This is based on a recognition of the social obligation of all members of society to develop themselves as self-regulating subjects in the general social habitus. School is the social institution that has been established for the purpose of this development. It is thus a normative and, at the same time, autonomous institution that in and through its autonomy shapes that ability- and habitus-forming quality, or at least sets the conditions for it. The entire educational system of all developed industrial societies has been founded on this principle. The subject matter canon is not just the result of the educational ideas of one epoch about the range, structure, and unity of the knowledge that is to be passed on to the next generation. The subject matters are not just ordered schemata for the socially regulated appropriation of knowledge, they also establish the social conventions of its application in areas of social practice (Durkheim 1977; Bracht 1986). From this point of view the school is itself an objectified knowledge form of these societies with the cultural pattern that arose only with bourgeois society (Fichtner 1989; Engeström 1987) and that has shaped the development of all modern industrial states to the present time. If the development of the globalization of world capitalism (Pestel 1988; Gore 1992) really represents a new form of social organization, then it too will have — or already has had, in my view — effects on the quality, structure, and function of all aspects and forms of our knowledge, including the school, subject matter, communication, etc., even if this has not yet been openly discussed.

The Consequences for Research into Teaching and Learning

The question whether violence among children and young people can in fact be seen as a crisis of knowledge, as is my hypothesis, and the extent and quality of this crisis, seem to me among the most pressing issues for pedagogical research. The entire epistemological framework for school and learning in their historical form, together with the whole subject matter canon and its implied hierarchicalization, may be at stake. Neither the canon itself nor its hierarchy can be derived from some abstract subject matter system. Both have rather 'to be developed with a view to the educational tasks of our time' (Bracht 1986, 425). Subject matters are epistemological achievements of a particular historical situation. They organize 'historically developed problem areas of institutionalized precepts, substantively limited but oriented to specific goals'. 'The difficulty of subject matter development is that what ensues is its hierarchicalization on the basis of a social practice of classifying knowledge' (Bracht 1986, 425). And as the origin and change of knowledge becomes problematic, this hierarchicalization itself becomes obsolete.

The full importance of this becomes clear if one realizes the double character of the subject matter of instruction as described by Fichtner:

On the one hand it 'represents a certain societal knowledge form', in which social experiences are 'materialized' which are to be appropriated as knowledge and attitudes; it is a given fact, 'its reproduction is central'. At the same time, however, it is a task, 'its creative construction is central': That means 'It is to be produced from the viewpoint of the new, thus being a reason for the dialogue between the child and its future'. It is the 'old' and the 'new' at the same time. (Fichtner 1996, 198; my translation)

This contradiction between the demands of society and of culture (the 'objective meaning') and the demands of the child and his/her future (the 'personal sense') is a 'contradiction in principle' (as Fichtner emphasizes correctly). In consequence it cannot, and must not, be made to disappear didactically. To overemphasize its object side and to disregard its subject side would mean to overemphasize the reproductive functions and to disregard the productive-constructive functions of learning. In consequence this would lead to a fatal separation of knowledge and activity in the appropriation of the subject matter of instruction, resulting in severe limitations, respective impediments of the learning activity and to massive deficits in education. Fichtner (1996) describes the opposite quite vividly and comprehensibly, stressing the corresponding consequences:

Subject matter areas are ... perceived as a knowledge which is identified more or less totally with its definition. This means, to instruct is, above all, to explain. Here instruction aims at the 'argumentation' of a knowledge already finished. If knowledge is defined and explained in advance it loses its orientating, governing and developing function towards learning and, above all, towards the learner as a subject. Under this condition the subject matter content of instruction has a literally paralyzing effect. Knowledge becomes petrified as 'a dry content' and the pupil is being belittled to a storage-house. (Fichtner 1996, 210; my translation)

One can only agree with Fichtner's critical assessment of both misconceptions. But there is another aspect concerning the subject matter of instruction which is even more important: The origin of the 'new'. 'The new is not generated from the old but from the living movement leading away from the old' (Engeström 1987, 164). That means that the starting point of personal meaningful knowledge is the real societal life where human beings produce objective meaning in the form of personal sense by realizing their active subjectivity. This of course includes that existing objective meaningful knowledge (especially as traditional subject matter of instruction) can be and will be outdone by the vivid societal practice, thus becoming — in times of radical change — even anachronistic. Then the knowledge form of the content of instruction will constrain the current margin of the students' personal sense and their development of personality, not to speak of the perspectives of the future. It is obvious that knowledge in this form is 'old' and therefore unable to generate the required 'new'. Generating the new people cannot but start from the 'living movement' and so necessarily lead away from the 'old'. It is the central argument of Sandkühler that this hypothetical description is the harsh reality of the crisis of knowledge.

Subjects are specific knowledge forms themselves and as historical as those. So if we really are in a crisis, as described above, it is not sufficient at all just to think about new contents within traditionally organized subject matter areas and not about new forms of organizing them. The current hierarchicalization in major subject matter areas like maths and languages and minor ones like sports and arts is not only historic but corresponds to a historical knowledge form and a historical form of social practice. So, e.g., Norbert Bolz (1992): 'Books as information processing systems no longer measure up to the complexity of our social systems'. Jacques Derrida: 'What is to be thought today cannot be written down in the form of lines or books'.[8] Wolfgang Hagen: 'We are going to run into a process in which technical media more and more infiltrate and subvert the perception of ourselves and of the outside world. And at the same time we have less and less means to describe this process adequately. Our scientific organization as a whole comes from Humboldt and is based on an obsolete world model that is by no means adequate any more'.[9]

The real educational task of our time may possibly come from those fundamentally new mediational means like computers and computer networks which constitute — as the media theorists and media historians argue — a completely new space of knowledge, new forms of knowledge and correspondingly a new social practice.

On the research horizon of this hypothesis are questions like the following:

–   What knowledge is actually conveyed by our subject matter areas, and does any of this correspond to the new developments related to the 'global integration of humanity' (Elias 1988)?

–   What implicit forms of social behaviour does this knowledge contain, or what social practices are concealed in the hierarchies of the subject matters?

–   Within the context of our official notions of teaching and learning, what are the understandings of the subject matter content with which we approach our pupils?

–   With what understandings of ourselves do we stand before our pupils as teachers?

–   Are our forms of instruction, and the form in which our state schools have historically developed, appropriate for making knowledge real for the subject so that learning activity can develop?

–   What would these forms have to look like in order to do this with greater success under existing conditions?

–   What role is played here by extramural learning?

–   What significance do our successfully competitive media have for the appropriation of knowledge?

8. See Ulrich Schmitz (1997), http://schmitz.germanistik. uni-essen.de/papers/schriftl-texte.htm

9. Wolfgang Hagen (1997), http://www.hrz.uni-kassel.de/wz2/ mtg/hagen-htm.

– How do we distinguish between media-mediated knowledge and school knowledge?

– Is the status of perception changing relative to cognition with the aestheticization of the environment?

– In this context, what function is assumed by the computer as the 'dominant medium of our epoch' (Leeker 1993)?

– What are our subject matter areas of instruction doing for pupils' capabilities to develop personal sense?

– What are they doing about the multiplication, diversification, historicization and subversion of meaning systems by mass media (cf. Lyotard 1986)?

– Does the traditional structure of our instruction suit its actual function?

– What social hierarchy is implied in our classification of required and elective, general and vocational subjects (cf. Durkheim 1977)?

– What knowledge form is implied by the depreciation of art, music, and sport education in the context of the traditional curricula?

– What does it mean for an adequate education when the great key questions of global integration of humanity are not recognized as official subject matter, or as guides for instruction, or as the content of compulsory courses?

– Are optimal conditions provided by our rigidly frozen structures of space and time, grades and years, weekly and daily schedules, the concept of the classroom, the architecture of our buildings, or even our fixation on building itself?

– Is the state monopoly of the school still appropriate? Should the autonomy of the school be reviewed?

– Would its privatization be a good thing under certain circumstances (Hentig 1993)?

This catalogue of questions is nowhere near complete, nor is it meant to be. Its unsystematic and random nature is intended only to give a concrete picture of what the category of knowledge, or the thesis of the 'crisis of knowledge' could mean from a pedagogical point of view. And then it ought to indicate the direction that research programs in teaching and learning might take if guided by this thesis.

References

Beck, U. (1983). Jenseits von Stand und Klasse? Soziale Ungleichheiten, gesellschaftliche Individualisierungsprozesse und die Entstehung neuer Formationen und Identitäten. [Beyond class? Social inequalities, social processes of individualization and the development of new formations and identities.] In *Soziale Ungleichheiten*, vol. 2. Göttingen: Kreckel.

Beck, U. (1986a). *Risikogesellschaft. Auf dem Weg in eine andere Moderne* [The risk society. On the way to an other modern age]. Frankfurt: Suhrkamp.

Beck, U. (1986b). Die Zivilisation des Risikos [The Civilization of Risk]. *Psychologie heute* 11, 34-37.

Böhme, H. (1988). *Natur und Subjekt* [Nature and Subject]. Frankfurt: Suhrkamp.

Böhme, H. & Böhme, G. (1985). *Das Andere der Vernunft. Zur Entwicklung von Rationalitätsstrukturen am Beispiel Kants* [The other side of reason. On the development of the structures of rationality, discussed by the example of Kant]. Frankfurt: Suhrkamp.

Boltz, D.-M. (1993). Konstruktion von Erlebniswelten. Kommunikations- und Lernstrategien am Beispiel der Marketing-Kommunikation von Camel und Greenpeace [The Construction of worlds of experiences. Communication and learning strategies of the marketing communication of Camel and Green-peace]. Unpublished doctoral dissertation. Hochschule der Künste Berlin.

Bolz, N. (1992). *Die Welt als Chaos und als Simulation* [The world as chaos and as simulation]. München: Fink.

Bracht, U. (1986). Die gesellschaftliche Bedeutung des Fächerkanons [The Social meaning of the subject canon]. *Enzyklopädie Erziehungswissenschaft* 3, 419-34.

Bracht, U., Fichtner, B., Mies, Th. & Rückriem, G. (1990). Erziehung und Bildung [Upbringing and education]. In H.J. Sandkühler (ed.), *Europäische Enzyklopädie zu Philosophie und Wissenschaften*, vol. 1. Hamburg: Felix Meiner, 918-39.

Bundeskriminalamt. (1986). *Was ist Gewalt? Auseinandersetzung mit einem Begriff* [What is violence? The Discussion of a notion]. Wiesbaden: Verlag an der Ruhr.

Chorover, S. (1979). *From genesis to genocide*. Cambridge, Mass.: Harvard University Press.

Derrida, J. (1974). *Grammatologie*. [Of grammatology]. Frankfurt: Suhrkamp.

Dawkins, R. (1976). *The Selfish Gene* (2nd ed.). Oxford: Oxford University Press.

Durkheim, E. (1977). *Die Entwicklung der Pädagogik. Zur Geschichte und Soziologie des gelehrten Unterrichts in Frankreich* [The development of pedagogical science. On the history and sociology of learned teaching in France]. Basel: Weinheim.

Elias, N. (1981). Zivilisation und Gewalt [Civilization and violence]. In J. Matthes (ed.), *Lebenswelt und soziale Probleme*, 98-124. Frankfurt: Suhrkamp.

Elias, N. (1987). *Die Gesellschaft der Individuen*. [Society of Individuals]. Frankfurt: Suhrkamp.

Engeström, Y. (1987). *Learning by Expanding. An activity-theoretical approach to developmental research*. Helsinki: Orienta-Konsultit.

Fellsches, J. (1993). Didaktische Phantasie. Einführungen in Erziehungswissenschaft [Didactical imagination. Introduction to pedagogical science]. *Beiträge zu Theorie und Kultur der Sinne* 4. Essen: Verlag Die Blaue Eule.

Feltes, T. (1990). Gewalt in der Schule [Violence in school]. In H.D. Schwind, J. Baumann, F. Lösel, H. Remschmidt, R. Eckertr, H.-J. Kerner, A. Stümper, R. Wassermann, H. Otto, W. Rudolf, F. Berckhauer, E. Kube, M. Steinhilper & W. Steffen (eds.), *Ursachen, Prävention und Kontrolle von Gewalt* [Causes, prevention and control of violence], vol. 2. Berlin: Duncker und Humblot, 317-42.

Fichtner, B. (1989). Lernen und Lerntätigkeit. Phylogenetische, Ontogenetische und Epistemologische Studien [Learning and learning activity. Phylogenetic, ontogenetic and epistemic studies]. Unpublished doctoral dissertation, University of Siegen, Germany.

Fichtner, B. (1992). Erziehung und Bildung im Werk Diesterwegs [Upbringing and education in the works of Diesterweg]. In B. Fichtner & P. Menck (eds.), *Pädagogik der modernen Schule. Adolph Diesterwegs Pädagogik im Zusammenhang von Gesellschaft und Schule*. Weinheim und München: Juventa Verlag, 17-29.

Fichtner, B. (1996). *Lernen und Lerntätigkeit* [Learning and learning activity]. Marburg: Verlag Bund demokratischer Wissenschaftler.

Foucault, M. (1981a). *Archäologie des Wissens*. [Archeology of knowledge discourse]. Frankfurt: Suhrkamp

Foucault, M. (1981b). *Überwachen und Strafen* [Discipline and punishment] (4th ed.). Frankfurt: Suhrkamp.

Galtung, J. (1975). *Strukturelle Gewalt* [Structural violence]. Reinbek: Rowohlt Verlag.

Gallwitz, A., Paulus, M. & Gaal, F. (eds.), (1996). *Sexuelle Gewalt gegen Frauen und Kinder. Täter, Opfer, Tatabläufe* [Sexual violence against women and children. Perpetrators, victims and the circumstances of the offense]. Villingen-Schwenningen: Hochschule für Polizei.

Gewalt in der Schule (1997). *Eine Spezialbibliographie der psychologischen Literatur aus den deutschsprachigen Ländern* [Violence in school. A special bibliography from German speaking countries]. (Edited by A. Zimmer, Universität Trier).

Gore, A. (1992). *Wege zum Gleichgewicht. Ein Marshallplan für die Erde* [Ways to balance. A Marshall plan for the earth], Frankfurt: Fischer Verlag.

Gräning, A. (ed.), (1993). *Sexuelle Gewalt gegen Frauen — kein Thema?* [Sexual violence against women — no issue?]. Münster: Waxmann.

Groethuysen, B. (1978). *Die Entstehung der bürgerlichen Welt- und Lebensanschauung in Frankreich* [The development of the bourgeois view of world and life]. Frankfurt: Suhrkamp.

Gurjewitsch, A.J. (1978). *Das Weltbild des mittelalterlichen Menschen* [The worldview of people in Medieval times]. Dresden: Verlag der Kunst.

Gurjewitsch, A.J. (1986). *Mittelalterliche Volkskultur* [Medieval folk culture]. Dresden: Verlag der Kunst.

Hafer, H. (1990). *Die heimliche Droge Nahrungsphosphat.* [Phosphate in nutrition — the hidden drug] (5th ed.). Heidelberg: Decker und Müller.

Heitmeyer, W. (1992a). Desintegration und Gewalt [Disintegration and violence]. *Die deutsche Jugend* 3, 4-19.

Heitmeyer, W. (1992b, December 18). Die Ohnmacht der entsicherten Jugend [The helplessness of a disconcerted youth]. *Freitag* 52/53.

Heitmeyer, W. (1993a, January 14). Fremdenfeindlichkeit und Rechtsextremismus lassen sich nicht einfach verbieten [Xenophobia and right-wing extremism cannot be simply forbidden]. *Politik.*

Heitmeyer, W. (1993b). Gesellschaftliche Desintegrationsprozesse als Ursache von fremdenfeindlicher Gewalt und politischer Paralysierung [Social processes of disintegration as a cause of xenophobic violence and political paralysation]. *Aus Politik und Zeitgeschichte* 2-3, 3-13.

Hentig, H. von (1993a). *Die Schule neu denken* [Rethinking school]. München: Hanser.

Hentig, H. von (1993b). *'Humanisierung' — eine verschämt Rückkehr zur Pädagogik: Andere Wege zur Veränderung der Schule* ['Humanization' — a shy return to pedagogics: Other strategies of changing school]. Stuttgart: Klett-Cotta.

Judin, E.G. (1984). Das Problem der Tätigkeit in Philosophie und Wissenschaft [The problem of activity in philosophy and science]. In D. Viehweger (ed.), *Grundfragen einer Theorie der sprachlichen Tätigkeit*. Berlin: Akademie-Verlag, 216-70.

Kämper, G. (1993). Gewalt gegen Mädchen [Violence against girls]. *Pädagogik* 45, 3, 35.

Kamin, L.J. (1979). *Der Intelligenzquotient im Wissenschaft und Politik* [The IQ in science and politics], Darmstadt: Steinkopff.

Kamper, D. (ed.), (1987). *Die unvollendete Vernunft. Moderne versus Postmoderne* [The unfinished reason. Modern age versus postmodern age]. Frankfurt: Suhrkamp.

Kamper, D. (1990). *Zur Geschichte der Einbildungskraft* [The history of imagination]. Reinbek: Rowohlt.

Koppe, F. (1994). Jugend als Zwischenmündigkeit [Youth as as autonomy in transition]. In J.W. Erdmann, G. Rückriem & E. Wolf (eds.), *Jugend heute. Wege in die Autonomie.* Bad Heilbrunn: Klinkhardt, 171-80.

Krausch, Chr. (1990). Gewalt gegen Frauen [Violence against Women]. In H.J. Sandkühler (ed.), *Europäische Enzyklopädie zu Philosophie und Wissenschaften,* vol. 2. Hamburg: Felix Meiner, 448-54.

Leeker, M. (1995). *Mime, Mimesis und Technologie. Historisch-systematische Studien zur Mediatisierung von Körper und Mimesis* [Mime, mimesis and technology. Historical-systematical studies on the mediatization of body and mimesis]. München: Werner Fink.

Lektorsky, V. (1985). *Subject, object, cognition.* Moscow: Progress.

Leontiev, A.N. (1964). *Probleme der Entwicklung des Psychischen* [Problems of the development of the psychic]. Berlin: Volk und Wissen.

Leontiev, A.N. (1982). *Tätigkeit, Bewußtsein, Persönlichkeit* [Activity, Consciousness, Personality]. Köln: Pahl-Rugenstein.

Lewontin, R.C., Rose, S. & Kamin, L.J. (1988). *Die Gene sind es nicht. Biologie, Ideologie und menschliche Natur.* [Not in our genes. Biology, ideology, and human nature]. München: Psychologie-Verl.-Union.

Lumsden, C.J. & Wilson, E.O. (1981). *Genes, Mind, and Culture.* Cambridge, Mass.: Harvard University Press.

Lyotard, J.-F. (1986). *Das postmoderne Wissen. Ein Bericht.* [The postmodern condition. A report on knowledge]. Graz, Wien: Böhlau.

Mittelstraß, J. (1982). *Wissenschaft als Lebensform* [Science as a way of life]. Frankfurt: Suhrkamp.

Nicklas, N. (1984). Erziehung zum Ekel vor Gewalt [Educating in order to Distaste Violence]. In R. Steinweg (ed.), *Vom Krieg der Erwachsenen gegen die Kinder* [On adults' war against children]. Frankfurt: Suhrkamp.

Pestel, E. (1988). *Jenseits der Grenzen des Wachstums. Bericht an den Club of Rome* [Beyond the limits of growth. Report for the Club of Rome]. Stuttgart: Deutsche Verlagsanstalt.

Pilz, G.A. (1990). *Gewalt von, unter und an Kindern und Jugendlichen. Eine sozialhistorische Betrachtung der Gewaltproblematik in unserer Gesellschaft* [Violence from, between and against children and youth]. Dortmund: Pad-Verlag.

Rose, H.A. & Rose, S.P.R. (1969). *Science and Society.* Harmondsworth: Allen Lane.

Rose, S.P.R., Lewontin, R.C. & Kamin, L.J. (1984). *Not in Our Genes.* Harmondsworth: Penguin.

Rose, S.P.R. & Rose, H.A. (1986). Less than human nature: biology and the new right. *Race and Class* 27(3), 47-66.

Rose, S.P.R. (1987). *Molecules and Minds: Essays on Biology and the Social Order*. Milton Keynes: Open University Press.

Rückriem, G. (1992). Pädagogik als praktische Vermittlungswissenschaft. Versuch einer tätigkeitstheoretischen Interpretation F.A.W. Diesterwegs [Pedagogy as practical science of mediation. An activity theoretical interpretation of F.A.W. Diesterweg]. In B. Fichtner & P. Menck (eds.), *Pädagogik der modernen Schule. Adolph Diesterwegs Pädagogik im Zusammenhang von Gesellschaft und Schule*. Weinheim: Juventa.

Rückriem, G. (1993). Gewalt — ein Bildungsproblem? Zur Bedeutung der Gewalterscheinungen für die Diskussion der Bildungsinnovation im vereinten Deutschland [Violence — a problem of education? On the importance of violence for the discussion about a new education in unified Germany]. In L. Lambrecht & E.M. Tschurenev (eds.), *Geschichtliche Welt und menschliches Wesen. Beiträge zum Bedenken der conditio humana in der europäischen Geistesgeschichte*. Frankfurt: Peter Lang.

Rückriem, G. (1994). Sinnkrise des Wissens [The Crisis of knowledge]. *Lern- und Lehr-Forschung. Berichte des Interdisziplinären Zentrums für Lern- und Lehrforschung der Universität Potsdam* 8, 2-33.

Sahlins, M. (1986). *Kultur und praktische Vernunft* [Culture and practical reason]. Frankfurt: Suhrkamp.

Sandkühler, H.J. (1991a). *Die Wirklichkeit des Wissens. Geschichtliche Einführung in die Epistemologie und Theorie der Erkenntnis* [The reality of knowledge. A historical introduction into epistemology and the theory of cognition]. Frankfurt: Suhrkamp.

Sandkühler, H.J. (1991b). Die Wirklichkeit des Wissens und das epistemische Menschenrecht [The reality of knowledge and the epistemic human right]. *Dialektik. Enzyklopädische Zeitschrift für Philosophie und Wissenschaften* 1, 13-34.

Schirb, H. (1989). Gewaltverhältnisse in der Schule? Ursachen und Effekte institutioneller Zwänge und Strukturen [Violent structures in school? Causes and effects of institutional structures]. In W. Heitmeyer, K. Möller & H. Sünker (eds.), *Jugend — Staat — Gewalt. Politische Sozialisation von Jugendlichen, Jugendpolitik und politische Bildung*. Weinheim und München: Juventa.

Schmale W. & Dodde, N.C. (1991). *Revolution des Wissens? Europa und seine Schulen im Zeitalter der Aufklärung (1750-1825). Ein handbuch zur europäischen Kulturgeschichte* [Revolution of Knowledge? The Schools of Europe in the Age of Enlightenment (1750-1825). A handbook of the history of the European culture]. Bochum: D. Winkler.

Schmale W. (1991). Einleitung [Introduction]. In W. Schmale & N.C. Dodde (eds.), *Revolution des Wissens? Europa und seine Schulen im Zeitalter der Aufklärung (1750-1825). Ein Handbuch zur europäischen Kulturgeschichte*. Bochum: D. Winkler, 5-46.

Schwind, H.-D., Baumann, J., Lösel, F., Remschmidt, H., Eckertr, R., Kerner, H.-J., Stümper, A., Wassermann, R., Otto, H., Rudolf, W., Berckhauer, F., Kube, E., Steinhilper, M. & Steffen, W. (eds.), (1990). *Ursachen, Prävention und Kontrolle von Gewalt* [Causes, prevention and control of violence] (4 vols). Berlin: Duncker und Humblot.

Sperling, U. & Tjaden-Steinhauer, M. (1992). Die Modernisierung patriarchalischer Herrschaft in der kapitalistischen Industriegesellschaft [The Modernization of patriarchalic domination in capitalist Industrial Society], *Dialektik. Enzyklopädische Zeitschrift für Philosophie und Wissenschaft*, 2, 81-94.

Spiegel-Verlag (ed.), (1991). *Die globale Revolution. Bericht des Club of Rome* [The global revolution. Report of the Club of Rome]. Hamburg: Spiegel-Spezial.

Steinweg, R. (ed.), (1984). *Vom Krieg der Erwachsenen gegen die Kinder* [The adults' war against children]. Frankfurt: Suhrkamp.

Stellmach, C. (1994). Rassismus und Eugenik in Begriffen. Konstitutive Elemente neuzeitlicher Wissenschaftsentwicklung [Racism and eugenics in notions. Constitutive elements of modern development of science]. *Forum Wissenschaft*, 11(1), 44-49.

Tenorth, H.-E. (1989). Kulturphilosophie als Weltanschauungswissenschaft. [Philosophy of culture as science of world-views] Zur Theoretisierung des Denkens über Erziehung. In R. vom Bruch, Fr. W. Graf & G. Hübinger (eds.), *Kultur und Kulturwissenschaften um 1900. Krise der Moderne und Glaube an die Wissenschaft*. Stuttgart: Franz Steiner Verlag, 152-67.

Tremmel, J. (1996). *Der Generationsbetrug* [The generation betrayal]. Frankfurt: Eichborn.

Weingart, P., Bayertz, K. & Kroll, J. (1988). *Rasse, Blut und Gene. Geschichte der Eugenik und Rassehygiene in Deutschland* [Race, blood and genes. A History of eugenics and race hygienics in Germany]. Frankfurt: Suhrkamp.

Wilson, E.O. (1975). *Sociobiology: the new synthesis*. Cambridge, Mass.: Belknap Press of Harvard University Press.

Wilson, E.O. (1978). *On Human Nature*. Cambridge, Mass.: Harvard University Press.

Winkel, R. (1993). *Der gestörte Unterricht* [Disturbed instruction] (5th ed.), Bochum: Kamp.

Wulf, Ch. & Gebauer, G. (1992). *Mimesis: Kultur, Kunst, Gesellschaft* [Mimesis: Culture, art, society]. Reinbek: Rowohlt.

Zygowski, H. (1989). Medizinisierung als professionelle Strategie. Entwicklungstendenzen im Psycho-Sektor [Medicinalization as a professional strategy. Tendencies in the psychological field]. *Widersprüche* 30, 31-37.

6 What is Real Learning Activity?

Vasily V. Davydov

Introduction

It is well-known that every human being is appropriating knowledge and skills throughout his/her entire life. Particularly during childhood the process of learning is rather intensive: through communication with other people, through play, through games and sport, and through obligations to work. Often the child is not even aware that he/she is learning in such situations. Learning processes are usually connected and legitimatized with special institutions, namely schools, or, as expressed in pedagogics, connected with the educational system. Today, in many countries, new content and new methods of school education are being sought. But the main task of deep-going analyses of the core of 'school learning' still exists, so that the specificity of the learning process based on modern philosophical, psychological and pedagogical concepts can be understood. One such new multidisciplinary concept is the notion *activity* and a number of derived, specific concepts such as art activity, play activity, learning activity, labor activity, etc.

In this paper I will start by giving a brief explanation of what is meant by activity. Then I will describe the characteristics of the concept of learning activity as derived from the activity concept. This will be followed by a characterization of the central content of that activity which is theoretical knowledge. Approaching learning activity, the most important aspect is to understand the conditions of its right organization in classrooms. Such conditions will be described in a special section. The system of different actions shaping learning activity as a whole will be considered next. One of the complicated problems concerns the individualities of theoretical consciousness and thinking emerging and intensively developing in the very process of accomplishing learning activity in students. Therefore that problem will be discussed. Putting into practice this activity presupposes new content and new curricula for the teaching-learning or educational process. This problem will also be briefly discussed. Last, but not least, some words will be said about how new curricula, built on our learning approach, are used in Russian education (Davydov 1988, 1990).

The Content of the Activity Concept

Positive changes in the modern educational system depend primarily on how pedagogues will be able to organize anew the whole process of teaching and upbringing in school. This last aspect depends, in our view, on how the very learning-teaching activity is organized and how skill and knowledge can be appropriated by school children. One might then ask 'What is learning-teaching activity?' To answer this question we must first address the more general concept of activity.

Within the philosophical-pedagogical area, the notion of activity is understood as the process in which the surrounding reality is transformed by men's creative efforts. Labor is the original form of such transformation. All kinds of material and mental human activity are derivatives from labor and keep its main characteristic features which is transformation of reality and person(s) as acting.

While studying concrete structures of human activity, the Russian psychologist, A.N. Leontiev and his followers suggested that the main components of such activity are needs, motives, goals, conditions, means, actions and operations.

One important characteristic feature of activity is the fact that it is always, whether explicitly or implicitly, object-related. This implies that all its components have some object-related contents and that the activity itself is necessarily directed toward the creation of some material or spiritual product (thus, for example, during their activities industrial workers' create real machines and buildings; writers and artists produce artistic work, etc.).

If we intentionally use the term 'activity' with regard to the particular spheres of human life then we need to realize clearly what kind of objective content is involved in its components and final products. At the same time, if in the real life, which we observe around us, we are not able to select and define components that are involved in the activities, then we cannot trace how real transformations of particular material or mental activity occur, and, consequently, we should not apply the term of 'activity' to the events observed.

A General Characterization of Learning Activity

The above characteristic can be directly related to what should be called 'school children's learning activity'. First, this kind of activity involves all the features listed above, characteristic of the general concept of activity. Second, this activity also has a specific object-related content by which it differs from any other kind of human activity (e.g., games or work). Third, learning activity necessarily involves some creative or reforming elements. If the listed components are not present in actually observed lessons, then we can state that in such lessons the proper learning activity is not realized at all or realized quite imperfectly (a case which is not rare in school).

In its historical origin, however, properly organized school learning is the core of children's learning activity. We speak here of the origin, because in more recent history school education has had long periods when children's presence in the classroom was not connected to proper learning activity. In order to learn while in class, the children should learn and appropriate knowledge and skills in the process of full-fledged learning activity; such activity should be *properly arranged*. What then is the idea of such an *adequate arrangement*?

Children can only appropriate knowledge and skills through learning activity when they have an internal need and motivation to do so. Learning activity involves transformation of the material to be appropriated and implies that some new mental product, i.e., knowledge, is received.

Learning needs and motives orient children toward appropriation of knowledge as a result of transformations of a given material. These transformations reveal certain relevant internal relations of the material. Through the study of this transformation, school children can trace how external appearances of a material have developed and depend on the internal relation of the material. The *origin* of the appearance can then be traced. Learning need orients pupils towards making real or imaginary experiments with a particular material in order to divide the material into general core aspects and particular aspects, and to see how these aspects are interrelated.

It should be noted that, in logical science, knowledge about the interrelation between general and particular core aspects — is referred to as *theoretical* knowledge. Children's need in learning consists then in their strivings to obtain knowledge about general aspects of an object, that is theoretical knowledge through experimentation and exploration. Making experimentations and transformations with objects necessarily involves creativity. When the teacher systematically directs the situation in the classroom so that it would require that the children obtain knowledge about a certain object by means of experiments with the object, the children face tasks requiring learning activity.

When children have to appropriate a certain knowledge that has already been formed and is offered to them as something ready-made, their learning activity cannot be realized even if they actually fulfill some 'learning work'. Many traditional textbooks and learning techniques presume exactly this kind of 'work' that does not involve any large-scale components of school children's activity. One characteristic feature related to the new pedagogical way of thinking which may contribute to the overcoming of these negative traditions consists in the requirement that the activity approach has to be applied to the organization of the learning-teaching process.

How are 'appropriation' and 'learning' interrelated in 'learning activity'? Children and adults continuously appropriate knowledge while performing different activities (such as play or work). If 'ready-made' knowledge is appropriated, the learning process may not require that any object-related or mental experiments be conducted by the learning person. Consequently, the learning activity that involves appropriation processes is performed only when these processes take the form of goal-directed transformation of a particular material. First of all, since both 'appropriation' and 'learning' can occur, not only in learning activity but also in other kinds of activity and, secondly, material can be appropriated without any transformation, then these concepts should not be identified with learning activity only.

We must emphasize that learning activity and learning goals, respectively, are connected, first of all, within the process of transformation of material in which a learning person can study, detect and fix some core components that underlie many external features of a material and, by doing so, the learning person comes to understand the relation between a material's external appearances and changes in appearances.

Characteristics of Theoretical Knowledge as Content of Learning Activity

Knowledge that represents interrelations between internal and external, between entity and appearance, between original and derived is called *theoretical* knowledge. Such knowledge can be appropriated only if one reproduces the very process of its *origination*, receiving, and arrangement, i.e., when one transforms material. Then the material acquires a learning-directed purpose because now it is intended only for repeating the acts that have once led people to discover and conceptualize theoretical knowledge.

Learning-directed experiments is the only way for school children to trace the interrelations which exist between the internal and external content of material to be appropriated. Such experiments always involve creative features. In our opinion, human personality manifests itself in the creative deeds of a person. Therefore, when we form in school children a need for learning activity and the very ability to perform such activity we thereby contribute considerably to their personal development.

The Organization of Students' Learning Activity

Now let us consider the issue of what the 'proper arrangement' of school activity is? First of all, the teaching-upbringing process should rely heavily on the need of pupils to appropriate mankind's spiritual heritage (including, in particular, communication skills that utilize moral values and legal norms). 'True' organization of teaching-learning activity starts by gradually, yet persistently, inculcating such needs in school children. Learning activity just cannot exist without this basic component; however, the issue of *how* to inculcate such needs in children requires special discussion.

Nobody can force a small child to play. The child should feel the need to play. Equally, we cannot force school children to enter into learning activity if they do not have the need to do so. Although school children, without having such needs, can in fact learn and appropriate various knowledge (and indeed appropriate very well), they are not able to transform learning material creatively because they do not have the ability to formulate such critical vital questions that can be answered only by means of secret-revealing experiments.

The second condition needed to arrange proper learning activity is the formulation of learning tasks for pupils which would require their making experiments with the material to be appropriated. The learning tasks should be formulated in such a way that transformation is required. For example, in a lesson on mathematics in primary school, the following learning task was formulated for the pupils (of course, this task included sequences of minor exercises):

If we want to measure a very large object and only have a small measuring device, how could we then reduce the time of measuring and yet present the result by means of this device?

To solve this task, the children should make a series of experiments. In particular, they needed to be introduced to a wide range of large measurement exercises as part of the major task.

In short, learners should act in the following order: First, they realize that to reduce the measuring time some type of large-scale measuring device would be required; then (with the help of their teacher) they understand the need to know the relationship between small and large measurements. Finally, the children having understood this connection and working with a large measuring device, can quickly measure the large object and present the result in the units of the small measuring device.

Although the children solve the task with the help of their teacher, they actually discover for themselves the need to use the mathematical action of multiplying in order to find out the answer to a practical question (getting this kind of answer means orienting children towards the relationship between different scales of measurement).

Learning tasks, whose solution implies a full-scale learning activity, require that pupils analyze the conditions in which the particular concepts of theoretical knowledge originated, and that they appropriate generalized ways of acting. In other words, while solving learning tasks school children discover original or relevant relationships inherent in the respective material.

Metaphorically speaking, one should not study a particular 'tree' as such, but instead one should first address the tree's universal germ cell, the seed, and only then should one try to relate different trees to one another. Here we do not speak of the tasks that the teacher formulates for the children in the lesson (such as to solve a particular task or re-tell some text). Instead, a 'proper' arrangement of learning activity implies that the teacher should formulate a goal for the children in such a way that in trying to achieve it the children would analyze the 'seed' first, and only then trace how the seed could be transformed into a 'tree' by means of material or mental experiments.

To formulate and solve learning tasks one needs to use such material that the children could perform the respective transformations and make object-related or mental experiments with this material. Current learning material of school subjects such as physics, chemistry, or biology meet these requirements rather badly. With the proper organization, however, good opportunities can be found in subjects like history, literature, native language, arts, etc. Thus, languages could be taught by means of for-mulating learning tasks for the children. These tasks should engage the children and at the same time lead to actions of transforming words and phrases, enabling the children to appropriate norms that rule speech construction (Poluyanov & Matiss 1994). A similar way of teaching involves a learning task that implies how experimentation and transformation could be organized in mathematics, work training, and other school subjects.

Basic Learning Actions

Large-scale teaching and learning activity in both natural-scientific-mathematical and humanistic school subjects implies that the teacher should give special attention to how fully and correctly the school children perform the necessary actions in order to solve the learning tasks successfully. A number of such actions are known today. Let us consider them in detail. The first and major learning action is the one in which pupils have to transform the terms of a task when the task cannot be resolved in the ways they have already been taught. The goal of this action is to search for and characterize the basic features of the same kind of tasks. It is the kind of action that younger school children would perform in order to solve the above-mentioned mathematical task of multiple measurement relations.

The second learning action requires the student to make models that represent already known relations of the material in the learning task. These models have to be represented either in object-based, sign-based, or graphical form (for the above-mentioned task this kind of relation is modeled in sign-numerical form). This does not mean that any special form of representation can be called a model. For a *representation* to become a *model*, it should reflect some general (fundamental) relations between the elements of the task to be solved.

A special learning action consists in transformation of the very model in order to study carefully the properties of the general relation already found. Another learning action consists in a concrete definition of the system of relations found in the various specific tasks that are uniform to the learning task (in the cited mathematical task such concretization occurs when pupils discover the possibilities of using multiplication in all situations where it is difficult to compare the measuring device at hand with the object to be measured).

Learning actions also include actions like control and evaluation. Control gives school children a possibility for correcting their execution of learning actions and evaluation enables them to determine if a general way of solving the given learning task is appropriated (and to what extent) or not.

Thus, a proper arrangement of learning activity requires that the teacher, relying on the children's need and readiness to appropriate theoretical knowledge, would be able to formulate, on the basis of specific material within a subject matter area, a learning task that can be resolved by means of the actions discussed above (i.e., the teacher should use definite means to promote the children's existing need and ability to receive a learning task and perform learning actions). In this case, the teacher instructs the respective subjects in accordance with the requirements of learning activity (i.e., by means of pupil's solving learning tasks).

As observations show, some teachers, whether consciously or spontaneously, utilize these techniques in their practical work, though often not in full sequences and therefore not completely successful. Often the instruction is not successful because textbooks and methodical recommendations for the instruction of particular school subjects do not meet the requirement of the very learning material and the intended way of how to introduce the subject into the teaching/learning process. Neither do the textbooks or methodological recommentations meet the requirements of the full sequences of learning activity and the method of solving learning tasks. To overcome these serious shortcomings we need some special kinds of research to be carried out which include work by logicians, psychologists, specialists on didactics and learning experts.

Learning Activity as Basis for Developing Theoretical Thinking

Another issue related to developmental teaching is that any teaching to a certain degree is directed toward development of consciousness and personality of learners. In a goal-directed way, large-scale learning activity forms and develops in school children a background of theoretical knowledge and thinking and contributes to their personal development. Usually, teachers believe that theoretical consciousness and thinking represent an abstract attitude to real life and are often connected to verbal knowledge only. This is clearly a misunderstanding, undoubtedly related to obsolete philosophical and psychological views.

First of all, theoretical consciousness and thinking is realized in an action-performance-visual, visual-image, and verbal-discursive form. Second, it is represented in the sciences and arts, moral practices and law. Third, it consists in humans' rational attitudes to real life, in humans' ability to resolve rationally both abstract and practical everyday tasks. Here, we do not mean just *any* tasks, but the ones which, in order to be solved, require from humans (including, of course, school children) the ability to distinguish between internal and external, appearance and essential. It is well-known that external appearances of things differ from the internal core of things. Only dialectical consciousness and thinking can resolve these conflicts. Therefore, the commonly used term *theoretical thinking* is, at the same time, *dialectical thinking*. Theoretical consciousness directs the attention of humans toward the need to conceive of one's own cognitive actions, to consider knowledge itself. In philosophical terms this is referred to as reflection.

We have called theoretical consciousness and thinking *dialectical* or *reasonable* (as compared with rational or intellectual).[1] The task of studying this *type* of consciousness and thinking has a very high philosophical and psychological significance. Its solution allowed us to formulate the concept of 'learning activity', which may exist only where dialectical (theoretical) consciousness and thinking have developed and are functioning.

Modern philosophy and psychology claim that humans have two basic types of consciousness and thinking (the details of the differences between consciousness and thinking will not be described here, only thinking will be touched upon).

At first, humans possess empirical-rational thinking allowing them to group and classify things and phenomena of the surrounding world by comparing and pointing out the interrelations of genus and kind. This type of thinking makes it possible to solve the tasks of relating things to a certain class (genus) or, vice versa, divide a class into certain subclasses or kinds.

Second, humans are often confronted with tasks that require analysis of a system of things under observation where the demand is to distinguish between main and second order aspects, basic and derived aspects, general and particular aspects, essence and phenomenon. Very often the task is not only to point out such characteristics of a system, but also to link them together mentally, to construct a phenomenon derived from its general core, a particular feature from a general feature. On the contrary, in other cases, it might be necessary to understand the core, i.e., the general and

1. This problem was discussed in detail in chapter VII of my book, *Types of generalization in instruction*, published in Moscow in 1972 and translated into English and published in the USA (Davydov 1972, 1990) as well as in several other publications in Russian and English (see, e.g., Davydov 1988a, 1988b, 1988c).

most important characteristic relying on particular phenomena. Quite clearly the phenomenon and core (particular and general, etc.) of a system are not similar. They characterize different contents of that system and are *contradictory* to each other. In a lot of different life situations it is necessary to find out and to cope with such leading contradictory characteristics of systems of objects. For instance, ordinary (and often observed) bulbs are particular and concrete phenomena of electricity, but the essence of that system is the 'movement of electric power' between the poles 'plus' and 'minus', which is *not* visible to the human eye.

Thus, there are tasks of deriving phenomena out of core characteristics (i.e., essence) and tasks of tracing back phenomena to core characteristics (e.g., essence) — that is, understanding certain particular characteristics of a system by means of attributing them to its general characteristic. Humans solve all these tasks by means of dialectical/ theoretical thinking within which contradictions can be handled in objective systems, to find mutual relationships and transitions in such holistic systems. Analyzing the mutual connections and transformations of phenomenon and essence is, at the same time, the process of studying their *development*. Tasks of this type cannot be solved by the first type of thinking. A dialectical solution of tasks presupposes for its functioning two further mental actions (besides analysis) — planning of mental movement and reflection, that is the inspection of different bases of that movement.

Many people believe that dialectical thinking is a quality known only in a small group of particularly bright humans. This is *not* the case: A large part of the population have spontaneously acquired this type of thinking through difficult life practices (e.g., by solving complicated moral problems). However, a certain percentage of the population has not acquired the capacity for this kind of thinking at all (which is caused, above all, by the education they received or by a 'conflictless' life) or they have to a very small extent demonstrated this kind of thinking and are not theoretically orientated in complicated situations. Our theory of learning activity — put into practice in the right way — is aimed at the goal of educating and developing all school and college students' capacity for dialectical thinking in *all* matters.

Dialectical thinking can and should be formed in school children at all educational stages. Their development of creative abilities, initiatives, self-understanding, and, finally, the development of their personality depends on it. A proper organization and implementation of learning activity contributes to this aim. The developmental influence of learning activity will increase considerably if combined with school children's labor activity and productive work which is related to the origins of genuine, creative transformations and experiments with objects. Combinations of learning experiments with labor activities provide new sources for developing school children's creative potential, i.e., their personality.

One may ask: Can theoretical consciousness and thinking not be formed in school children who study common textbooks and techniques? I will reply directly: Yes, it can. But it will be formed spontaneously, not to a full scale, and not necessarily for all children. And when it happens, it happens *in spite of* the many recommendations of commonly accepted didactic and methodical principles which varies within the real practice of different teachers.

Elaboration of new Curricula Based on Learning Activity

The theory of learning activity underlies elaboration of a new kind of curriculum (Petrovsky 1989). It is well-known that a curriculum, or a teaching program, describes intended *contents* of school subjects (such as mathematics, biology, history, etc.); a hierarchical listing of concrete knowledge and skills which are relevant to separate subjects and how they should be developed in time. Problems related to curriculum design are not particularly technical issues. Instead, such problems mostly constitute general and basic issues for the entire educational system. The reform in the Russian educational system is closely connected to the design of a new kind of curriculum (i.e., learning programs that strongly differ from the programs commonly accepted in traditional schools.)

Here are the basic statements suggested by the new pedagogical psychology of our general direction in relation to curriculum design:

First Statement

In traditional schools, curricula are designed according to the requirements based on the formal-logical views of human thinking. In these programs learning material is arranged so that in order to appropriate it the learner's thoughts should move from *observing many particular* appearances of an object to detecting in these appearances certain identical, similar, or *common* components that are designated by word(s). In this case, learners appropriate 'general knowledge' as a result of comparison between particular phenomena. The learners' thoughts move *from the particular to the general aspects* of the problem area. Teaching programs that provide for such direction of thought in the process of appropriation are, in fact, a kind of catalog, categorization, or conglomeration of knowledge. The *discursive* speech of learners plays a major role in appropriation of such knowledge.

One example of such curriculum design on mathematics is related to how children appropriate the *notion of number*. As is well-known, to make children familiar with the notion they are shown sets of objects (such as sets of sticks, balls, toy cars, etc.). The children observe these sets, compare them in numbers, abstract the characteristic features of these sets, extract the identical or common numerical characteristics, and name them with word-numerals. As a result, one set can be named with the numerical word 'two', another set — 'three', and so on.

The cited example illustrates how the notion of number is formed in children on a formal-logical basis. This is the scheme of how mathematical concepts are formed in children, and which is included in traditional programs of mathematic teaching. And this is not only used for mathematics, but also for other school subjects!

Second Statement

Systematic schooling that follows traditional programs, on the one hand, forms in children *empirical concepts* and notions about various domains of real life and, on the other hand, cultivates an *empirical way of thinking*. By means of such thinking we can classify manifold objects existing in the spheres of life and solve various tasks based on gender-specific relations between objects.

Due to empirical thinking we can orient ourselves well in the events of everyday life. Such thinking corresponds to 'commonsense'. Empirical thinking is developed in humans *without* any schooling; schooling only supports the further utilization and cultivation of this form of thinking.

Therefore, however paradoxical this may seem, schooling that follows traditional programs *does not promote the development* of the learners. To be more precise, traditional teaching forms the background for any other kind of thinking apart from the empirical one. Empirical thinking appears in human beings *outside* school and can, to a certain degree, be developed *outside* school.

Third Statement

Systematic schooling that follows our school programs is based on the dialectical understanding of thinking. First of all, learners *actively transform* the learning material included in these programs by means of certain object-related or mental actions. In the process of this kind of transformation, learners discover and distinguish in the learning material some essential or *general relationship*, and when they study it they can discover many particular appearances of the material. In this case learners appropriate 'general knowledge' straight away through their activity-analysis of the material. The particular appearances of the material are derived from the 'general knowledge'. The learner's thought moves 'from the general to the particular within a material'. Curricula that provide for such directions of thought help to establish relationships with integrated systems of knowledge. The leading role in the appropriation of such knowledge belongs to the learners' *actions*.

The next illustration from our curriculum shows how children are introduced to the notion of number (Davydov 1990). At first the children become familiar with the mathematical notion of quantity (it is defined by three difference relations: a=b, a<<b, a>>b. With this notion children can directly equalize physical values. Thus, for example, they can use a sample of wooden segment to make many such segments from a big wooden plank.

There are situations, however, in which equalization of quantity can be made but only *in a mediated way*. Thus, for example, in one task one needs to fill a vessel with the same quantity of water as is found in the vessel of another shape. To solve the task one needs to know how to *measure quantities* with numbers. In the curriculum built on our principles, the teacher formulates for the children a task that requires making measures. The children get the idea that to implement such action they need to find a special *means* (for example, a small mug to measure water) and, also, appropriate special rules for using it (for example, how to fill the mug with water).

With the help of their teacher, the children find *a means of measuring*, appropriate principles for using this means and discover that the very *act* of measuring represents a search for the *multiple relation of values*, resulting in a particular number. Then the learners can write down in literal form the *general* formula of this relation as follows:

A:b = N, where A is the value to be measured; b is the means of measuring; N is the multiple relation as a result of the measuring action represented in number.

Having appropriated the general idea of this formula, the children then become able to implement all kinds of particular measurements and receive concrete numbers; with these numbers they can now perform mediated equalization (e.g., solve the task of equalizing water in vessels with different shapes).

The above illustration is a very brief presentation of how the notion of number is formed in children on the basis of dialectical understanding of thinking. This scheme can also serve to form in school children other mathematical conceptions, if children study in a program of our kind (Davydov 1996). By means of this kind of scheme one can also form in children the notions involved in other school subjects, such as physics, chemistry, geography, and others. The main characteristic of these principles is the idea that first the children implement the action of distinguishing some general relationship and then they try to find out various particular appearances of the relationship. In other words, by means of their actions the children trace the conditions in which particular conceptions *originate*.

Fourth Statement

As special pedagogical-psychological studies show, systematic teaching in accordance with our program develops school children's theoretical notions and theoretical thinking that direct the search for the conditions and origin of relationships within a material. Theoretical thinking helps students to orient among general relationships and allows them to derive from these relationships various specific consequences. Such thinking does not remove the need for empirical thinking — this kind of thinking should be seen as a kind of thinking directed at other kinds of tasks.

Theoretical thinking does not originate and does not develop in people's everyday life. It develops only in the kind of teaching that uses a curriculum based on dialectical concepts of thinking. It is the latter kind of teaching that has *developmental* effect. The Russian educational system is now in the process of reform and directed at developing the intellectual potential in young people; hence the need to implement and elaborate systems of promoting theoretical thinking. (Davydov 1988).

Practical Application of the New Curricula

We would like to note that our theory of learning activity and developmental education in Russia today finds considerably wide usage. At present, many schools in the cities and the countryside in various regions of Russia (like Siberia, Povolzh'e, Ural, and others) utilize curricula based on our theory. These curricula involve programs on mathematics (Davydov 1990; Davydov 1996) and physics, Russian language and literature (Poluyanov & Matiss 1994; Davydov, Gorbov, Mikulin & Savel'eva 1996), art (Kudina & Novyanskaya 1992-96), labor practice, chemistry, and grammatics. These programs are used in primary and secondary schools.

Thus, the resolute reform of the educational system that occurs in Russia today rests heavily on new pedagogical ideas (Davydov, Gorbov, Mikulin & Savel'eva 1996) and utilizes new programs based on new pedagogical psychology. The process of reforming has started quite recently and the considerable efforts of scientists and practical teachers are needed for its successful realization.

References

Davydov, V.V. (1988a). Problems of developmental teaching. *Soviet Education* 30 (8), 15-97.

Davydov, V.V. (1988b). Problems of developmental teaching. *Soviet Education* 30 (9), 3-83.

Davydov, V.V. (1988c). Problems of developmental teaching. *Soviet Education* 30 (19), 3-77.

Davydov, V.V. (1990). *Types of generalization in instruction: Logical and psychological problems in the structuring of school curricula* (J. Teller, trans.). Reston, Va.: National Council of Teachers of Mathematics. (Original work published 1972)

Davydov, V.V. (1996). *Teoria razvivayushchego obuchenia* [The theory of developmental teaching]. Moscow: Intor.

Davydov, V.V., Gorbov, S.F., Mikulin, G.G. & Savel'eva, O.V. (1996a). *Matematika, 1. klass* [Mathematics Textbook for first-graders]. Moscow: Miros.

Davydov, V.V., Gorbov, S.F., Mikulin, G.G. & Savel'eva, O.V. (1996b). *Matematika 2. klass* [Mathematics Textbook for Second-graders]. Moscow: Miros.

Kudina, G.N. & Novyanskaya, Z.N. (1992-96). *Literatura 1.-5. klass* [Literature Textbook for 1st-5th grades]. Moscow: Intor.

Petrovsky, A.V. (ed.), (1989). *Novoe pedagogicheskoe myshlenie* [New Pedagogical Thinking]. Moscow: Prosveshchenie.

Poluyanov, Yu. A. & Matiss, T.A. (1994). *Metodicheskoe rukovodstvo po obucheniyu iskusstvu, 1. klass* [Methodical manual on teaching art. First grade]. Moscow.

Uchebnye programmy po russkomu yazyku i matematike, 1.-5. klass [Curricula for Russian and mathematics, 1st-5th grades]. Moscow: Prosveshchenie, 1992.

Repkin, V.V. (1991). *Russky yazyk 1.-3. klass* [Russian Language, 1st-3rd grade]. Tomsk: Peleng.

7 Learning Activity and its Formation: Ascending from the Abstract to the Concrete

Joachim Lompscher

Introduction

The concept of learning activity was formed within the framework of cultural-historical theory as a concretization of the general concept of activity. The concept has its roots in the philosophical ideas of Kant, Fichte, Hegel and Marx, and was elaborated in its philosophical and psychological aspects particularly by Ilyenkov, Lektorsky and Leontiev. Learning activity is not identical with learning processes as such, but represents a special kind of activity. Learning is always connected with activity, but in different ways: It may occur as an aspect of several activities or as a special activity.

In the first section of the paper I shall try to briefly outline which implications the concept of learning has as a special kind of activity for how teaching is conceptualized and for its interrelations with learning and development. Learning activity is not given 'from the beginning' and it does not emerge and develop spontaneously. As a significant component of societal culture, it has to be acquired by individuals as other content and forms of culture as well (i.e., it has to be systematically formed in order to make learners able to meet the challenges of their present and future lives).

An activity-theoretical approach is directed towards the formation of consciousness rather than simply concentrating on describing what can be found in schools or elsewhere. Therefore, teaching strategies — their theoretical foundation and practical implementation, their prerequisites and results — play an important role in this concept. The teaching strategy of ascending from the abstract to the concrete — as one form and possibility of putting into practice the 'activity-and-formation strategy' — is the topic of the second section.

Finally, in the third section, I report on our first steps of studying learning strategies which are the 'pendant' of teaching strategies and represent an important aspect or component of the psychic regulation of learning activity. In order to be successful in forming an effective learning activity in learners (in teaching them to learn), teaching strategies have to correspond to the learners' subjective prerequisites, one of them being their learning strategies. A lot of work has to be done yet in order to analyze the functioning and relationships of learning strategies with other regulation components and with teaching strategies. An important condition for that work is the synthesis of what has been found in different scientific 'schools' or directions as, for instance, cultural-historical and cognitive-psychological research.

Learning Activity and Teaching

Learning activity, as it was characterized in the Introduction to this volume and in the paper by Davydov, does not develop spontaneously. It develops as a function of societal conditions, first of all, on the quality of teaching activity. Wide-spread teaching strategies aimed at the transmission of ready-made knowledge to the learners (found, e.g., in cross-cultural studies by Anderson, Ryan & Shapiro 1989) or the orientation towards the so-called free development of personality (implemented by some reform-pedagogical directions and represented, e.g., in the view that children themselves know best what is necessary for their development) are unable to form or promote learning activity. These two kinds of teaching strategies represent the extreme poles of a wide continuum. In real teaching practice, a great variety of different strategies can be found depending on goals and content of instruction, preferences and pedagogical abilities of teachers, level and diversity of learners' development, conditions of school context, etc. Here we are only interested in one aspect of that very complex problem, namely in the appropriateness of teaching strategies for pro-moting the development of learning activity in the discussed sense.

For this aim we need teaching strategies oriented towards the learner's own activity and, at the same time, towards the conscious and systematic formation of that activity. Comparing with the above mentioned strategies, I use the label 'activity-and-formation strategy' (Lompscher 1995) and will characterize its main positions or principles as follows:

1) Learning is based on a subject's own activities (interacting with others) directed towards accomplishing tasks under concrete conditions and with concrete means. Therefore, the didactic organization of learning processes must not be oriented simply towards the material to be learned, its pre-

sentation, and the teacher's actions, but it has to be oriented towards the learners' activity, which is necessary for mastering the learning material, and towards the psychic regulation of that activity. This statement does not mean a negation of the concrete learning material, because there is no — and cannot be any — activity without object or content. What I am stressing is the necessity of considering a teaching object or subject matter material in close connection with the respective activity. The learning material is not acting upon the learner, the learner can acquire the material only by actively working with it. Therefore, the teaching material has to be transformed into a learning object, i.e., to be presented and shaped in a form appropriate to learning activity. The first question is which kind and structure of learners' activity is necessary and how can it be provoked and promoted to ensure a certain learning result. (The advanced learner will ask such questions himself concerning self-set learning goals.)

2) Learning activity is characterized by a fundamental dilemma: As a rule, the activity necessary for mastering a new learning object (a subject matter area) has not yet been — or only insufficiently — acquired by the learners. Thus, learning actions, motives, etc., adequate for concrete objects (subject matter materials), conditions, and goals have to be formed specifically. But this cannot be done independently of the respective object — because there is no activity without object or content and one essential feature of any activity consists in the fact that its structure and course depends on its object! Acquisition presupposes adequate activity, but that activity cannot emerge and develop outside of the respective acquisition process. There is only one way of resolving this contradiction: Learning activity and learning object have to be considered and organized as a unity. The didactic organization of learning processes, i.e., planning, designing and implementing instructional arrangements, has to have in mind, and to connect with each other, three different 'logics': The first one is, of course, the logic of the teaching object (the system, structure, character of the respective subject matter area), the second is the logic of the acquisition process concerning the specific subject matter area (teaching object), (e.g., prior knowledge, approaches and learning actions necessary for transforming the teaching object into a learning object, for studying it and for constructing new knowledge, skills and motives), and the third is the logic of psychic development (levels and qualities of cognitive operations and structures, emotional and motivational levels, their interrelations etc.). The predominant and one-sided orientation towards the content, the teaching material

by the majority of teachers, curriculum and text book specialists and other people engaged in instructional processes is a serious obstacle for turning to the described approach.

3) The formation of an appropriate activity necessary for the acquisition of a learning object (the material to be learned) presupposes the analysis of the interrelationships between objective demands and subjective pre-requisites: The specific content, structure, complexity, etc. of a learning object make objective demands to be accomplished by the learner in order to acquire respective knowledge and skills, to become able to solve respec-tive tasks, etc. Handling these demands, in turn, presupposes objectively necessary subjective prerequisites in the learner. He/she must have certain knowledge, skills, capabilities, etc. in order to find and conduct an appro-priate approach to the learning object. But very often, learners really do not know and are not able to do what would be required for further learning. There is quite a large gap between really existing subjective prerequisites and objectively necessary prerequisites which are also subjective ones. This gap can serve as a starting point for systematic formation of learning activity through the formulation of hypotheses about learning actions, which are necessary for bridging that gap through one's own activity. Teaching goals and methods have to be determined not only with respect to the teaching object and its presentation, but particularly with respect to the necessary activity and the conditions, under which it may be formed and carried out. Putting into practice such hypotheses requires a differentiated approach, stepwise formation, and long-term experimentation with continuous evaluation in order to find out optimal conditions of that process. It should be stressed that the formation of subjective prerequisites for a certain learning activity can be reached only through that very activity itself — neither by development of internal programs as such nor by projection and transmission from outside. The crucial point is the own activity of the learner based on the interaction of internalization and externalization under concrete conditions ('self-development').

4) Activity and self-development presuppose appropriate motivation. As indicated by Leontiev (1979), activities differ, first of all, with respect to their motivation. Learning motives cannot be transmitted to the learner, they can only emerge in the respective activity. Didactic organization of learning has to start from the learners' experience, interests, questions, and needs, etc.; it has to stimulate and use cognitive conflicts, stimulate

reflection on objective demands and subjective prerequisites as a basis for the formation of learning goals, make pupils aware of successes as well as failures, etc., and it has to support the learners' self-confidence and self-efficacy.

5) Psychic structures and functions develop depending on how they are used as means and components of activity regulation. Didactic organization of learning and/or other kinds of activity aimed at the stimulation and promotion of psychic development has to be oriented towards the learners' 'zone of proximal development'. As indicated by Vygotsky (1934, 1956), a given level of development is characterized on the one hand by a set of real, independent performances and, on the other, by possibilities arising beyond that performance level. The transformation of such possibilities into the reality of practical or cognitive or social processes needs two inter-related conditions: first, a model, instruction or help by others; and second, a person's own activity. The interrelations between guidance and independence and their quality are continuously changing in the process of transition from a zone of proximal development to a zone of actual performance, thus opening up a new zone of proximal development and so forth.

This teaching strategy may have different forms of implementation. It serves as a general 'orientation basis' (sensu Galperin, 1989, 1992) for designing and practicing concrete teaching actions and instructional models. There are other concepts elaborated with the same goal of overcoming weaknesses of traditional teaching and strengthening the role of learners' own activity. Of special interest among them are, in my opinion, the concepts of situated learning (Greeno 1992, 1997; Lave 1992; Lave & Wenger 1991; Spiro, Feltovich, Jacobson & Coulson 1991), guided participation (Rogoff 1990, 1992, 1995), reciprocal teaching (Brown & Palincsar 1989), cognitive apprenticeship (Collins, Brown & Newman 1989), and anchored instruction (Cognition and Technology Group at Vanderbilt, 1993, 1996). These and some other concepts, as well as much effort directly made by practitioners in schools, show more or less far-reaching similarities with the 'activity-and-formation strategy', although, as a rule, they only stress certain aspects of learning and do not try to consequently grasp and to form learning activity in its whole complexity.

This is not the place to go into detail, but it is worthwhile considering the widespread efforts of designing new conditions and forms of teaching and learning based on ideas about learners as subjects cooperating with others, actively acting upon learning objects and each other, regulating and forming their activity under guidance and becoming more and more independent and self-responsible in this process.[1]

The Teaching Strategy of Ascending from the Abstract to the Concrete

This teaching strategy is one form or possibility of implementing the above characterized 'activity-and-formation strategy'. Beginning with the late 50s, Elkonin and Davydov (1962, 1966) elaborated a teaching concept based on Vygotsky's cultural-historical theory and Leontiev's activity theory and put it into practice in the laboratory school No. 91 in Moscow and later in other schools as well (Davydov 1969, 1988a, 1988b, 1988c, 1996, Davydov & Vardanjan 1981, Davydov & Rubtsov 1995, etc.).[2] Following them and cooperating with them (e.g., Davydov, Lompscher & Markova 1982), we organized teaching experiments in grades 4-6 (10 to 12-year-old learners) with the teaching strategy of ascending from the abstract to the concrete (Lompscher 1984, 1985, 1989a, 1989b). The aim was to find ways for and to show possibilities of promoting elementary theoretical thinking and cognitive motivation at an age level which is more or less still characterized by concrete operations (in Piagetian terms).

Traditional instruction very often begins with different concrete phenomena and tries to transmit to the learners what is essential in these phenomena, but the learners do not yet have an idea of that essence and

---

1. It is not surprising to state similarities between these concepts: Particularly, during the 80s and 90s a certain kind of convergency could be observed between activity theory (or broader: cultural-historical theory) on the one hand, and some other directions, especially, cognitive psychology, on the other, in the fields of learning, instruction, development, etc. (see, e.g., Billett 1996; de Corte 1992; Engelsted, Hedegaard, Karpatschof & Mortensen 1993; Hildebrand-Nilshon & Rückriem 1988; Resnick 1989; Resnick, Levine & Teasley 1992; Säljö 1991; Oers 1990; Vosniadou 1996). Especially, the study and discussion of Vygotsky's ideas and works stimulated this process (e.g., Das & Gindis 1995; Engeström 1987; Lompscher 1996a; Moll 1990; Newman & Holzman 1993; Tharp & Gallimore 1988; Veer & Valsiner 1993; Wertsch 1985a, b). The centenary of Vygotsky's birthday in 1996 brought a lot of conferences, publications and other activities, which strongly contributed to a wide acquaintance with his work and, partially, with what was done on this basis during the following decades after his death in 1934 (see, e.g., Lompscher 1996b; Tryphon & Voneche 1996).
2. Nowadays, based on the International Association of Developmental Teaching founded in 1994, this conception has been adopted by a huge number of teachers, principals, authors of teaching material etc. in Russia and some other countries.

cannot get it, because they do not have any means of achieving that goal. When comparing concrete phenomena without such a cognitive tool, learners will predominantly see the surface features and relationships and not go beyond them, because they cannot differentiate between general and essential features (general features may not be essential with respect to a certain question or aim, whereas essential features, in a certain respect, are general necessarily for a corresponding class of objects, events or processes). The teacher's verbal explanations may be adopted, but not understood by the learners. Thus, they have to keep in mind a lot of concrete phenomena and isolated facts overloading their memory instead of subordinating them under an appropriate abstraction containing the essential features and relationships of a respective whole class of objects, events or processes. Such an abstraction would function as an orientation basis (sensu Galperin) to uncover what is essential regarding different concrete phenomena and serves as an anchor for storing them in memory.[3] But, of course, it only functions if it is itself formed appropriately. The teaching strategy of ascending from the abstract to the concrete is directed towards solving this problem and contradiction.

This strategy is often misunderstood as deductive teaching or negation of an iconic, concrete basis of learning and the like, as overstraining the children by going beyond their cognitive capacity. This would be correct from a point of view according to which instruction has to *follow* development and has to wait until the prerequisites for a higher level of cognitive performance have developed. From a Vygotskian point of view, we have to determine the zone of proximal development (ZPD) being opened in a new social situation of development and to elaborate and organize teaching *in advance of* development in the very sense of ZPD. The beginning of school and primary education is such a new social situation for developmental potentialities which are often — especially in traditional public schooling — underestimated or not seen at all. The results of Davydov and others have convincingly shown these potentialities.

The strategy of ascending from the abstract to the concrete has two main steps. The first step is the formation of the so-called starting abstractions, the second is the study of the concrete material by means of the abstractions corresponding to the instructional goals and content as far as the starting abstraction allows (Fig. 7.1). In this process of ascending, the

3. Here a connection exists to the somewhat vague schema concept as it has been developed in cognitive psychology (see, e.g., Aebli 1980/81; Anderson 1983; Bartlett 1932; Piaget 1937; Rummelhart & Norman 1978).

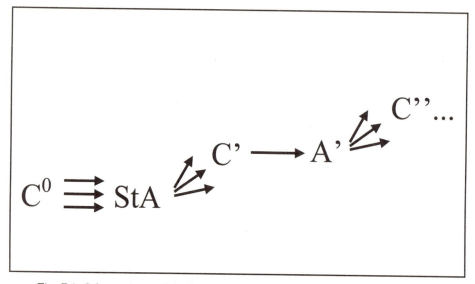

Fig. 7.1. Schematic model of ascending from the abstract to the concrete.

concrete variety is cognitively penetrated and the abstract conceptualization itself is changed and enriched by the concrete content. The starting abstraction contains only the most important features and relations of the learning object and forms a kind of wholistic frame into which the concrete details may then be integrated and stored in memory.

Essential features and relationships can be found out by the learner by actively modifying the learning object or its representatives, because in this case he/she will discriminate varying features from invariant ones. The latter ones constitute what is necessary for the object to remain itself in different concrete variations. This calls for appropriate actions upon the learning object, adequate to the substance of that object or domain, and for the learners' qualification to carry out these actions appropriately. Thus, the formation of starting abstractions — as a first step or stage in the acquisition process — does not mean transmitting them to the learners in a ready form. They have to be found out and formed by the learners themselves in the process of actively working with concrete phenomena in the domain of the learning object. Learners need guidance and cooperation with others in order to achieve this goal. In this context, starting abstractions are not the real starting point of the whole learning process: As a result of the learners' own activity, they represent the starting point for the ascending to the concrete — a phase which is often underestimated in teaching, when the formation of abstractions is seen as the very goal of instruction. On the contrary, in our conception abstractions are necessary means for penetrating into the learning material and constitute only intermediate learning results.

What has been said so far becomes a real teaching strategy only if the following characteristics or principles are considered and implemented in the learning-teaching process:

Formation of Learning Goals

Learning activity, in the sense discussed here, will be carried out and formed under the condition of the learner's own motivation only. Teaching has to make the learners' problems, questions, interests, and experience the starting point for learning. One of the preferred ways of doing so is to create task situations in the ZPD, which means that the learners have the sufficient prior knowledge to understand the situation, but not to solve it. Such a situation serves as a starting point only, if it meets existing motives and supports them further. After several trials to solve the task, the learners are stimulated to analyze the demands of the task in relation to their own prerequisites and to determine 'what we do not know and cannot do' in order to solve the task. Thus, jointly discussing and evaluating their own knowledge and skills in relation to the task, the learners, under guidance and in cooperation with each other, determine the learning goal, but only in a general form, because what is unknown one cannot say concretely and differentiatedly. Such a learning goal is then step-by-step concretized into sub-goals and serves as a learning perspective and a criterion for the permanent evaluation of the learning progress. In our teaching experiments, such a starting point was, for example, the task of explaining the ancient claim of Heraclitus that nobody is able to go twice into the same river. Through the discussion students become aware that nature consists of processes, even when we do not consider them directly. This led to the formulation of a learning goal 'How can we study processes in nature'.

Formation of Learning Actions

As mentioned above, essential features and relationships constituting the substance of a learning object can be uncovered only by actions modifying the object or its representatives in one way or the other. Here, another contradiction of learning activity has to be solved. As a rule, learners do not have available actions adequate for a new learning domain or a new quality of dealing with it, and they cannot aquire them without acting adequately upon the learning object. Therefore, it is necessary to jointly seek for appropriate actions or to demonstrate them as means for attaining the learning goal and to organize adequate actions, which have first to be a learning object themselves in order to serve then as means for further learning activity. In other words, learners can adequately use the necessary actions only if they have acquired them. In this context, the findings of Galperin (1969, 1989, 1992) about orientation basis and types of orientation, of stepwise formation and interiorization of actions are of high value. In our teaching experiments in introductory science instruction, for instance, observation and experimentation were systematically developed as central actions in this domain. In order to become able to formulate questions concerning phenomena or processes in nature and in order to find answers via experimenting, the learners had not only to perform the necessary steps (and not only once), but they also had to discuss and state reasons for their concrete actions. While learning to plan experiments, they, at first, determined the steps, having all necessary materials and devices at hand, then they had to select them out of a large amount of things or corresponding symbols. A higher level was reached when they began to plan experiments based on rough outlines or verbal explanations only. In each domain, the necessary learning actions had to be determined on the basis of an analysis of the learners' prerequisites in relation to the demand structure of the learning object. These learning actions have to be formed very carefully, because this is the basis of any learning progress.

Formation of Learning Models

When acting upon learning objects and observing their changes, learners under guidance gradually become conscious of the invariants as well. If they have not lost their learning goal in this process (which might also happen), they feel the need to fixate that new knowledge in a form free from and independent of the varying phenomena. Here, the transition from the concrete to the abstract takes place. The learners form abstractions containing essential features and relationships, though in an elementary and incomplete form. These abstractions are formulated verbally, but this

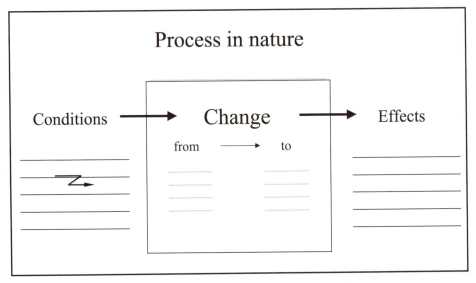

Fig. 7.2. Learning model for studying processes in nature.

is not sufficient in order to make them a special learning object and to complete them, thus making them the starting point of and means for the ascending to the concrete. To achieve this goal, learning models (i.e., simple and easy-to-handle graphical schemata containing only the most essential features and relationships found by the learners) are very helpful. An important demand concerning such models consists of fixing the abstract structure of the learning object together with the principal way in which it is and has to be uncovered. The formation of scientific, although elementary concepts is thus closely connected with the corresponding method — concept and method represent a unity. For the starting abstraction 'process in nature', our elementary school children found — again under guidance — a graphical presentation containing the changing state (from one state to another), consequences for that change and conditions of it, especially energy, and some ways humans use their knowledge about nature (Fig. 7.2, Hinz 1989). This model was modified when we turned to the study of physical processes where special emphasis was put on the explanation of changes by means of the model of elementary particula, the differentiation between the descriptive and the explanatory level and their correspondence.

Working with Series of Concretization

When a starting abstraction is formed appropriately for further learning, it has to be applied to different concrete objects, processes or aspects of the respective domain. It now serves as a tool for the study of the concrete under the aspect of the abstract. This ascending from the abstract to the concrete takes time and effort. It does not mean a formal subordination of different concrete phenomena under a general label in a sense of 'all is the same', but a real exploration in order to understand and explain the particularities within the framework of the essence of the domain. Therefore, the learner has to apply and modify his learning actions in correspondence with the characteristics of the concrete objects under study. This will continue until the starting abstraction loses its explanatory power and/or the learner reaches his learning goal or loses his learning motivation (including goal setting) and/or the teaching goal is reached, etc.

The starting abstraction of process in nature mentioned above was used, for instance, as a cognitive tool for the study of the circular course of water, the emergence of wind and rain, elementary life processes in plants and animals.

Problem Solving as a 'Red Thread' of Learning and Teaching

As follows from what has been said so far, solving problems is a preferred kind of formation of learning activity in this teaching strategy. Neither the formation of learning goals nor the formation of starting abstractions and their application as tools of ascending to the concrete could be successfully put into practice without problem solving. It functions as an important source of motivational and cognitive activation. What is found by one's own practical and cognitive efforts is more or less deeply understood and can be stored in the long-term memory, especially within a framework based on a broad starting abstraction. Besides that, problem solving is an end in itself as well. The development of problem solving strategies — of domain specific ones as well as of more or less general heuristic ones — is a necessary aspect of the development of learning activity as a whole, especially with respect to the development of growing independence and people's life-long learning. In the course of our science instruction, the goal-means-conditions analysis of problems played a significant role in the students' learning.

Reflection and Verbalization

Learning activity is conceptualized as an activity of a conscious subject on a concrete level of physical and psychic development. Provided the learner works actively on the learning objects, while interacting with others, he/she is permanently stimulated to reflect upon the 'What', 'How', and 'Why' of what he/she is doing, or has done, concerning successful actions as well as mistakes, complications etc. Verbal comments, questions, statements, and explanations are necessary components of that learning activity. Cognition, metacognition, and motivation may be topics of different psychological domains and theories, but in the reality of activity they form an inseparable unity. When aiming at the development of students' problem solving capacities, we tried to support and promote the development of this unity by creating attractive and cognitively affording problem situations and by stimulating reflection upon their respective experiences, difficulties, ideas, etc. On this basis, a learning model for problem solving was elaborated in an iconic and schematic form representing the main steps of problem solving in connection with the main contradictions of this process. Again, the model was a result of learning activity and then became a means of orientation for further learning in the concrete form of problem solving.

Social Interaction

This is another 'red thread' in the formation of learning activity by ascending from the abstract to the concrete. The genetically primary action — in the sociogenetic as well as in the ontogenetic respect — is the joint action. Concerning learning activity, that means immediate and more or less mediated forms of guidance by teachers and, at the same time, a great variety of forms of communication and cooperation among the learners themselves and with other people inside and outside of the classroom and of school. Cognitive and social aspects of learning are closely connected here. The potentialities of this basic process for personality development and learning are not yet fully uncovered and used, although it has become a more differentiated research topic during recent years. Conducting experiments and observations in science lessons, students at the same time learned to cooperate with each other.

Our research team carried out teaching experiments in different learning domains (science, geography, history, maths, native and foreign languages) in grades 4 to 6. As a rule, the experiments lasted about 30 lessons during 3 to 4 months, in some cases lasting a whole school year or more. Some of these experiments were conducted several times. However, this is not the place to describe in detail the course and results of the teaching experiments. In general, the experimental classes (being taught under normal school conditions) always surpassed the respective control classes, even older ones, with respect to the amount and quality of knowledge. For instance, in physics our 5th grade students discriminated description and explanation and explained physical phenomena much better than 6th grade students of control classes having learned the same material (Giest 1985).

Our students' elementary theoretical thinking and cognitive motivation also reached a higher level than that of the control classes. But, in this respect, we found differing results with regard to different domains and groups of learners. For instance, in science lessons in grade 4, the children learned to analyze different processes in nature. Among other results, the ability to draw analogies in this domain was tested. All performance groups within the experimental classes gained significantly from the teaching experiment, but to a differing extent (Jülisch 1989). High performance students gained substantially more in that respect than low performance students. In other experiments, for instance in math, the latter group had high gains as well.

The science experiment was carried out several times. In each case, some of the low performance pupils did not fully reach the respective learning goals. An experiment was then performed only with students of the same category in small groups, about 4 students per group (Böhme 1989). The learning program and material and the time available were the same, but under these conditions, the social position and communication among the learners and with the teacher changed essentially and it became easier to consider and activate their prerequisites. In this case, low performance students significantly outperformed their peers in the normal classroom and reached a level of medium performance in concept acquisition as well as in recognition of causal relations.

These few examples from the respective investigations show the potentials of the teaching strategy of ascending from the abstract to the concrete with respect to knowledge acquisition and psychic development, especially cognitive and motivational aspects. The latter aspect as well as the problem of inter-individual differences, the social conditions and some other problems still remain unsatisfactorily resolved in the context of that teaching strategy. So, the study of teaching strategies has to be completed more consequently by the study of students' learning strategies in order to better grasp the unity and mutual dependency of learning and teaching.

Investigations into Learning Strategies

The problem of learning strategies is the problem of how to learn and — in this context — of learning to learn. This is an old problem studied and treated using different terms such as methods, procedures, techniques, skills, plans etc. In the activity-theoretical tradition it was and still is one of the aspects of the formation of learning activity (Davydov 1972, 1988a, 1988b, 1988c; Galperin 1969, 1989, 1992; Kabanova-Meller 1968; and many others). When cognitive psychologists began to understand humans and especially learners as active subjects (not only as information processing systems operating with symbols), learning strategies became an important topic in that framework as well.[4] During the 80s and 90s a real boom of investigations into learning strategies could be observed (see, e.g., Biggs 1993; Bjorklund 1990; Braten 1993; Colley & Beech 1989; de Corte 1992; Jones & Idol 1990; Klauer 1988; Schmeck 1988; Segal, Chipman & Glaser 1985; Weinstein, Goetz & Alexander 1988).

From an activity-theoretical point of view (Leontiev 1979; Davydov 1991, 1993), learning strategies may be defined as complex and generalized, consciously or unconsciously used procedures for reaching learning goals, for mastering learning tasks. This definition includes the following implications:

1) Learning strategies refer to the individual way of performing learning actions.
2) They are imbedded in a structure and in a context of an activity with concrete motives, means, and conditions.
3) They are a result of learning processes during different activities as well as a subjective prerequisite of learning.
4) They emerge either from an unconscious adaptation to the conditions of an activity or from a conscious orientation towards goals and tasks (these are opposite ends of a continuum).

---

4. One of the reasons of that turn was the students' low level of knowledge and skills, especially college students who needed additional instruction in reading scientific texts, etc.

5) Depending on the conditions of emergence and implementation, they may develop in different directions — generalization or specialization, unfolding or reduction, awareness raising or automatization.

6) As components to regulate psychic activity, they interact with motivational, emotional, volitional, and cognitive components.

7) They may be promoted as well as restrained by pedagogical or other arrangements of the learners' activity.

This strategy concept leads to several consequences concerning the analysis and formation of learning strategies. First of all, an essential access to learning strategies should be the analysis of the learners' real actions via observation, experimental and quasi-experimental procedures — qualities of performance, structures, processes, and results of actions etc. There are some examples of such an approach in the literature, but it is very time- and effort-consuming. Most investigations in this field use questionnaires (e.g., Geisler-Brenstein & Schmeck 1996; Garcia & Pintrich 1996; Vizcarro, Bermejo, Castillo & Aragones 1996). By this way, strategy knowledge and the level of consciousness concerning one's own learning activity may be studied. Doubtless, this is an important aspect and a starting point for the formation of learning strategies. But it is not identical with the access to and the use of strategies in real learning situations. Therefore learning strategies should be studied on both levels — on the action level and on the reflection level including the interrelations between them.

Learning strategies are directed towards mastering learning tasks — independently of whether they are defined and given by others or by the learner himself (in each case active learning presupposes a person's own motivation and goal-setting — cf. above). Therefore they have to be studied in the context of concrete learning tasks (such as problem solving, text processing, memorizing etc.) in different learning domains (subject matter areas) and conditions (classroom learning or home work, individual or cooperative learning etc.). Since learning strategies are only one component of the psychic regulation of learning activity, they must not be studied in isolation. Their use and value for the learner depends on his/her concrete learning motives and goals, self-efficacy, domain specific and strategy knowledge and other components.

These consequences ask for a long-term systematic research. We made the first steps only. In a relatively complex study with fourth, sixth, and eighth grade students (n = 260) we administered a learning strategy ques- tionnaire, several instruments for emotional, motivational and cognitive aspects and carried out individual video-taped sessions with real learning actions and interviews (Lompscher 1998; Artelt, Schellhas & Giest 1996).

The questionnaire 'How do you learn?' is structured by different learning task classes: text processing, instructional communication, problem solving, memorization/recall, organization of one's own learning activity, cooperation in learning. Each task class is represented by items of different strategy dimensions: Surface strategies, deep structure strategies, meta-cognitive strategies, and learning techniques (formulated from the student's point of view and to be rated on a 4-point scale from 'is mostly true' to 'is not true at all'). The questionnaire has been validated and revised several times, the internal consistency values (Cronbach alpha) ranged from .75 to .87 for the learning task scales and from .75 to .92 for the strategy dimen-sion scales (similar alphas were obtained for an English version admini-stered by Adey in London). Standardized instruments for cognitive abili-ties, performance motivation, self-efficacy, and school anxiety were used and school marks were registered. In individual sessions, the students were confronted a) with a problem of interest to the majority of them (an ecological problem situation) and b) with different texts from which one should be chosen depending on individual interests and read with a view to answering questions about it. Afterwards, the students were asked to describe and give reasons for their strategies. Here only a few results can be reported.

The students' agreement vs. disagreement with different strategy dimensions in the text processing scale of the questionnaire is shown in Fig. 7.3. Each strategy dimension was represented by four items (two options for agreement and two for disagreement computed from 1 to 4 points, in sum 4 to 16 points per dimension, 10 points marking a neutral or undecided position). The percentage of the neutral positions in the sample is marked in the middle of the columns, the upper part shows agreement, the lower one disagreement. The differences between grades are relatively small (the same is true for a comparison between girls and boys). A majority agrees with deep structure and metacognitive strategies and more often refuses surface strategies (though they do not present an alternative for the students), but most of the students reject learning techniques concerning text processing (such as note-taking, underlining etc.).

Problem solving presents a somewhat different picture in this regard (Fig. 7.4). Obviously, students discriminate the task domains and their strategies in dealing with them.

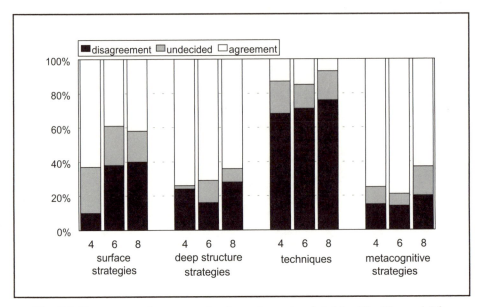

Fig. 7.3. Text processing strategies (questionnaire data) in 4th, 6th, and 8th grade students.

Factor analyses support this result. In text processing, we extracted four factors, two of which could clearly be interpreted as deep structure strategies, on the one hand, and surface strategies, on the other. The other factors showed a combination of metacognitive and deep structure strategies and learning techniques. In the process of accomplishing learning tasks, these three dimensions are closer connected with each other than with surface strategies, but the latter ones are not understood as opposite to those — the preference for this or that strategy depends on the concrete task demands in relationship to the subjective prerequisites and goals. The factor analysis concerning problem solving showed five factors — one for deep structure strategies, another for surface strategies, a third one for learning techniques, a fourth one for a combination of metacognitive and deep structure strategies, and a mixed one. Thus, students are principally able to reflect on how they are approaching different task classes. The discrimination between the strategy dimensions is more evident concerning surface and deep structure stategies than concerning metacognitive strategies and learning techniques.

The data do not show a clear development from younger to older students with regard to the reflection of learning strategies. This raises questions about the role and quality of school instruction in this respect

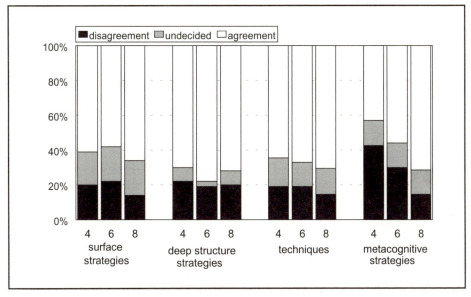

Fig. 7.4. Problem solving strategies (questionnaire data) in 4th, 6th and 8th grade students.

and about the development of individual strategy repertoires in general as well as concerning different task classes and content domains. There are some hints in the literature that a more or less developed repertoire emerges around the age of 16 (in the case of 'normal', more or less spontaneous development without special developmental teaching activities). Further, our data do not show a complete correspondence between the hypothetical structure of learning strategies implemented in the questionnaire and the students' preferences/refusals. The analysis of learning strategies on the reflection level should be continued and deepened with regard to the dimensions and concrete items, their application to different learning situations and domains.

Verbal statements or agreement/disagreement with statements about learning strategies show a certain level of consciousness and give some hints concerning the deficits or advantages in strategy development to be considered by a teaching strategy of systematic formation of learning activity. But, of course, they are not identical with real strategy use. On the action level, students are confronted with concrete situations, task demands and conditions; on the reflection level, strategies refer to more general and less defined situations etc., and, as a rule, the task is less obligatory (though for some students such a questionnaire is like an exam!). Therefore differences between these two levels have to be expected (Artelt 1998).

Concerning text processing, correlational analyses and the application of structural equation models showed no significant correspondence between the two levels. On the action level, we found a clear tendency in groups of students to prefer surface or deep structure strategies, whereas on the reflection level, a tendency dominated to prefer both surface and deep structure strategies. To a certain extent, these differences may be explained by other variables. School anxiety, especially test anxiety influences the use of deep structure strategies negatively on the action level, but even increases the preference of these strategies on the reflection level. Selected cognitive variables are positively related with the use of deep structure strategies on the action level, but not on the reflection level. A similar relation was found for motivational variables. A close connection was found between the use of deep structure strategies in the real action situation and academic performance. It is much easier to reproduce strategy knowledge or to give a positive statement concerning deep structure strategies described verbally than to use them appropriately in real task situations. For instance, the majority of our students stated that they use a dictionnary if words in a text are unfamiliar, but only a few of them were able to do so while working on the concrete text.

Similar results were reached with respect to problem solving. But a number of different strategy items (not their aggregation in strategy dimensions) showed plausible relationships between reflection and action level. For instance, preference of several deep structure and metacognitive items of the problem-solving scale in the questionnaire is positively related with self-confidence in the real problem situation; students who prefer help from other people have greater difficulties finding a problem solution; students who prefer the technique of imaging, solve a real problem more independently and with better quality than others. Girls show a closer correspondence between the two levels — boys tend to overestimate themselves more, girls are more realistic in their self-esteem. Between 4th, 6th, and 8th grades, no significant differences concerning problem solving could be found in a real situation. Again, the question arises how school and instruction is really promoting the development of learning activity, especially with respect to problem-solving capacities.

Obviously, the relationships between action and reflection level of learning strategies are contradictory, complicated and mediated by different psychic variables. A study of learning strategies relying only on one or the other of these levels (e.g., by means of questionnaires) is necessarily one-sided. Research activities have to find out more differentiated and precise methods and conditions for investigating learning strategies on these levels including their relationships. For instance, we are preparing investigations with hypermedia learning environments in different domains which allow students to freely select their ways of dealing with the topic and the different modes of presentation. Strategies used under these conditions are accurately recorded in an on-line protocol and the students can be confronted with it afterwards as a basis for reflection. These data will be compared with data obtained from open and closed forms of questionnaires. Thus, we hope, in time, to get a more reliable basis for the formation of learning strategies, the latter understood not as an end in itself, but as one component in the regulation structure of learning activity. Therefore we cannot accept 'pure', isolated strategy training. Learning strategies will be formed in the context of the formation of learning activity in concrete learning domains (see above). Investigations into learning strategies and their interrelations with other psychic variables will help to elaborate a more differentiated basis for this aim.

Some Prospects

Activity theory has shown its methodological potential in different fields, learning activity is one of them. During the last years, even a kind of convergence with other different theoretical and methodological traditions can be observed, e.g., with parts of cognitive psychology, ecological developmental psychology, etc. This opens up an opportunity for using models and methods of different scientific streams better in joint endeavors to uncover mechanisms and conditions of learning, teaching, and development. The recent activities to use the theoretical and methodological heritage of Vygotsky and others support these prospects.

A detailed and intensive study of learning activity and of the conditions of its development and formation needs long-term research based on the causal-genetic method (unity of formation and analysis) and a combination of cross-sectional and longitudinal developmental investigations using different instruments completing each other. Too often results are obtained by short and superficial surveys not going beyond certain phenomena.

Prospects of our research on learning strategies concern such problems as interrelations between learning and teaching strategies (correspondence, compatibility or contradictions), conditions and regularities of development and formation of learning strategies as components of learning activity as a whole. In this context, it is worthwhile to further develop and use the 'activity-and-formation strategy', especially the teaching strategy of ascending from the abstract to the concrete. One of the most important conditions of this work is the full use and further improvement of modern methodology and methods.

References

Aebli, H. (1980/81). *Denken: Das Ordnen des Tuns* [Thinking: The regulation of acts]. Vols. I & II. Stuttgart: Klett-Cotta.

Anderson, L.W., Ryan, D.W. & Shapiro, B.J. (eds.), (1989). *The IEA classroom environmental study*. Oxford: Pergamon Press.

Andersson, J.R. (1983). *The architecture of cognition*. Cambridge, Mass.: Harvard University Press.

Artelt, C. (1998). Lernstrategien und Lernerfolg — Ein Methodenvergleich [Learning strategies and learning success — A comparison of methods]. *Lern- und Lehrforschung, LLF-Berichte* 18. Potsdam: University of Potsdam, 24-50.

Bartlett, F.C. (1932). *Remembering*. Cambridge: Cambridge University Press.

Biggs, J.B. (1993). What do inventories of students' learning process really measure? A theoretical review and clarification. *British Journal of Educational Psychology* 63, 3-19.

Billett, S. (1996). Situated learning: Bridging sociocultural and cognitive theorizing. *Learning and Instruction* 6, 263-80.

Bjorklund, D.F. (ed.), (1990). *Children's strategies*. Hillsdale, N.J.: Erlbaum.

Blumenfeld, Ph. C., Marx, R.W., Soloway, E. & Krajcik, J. (1996). Learning with peers: From small group cooperation to collaborative communities. *Educational Researcher* 25(8), 37-40.

Böhme, B. (1989). Besonderheiten leistungsschwacher Schüler 4. Klassen bei der Ausbildung von Lernhandlungen zum selbständigen Erkennen von Ursache-Wirkung-Zusammenhängen [Peculiarities of 4th grade low performance students in the formation of learning actions for independent recognizing causal relations]. Unpublished Doctoral Dissertation, Akademie der Pädagogischen Wissenschaften, Berlin.

Braten, J. (1993). Cognitive strategies: a multi-componental conception of strategy use and strategy instruction. *Scandinavian Journal of Educational Research* 37, 217-42.

Brown, A.L. & Palincsar, A.M. (1989). Guided, cooperative learning and individual knowledge acquisition. In Resnick, L.B. (ed.), *Knowing, learning and instruction*. Hillsdale, N.J.: Erlbaum, 393-451.

Cognition and Technology Group at Vanderbilt (1993). Designing learning environments that support thinking: The Jasper series as a case study. In Duffy, T.M., Lowyck, J. & Jonassen, D.H. (eds.), *Designing environments for constructive learning*. Berlin: Springer, 9-36.

Cognition and Technology Group at Vanderbilt (1996). Anchored instruction and situated learning revisited. In McLellan, H. (ed.), *Situated learning perspectives*. Englewood Cliffs, N.J.: Educational Technology Publications, 123-53.

Colley, A.M. & Beech, J.R. (eds.), (1989). *Acquisition and performance of cognitive skills*. Chichester: Wiley.

Collins, A., Brown, J.S. & Newman, S.E. (1989). Cognitive apprenticeship: Teaching the crafts of reading, writing and mathematics. In Resnick, L.B. (ed.), *Knowing, learning and instruction*. Hillsdale, N.J.: Erlbaum, 453-94.

Das, J.P. & Gindis, B. (eds.), (1995). Lev S. Vygotsky and contemporary educational psychology. *Educational Psychologist* 30(2).

Davydov, V.V. (ed.), (1969). *Psichologiceskie vozmoznosti mladsich skol'nikov v usvoenii matematiki* [Psychological potentials of young school children in acquiring math]. Moscow: Prosveshchenie.

Davydov, V.V. (1972). *Vidy obobscenija v obucenii* [Modes of generalization in instruction]. Moscow: Pedagogika.

Davydov, V.V. (1988a). Problems of developmental teaching. *Soviet Education* 30 (8), 15-97.

Davydov, V.V. (1988b). Problems of developmental teaching. *Soviet Education* 30 (9), 3-83.

Davydov, V.V. (1988c). Problems of developmental teaching. *Soviet Education* 30 (10), 3-77.

Davydov, V.V. (1991). The content and unsolved problems of activity theory. *Multidisciplinary Newsletter for Activity Theory* 7/8, 30-35.

Davydov, V.V. (1993). The perspectives of activity theory. *Multidisciplinary Newsletter for Activity Theory* 13/14, 50-53.

Davydov, V.V. (1996). *Teorija razvivajuscego obucenija* [Theory of developmental teaching]. Moscow: Intor.

Davydov, V.V., Lompscher, J. & Markova, A.K. (eds.), (1982). *Ausbildung der Lerntätigkeit bei Schülern*. [Formation of learning activity in students]. Berlin/Moscow: Volk und Wissen/Pedagogika.

Davydov, V.V. & Rubtsov, V.V. (eds.), (1995). *Razvitie ocnov refleksivnogo myslenija skolnikov v processe ucebnoj dejatelnosti* [Development of students' reflexive thinking in the process of learning activity]. Novosibirsk: Rossijskaja Akademija obrazovanija.

Davydov, V.V. & Vardanjan, A.U. (1981). *Ucebnaja dejatel'nost' i modelirovanie* [Learning activity and modelling]. Erevan: Luis.

de Corte, E. (1992). Acquiring and teaching cognitive skills: A state-of-the-art of theory and research. In Drenth, P.J.D., Sergeant, J.A. & Takens, R.J. (eds.), *European perspectives in psychology*, vol. 1. London: Wiley, 237-63..

Dienes, Z.P. & Jeeves, M.A. (1968). *Denken in Strukturen* [Thinking in structures]. Freiburg: Herder.

Elkonin, D.B. & Davydov, V.V. (eds.), (1962). *Voprosy ucebnoj dejatelnosti mladsich skolnikov* [Problems of learning activity in younger school-children]. Moscow: Akademija pedagogiceskich nauk.

Elkonin, D.B. & Davydov, V.V. (eds.), (1966). *Vozrastnye vozmoznosti usvojenija znanij* [Developmental possibilities of acquiring knowledge]. Moscow: Prosveshchenie.

Engelsted, N., Hedegaard, M., Karpatschof, B. & Mortensen, A. (eds.), (1993). *The societal subject*. Aarhus: Aarhus University Press.

Engeström, Y. (1987). *Learning by expanding*. Helsinki: Orienta-Konsultit.

Galperin, P.Y. (1969). Stages in the development of mental acts. In M. Cole & Maltzman (eds.), *A handbook of contemporary Soviet Psychology*. New York/ London: Basic Books, 249-73.

Galperin, P.Y. (1989). Mental actions as a basis for the formation of thoughts and images. *Soviet Psychology* 27(3), 45-64.

Galperin, P.Y. (1992). Stage-by-stage formation as a method of psychological investigation. *Journal of Russian and East European Psychology* 30 (4), 60-80.

Garcia, T. & Pintrich, P.R. (1996). Assessing students' motivation and learning strategies in the classroom context: The Motivated Strategies for Learning Questionnaire. In Birenbaum, M. & Dochy, F.J.R.C. (eds.), *Alternatives in assessment of achievements, learning processes and prior knowledge*. Boston: Kluwer, 319-93.

Geisler-Brenstein, E. & Schmeck, R.R. (1996). The revised inventory of learning processes: A multi-faceted perspective on individual differences in learning. In Birenbaum, M. & Dochy, F.J.R.C. (eds.), *Alternatives in assessment of achievements, learning processes and prior knowledge*. Boston: Kluwer, 283-317.

Greeno, J.G. (1992). The situation in cognitive theory: Some methodological implications of situativity. Paper presented at the meeting of APS, San Diego.

Greeno, J.G. (1997). On claims that answer the wrong questions. *Educational researcher* 26(1), 5-17.

Giest, H. (1985). Einführung der Schüler in die Physik nach der Lehrstrategie des Aufsteigens vom Abstrakten zum Konkreten [Introduction of students into physics based on the teaching strategy of ascending from the abstract to the concrete]. Unpublished Doctoral Dissertation, Akademie der Pädagogischen Wissenschaften, Berlin.

Hedegaard, M., Hakkarainen, P. & Engeström, Y. (eds.), (1984). *Learning and teaching on a scientific basis*. Aarhus: University of Aarhus, Department of Psychology.

Hedegaard, M. (1996). Vygotsky's theory of everyday and subject matter concepts applied to teaching/learning history for cultural minority children. In Lompscher, J. (ed.), *Entwicklung und Lernen aus kulturhistorischer Sicht — Was sagt uns Wygotski heute?* Marburg: Bund demokratischer Wissenschaftler, 403-16.

Hildebrand-Nilshon, M. & Rückriem, G. (eds.), (1988). *Proceedings of the 1st International Congress on Activity Theory*. Berlin: System Druck.

Hinz, G. (1989). Befähigung zum Erkennen und Lösen von Problemen [Qualification for recognizing and solving problems]. In Lompscher, J. (ed.), *Psychologische Analysen der Lerntätigkeit*. Berlin: Volk und Wissen, 137-81.

Jones, B.F. & Idol, L. (eds.), (1990). *Dimensions of thinking and cognitive instruction*. Hillsdale, N.J.: Erlbaum.

Jülisch, B. (1989). Analyse und Ausbildung von Begriffsstrukturen [Analysis and formation of conceptual structures]. In Lompscher, J. (ed.), *Psychologische Analysen der Lerntätigkeit*. Berlin: Volk und Wissen, 231-71.

Kabanova-Meller, J.N. (1968). *Formirovanie priemov umstennoj dejatelnosti i umstvennoe razvitie ucascichsja* [Formation of procedures of mental activity and students' mental development]. Moscow: Prosveshchenie.

Klauer, K.J. (1988). Teaching for learning-to-learn: A critical appraisal with some proposals. *Instructional Science* 17, 351-67.

Lave, J. (1992). Situated learning in communities of practice. In Resnick, L.B., Levine, J.M. & Teasley, S.D. (eds.), *Perspectives on socially shared cognition*. Washington, D.C.: American Psychological Association, 63-82.

Lave, J. & Wenger, E. (1991). *Situated learning. Legitimate peripheral participation*. New York: Cambridge University Press.

Leontiev, A.N. (1979). *Tätigkeit, Bewußtsein, Persönlichkeit* [Activity, consciousness, personality]. Berlin: Volk und Wissen.

Leontiev, A.N. (1983). *Izbrannye psichologiceskie proizvedenija* [Selected psychological works], vols. 1 & 2. Moscow: Pedagogika.

Lompscher, J. (1984). Problems and results of experimental research on the formation of theoretical thinking through instruction. In Hedegaard, M., Hakkarainen, P. & Engeström, Y. (eds.), *Learning and teaching on a scientific basis*. University of Aarhus: Department of Psychology, 293-357.

Lompscher, J. (1985). Formation of learning activity — a fundamental condition of cognitive development through instruction. In Bol, E., Haenen, J.P.P. & Wolters, M.A. (eds.), *Education for cognitive development*. Amsterdam: SVO/SOO, 21-37.

Lompscher, J. (1989a). Formation of learning activity in pupils. In Mandl, H., de Corte, E., Bennett, N. & Friedrich, H.F. (eds.), *Learning and instruction: Vol. 2.2. Analyses of complex skills and complex knowledge domains*. Oxford: Pergamon Press, 47-66.

Lompscher, J. (ed.), (1989b). *Psychologische Analysen der Lerntätigkeit* [Psychological analyses of learning activity]. Berlin: Volk und Wissen.

Lompscher, J. (1995). Unterschiedliche Lehrstrategien und ihre Konsequenzen [Different teachung strategies and their consequences]. In Ehlers, S. (ed.), *Lerntheorie, Tätigkeitstheorie, Fremdsprachenunterricht*. München: Goethe-Institut, 39-51.

Lompscher, J. (1996a). Ascending from the abstract to the concrete — learning and teaching in zones of proximal development. Paper presented at the 2nd Conference for socio-cultural research, Geneva.

Lompscher, J. (ed.), (1996b). *Entwicklung und Lernen aus kulturhistorischer Sicht — Was sagt uns Wygotski heute?* [Development and learning from a cultural-historical viewpoint — what has Vygotsky to say to us today?] Marburg: Bund demokratischer Wissenschaftler.

Lompscher, J., Artelt, C., Schellhas, B. & Giest, H. (1996). Lernstrategien — eine Komponente der Lerntätigkeit [Learning strategies — one component of learning activity]. *Empirische Pädagogik* 3.

Lompscher, J. (1998). Ergebnisse und Probleme der Potsdamer Lernstrategie-forschung [Results and problems of the learning strategy research in Potsdam]. *Lern- und Lehrforschung, LLF-Berichte* 18. Potsdam: University of Potsdam, 1-23.

Lompscher, J. (1999). Motivation and activity. *European Journal of Psychology of Education* XIV(4), 11-22.

Luria, A.R. (1987). *Die historische Bedingtheit individueller Erkenntnisprozesse.* [The historical determination of individual cognitive processes]. Berlin: Deutscher Verlag der Wissenschaften.

Mercer, N. (1996). The quality of talk in children's collaborative activity in the classroom. *Learning and Instruction* 6, 359-77.

Moll, L.C. (ed.), (1990). *Vygotsky and education. Instructional implications and applications of sociohistorical psychology*. Cambridge: Cambridge University Press.

Newman, F. & Holzman, L. (eds.), (1993). *Lev Vygotsky: Revolutionary scientist.* London: Routledge.

van Oers, B. (1990). The development of mathematical thinking in school: A comparison of the action-psychological and information-processing approaches. *International Journal of Educational Research* 14(1), 51-66.

Piaget, J. (1937). *La construction du réel chez l'enfant* [The child's construction of reality]. Neuchâtel: Delachauz et Niestlé.

Reinhold, J. (1988). Ausbildung der Lerntätigkeit im Mathematikunterricht des 4. Schuljahres zur Befähigung zum Lösen von Sach- und Anwendungsaufgaben [Formation of learning activity in math instruction in the 4th grade, qualification for solving text problems]. Unpublished doctoral dissertation, Akademie der Pädagogischen Wissenschaften, Berlin.

Resnick, L.B. (ed.), (1989). *Knowing, learning and instruction. Essays in honor of R. Glaser.* Hillsdale, N.J.: Erlbaum.

Resnick, L.B., Levine, J.M. & Teasley, S.D. (eds.), (1992). *Perspectives on socially shared cognition.* Washington, D.C.: American Psychological Association.

Rogoff, B. (1990). *Apprenticeship in thinking: Cognitive development in social context.* New York/Oxford: Oxford University Press.

Rogoff, B. (1992). Social interaction as apprenticeship in thinking: Guidance and participation in spatial planning. In Resnick, L.B., Levine, J.M. & Teasley, S.D. (eds.), *Perspectives on socially shared cognition,* (349-64). Washington, D.C.: American Psychological Association.

Rogoff, B. (1995). Observing sociocultural activity on three planes: participatory appropriation, guided participation, and apprenticeship. In Wertsch, J.V., Del Rio, P. & Alvarez, A. (eds.), *Sociocultural studies of mind.* New York: Cambridge University Press, 139-64.

Rumelhart, D.E. & Norman, D.A. (1978). Accretion, tuning, and restructuring: Three modes of learning. In Cotton, J.W. & Klatzky, R.L. (eds.), *Semantic factors in cognition,* (37-53). Hillsdale, N.J.: Erlbaum.

Schmeck, R.R. (ed.), (1988). *Learning strategies and learning styles.* New York/London: Plenum Press.

Segal, J.W., Chipman, S.F. & Glaser, R. (eds.), (1985). *Thinking and learning skills,* (vols. 1 & 2). Hillsdale, N.J.: Erlbaum.

Säljö, R. (ed.), (1991). Culture and learning. *Learning and instruction* 1(3).

Scribner, S. & Cole, M. (1981). *The psychology of literacy.* Cambridge, Mass.: Harvard University Press.

Spiro, R.J., Feltovich, P.J., Jacobson, M.J. & Coulson, R.L. (1991). Cognitive flexibility, constructivism and hypertext: Random access instruction for advanced knowledge acquisition in ill-structured domains. *Educational Technology* 31(5), 24-33.

Tharp, R.G. & Gallimore, R. (1988). *Rousing minds to life. Teaching, learning, and schooling in social context.* Cambridge: Cambridge University Press.

Tryphon, A. & Voneche, J. (eds.), (1996). *Piaget-Vygotsky. The social genesis of thought.* Hove: Psychology Press.

van der Veer, R. & Valsiner, J. (1993). *Understanding Vygotsky: A quest for synthesis.* Cambridge: Blackwell.

Vosniadou, S. (1996). Towards a revised cognitive psychology for new advances in learning and instruction. *Learning and Instruction* 6(2), 95-109.

Vygotsky, L.S. (1934). *Myslenie i rec* [Thinking and speech]. Moscow: Gosudarstvennoe socialno-ekonomiceskoe izdatelstvo.

Vygotsky, L.S. (1956). *Izbrannye psichologiceskie issledovanija* [Selected psychological investigations]. Moscow: Akademija pedagogiceskich nauk.

Vizcarro, C., Bermejo, I., del Castillo, M. & Aragones, C. (1996). Development of an inventory to measure learning strategies. In Birenbaum, M. & Dochy, F.J.R.C. (eds.), *Alternatives in assessment of achievements, learning processes and prior knowledge*. Boston: Kluwer, 341-61.

Weinstein, C.E., Goetz E.T. & Alexander, P.A. (eds.), (1988). *Learning and study strategies. Issues in assessment, instruction, and evaluation*. San Diego: Academic Press.

Wertsch, J.V. (1985a). *Vygotsky and the social formation of mind*. Cambridge, Mass.: Harvard University Press.

Wertsch, J.V. (ed.), (1985b). *Culture, communication and cognition: Vygotskian perspectives*. Cambridge: Cambridge University Press.

8 Psychological Mechanisms of Generalization

Nina F. Talyzina

Introduction

In this article a brief review of the approaches to the study of the problem of generalization will be given; this review will utilize experimental research. The author studied the dependence of generalized properties and their place in the structure of a subject's activity. The subjects were two groups of children aged from 5 to 6¾ years. The first group had a normal mental development, while the second had developmental delay. The results show that generalization takes place on those — and only those — properties of the objects which have entered the content of the orientation basis for actions. Thus it was shown that generalization was not determined directly by objects, but mediated by a subject's activity with objects.

In psychology, a large number of studies is devoted to the problem of generalization of knowledge and skills. In this chapter, I do not have the opportunity of making a review of the research carried out on this problem, but shall focus on the *basic approaches* used to carry out this research.

First approach: In these studies, major attention was paid to the properties of generalization: from the point of view of the importance of their physical nature, for problem solving, etc. (Shvachkin 1954; Boguslavskaja 1958; Skinner 1961; Oleron & Piaget 1963; Radford, Burton 1974, etc.).

Second approach: A significant amount of work was devoted to the study of the role of different factors during generalization: the role of words (Rosengart-Pupko 1948; Lublinskaja 1954; Fradkina 1960), and the role of insignificant attributes (Zukova 1950; Menchinskaja 1966).

Bruner, Goodnow, and Austin (1956) have found a large number of conditions influencing activity, which resulted in generalization: the peculiarities of the subject's understanding of a problem, the character of

examples which the subject meets during generalization; expected consequences from own actions; the character of restrictions, imposed on the
subject's activity; the peculiarities of estimation of own actions. Also the
study of conditions which affect the cognitive activity performed in the
course of generalization was continued in the works of Levine; Hunt;
Restle; Wason and Johnson-Laird, etc.

Third approach: This is characteristic of the supporters of the activity theory
approach in psychology — first of all, the Russian psychologists. In this
case, the researcher's attention was directed toward the content of the
subject's actions, which the subject performs with generalized objects. The
subject's action is the unit of psychological analysis in this particular
approach. Any action of the subject represents the whole system. The
following elements enter into its structure: object, purpose (aim), motive,
operations, realizing this action and the action's orientation basis,
containing information for the subject's fulfilment of the given action. At
a functional level, the action, as any system, includes working (executive)
and managing (orientation) parts, control and correction parts.

In the research based on the two first mentioned approaches, the subject's
activity remained unknown. In the first group of studies the attention of
the researchers was concentrated only on one element of action (i.e., on the
object of the subjects' activity). In the second group of studies the
conditions, positively influencing the activity, were investigated, but the
activity itself was not uncovered. In the activity theory approach the
research begins with revealing the content of the actions which the subject
carries out when solving a problem.

Research carried out from the activity theory approach of the process
of generalization, studies its dependence from structural and functional
parts of the subject's action. We have continued this line of research in our
study of the generalization process both in 5 to 6 year old children with
normal mental development, as well as those with developmental delay.

According to Zaporozhetz and his employees (Ruzskaya, Poddyakov
and others) the generalization process depends on the character of the
orientation actions which are directed toward demonstrated generalized
objects (Zaporozhetz et al. 1964; Poddiyakov 1977 and others).

Experimental Training of Children's Orientation Basis
for Simple Geometric Concepts

Our previous investigations have shown that the mere presence of common properties in objects does not result in the generalization of these properties, i.e., the process of generalization does not depend directly on the common properties of objects with which a person operates. The sixth and seventh-graders give an incomplete definition of concepts, such as adjacent angles, vertical angles, etc. Thus they skip essential attributes which can constantly be found in all objects relating to this concept. For example, in definition of adjacent angles they left out the attribute that these angles 'have a common part', although all adjacent angles with which the pupils dealt always had a common part, and they had perceived it. Moreover, they represented the adjacent angles without fail when asked to draw adjacent angles. Nevertheless it was not reflected and had not come into the content of a concept, there was no generalization of objects based on this representation (Talyzina 1981). Precisely the same results were obtained in the study we conducted together with Konstantinova (Talyzina 1957) on material of initial geometrical concepts: direct line, angles, perpendicular. The subjects were 25 fifth-grade pupils.

The peculiarity of training was that in all tasks with which the pupils dealt, the figures were represented on the drawings located strictly in the same spatial position. Thus, insignificant attributes such as the position in the space, constantly accompanied the essential attributes of the figures. The training was constructed so that from the very beginning the pupils would orientate to the entire system of essential attributes. In the control series, the tasks the pupils were given were, on the one hand, the objects relating to the given concepts, but having varied spatial positions. On the other hand, tasks were given relating to the objects having the same spatial position and looking similar to objects with which they had dealt at training, but not relating to the given concepts (for example, inclined, close to perpendicular lines). Besides, the subjects were asked to represent some few different objects related to learned concepts.

All subjects successfully coped with a control-series of problems. Out of 144 tasks, 139 concerned with the identification of a direct line were performed correctly (24 subjects participated, each performed 6 tasks). Upon fulfilling the tasks of identifying angles and perpendicular lines no error was found. The second kind of task was also performed successfully, i.e., each participant had represented at least three figures in various spatial situations.

Thus, providing an orientation to the system of essential attributes, the insignificant common attributes of the objects have not entered into the content of generalization, though they were present in all objects with which pupils worked.

The above-mentioned data have allowed us to put forward the following hypothesis: generalization of objects occurs only on those properties which are included in the structure of the orientation basis of a subject's actions directed towards these objects.

To check this hypothesis we have been carried out two studies: the first one together with H.Y. Lopes; the second one with N.W. Elfimova.

Study 1

The method of the research

We use Galperin's method of step-by-step formation of knowledge and skills.[1]

Experimental material: As experimental material we chose the geometrical figures, similar to those used in the Vygotsky and Sakharov studies. These figures were wood blocks that differed in the following aspects: the size of the figure's base, height, form and colour. Depending on their size, all figures, as well as in Vygotsky and Sakharov studies, were grouped in four classes: 'bat' (low figures with small base); 'dek' (high figures with small base); 'roz' (low figures with large base); 'moop' (high figures with large base). As investigations in child psychology have shown that colour and form are the most significant attributes for pre-schoolers, in our research we made them insignificant — but common and constant — properties for all objects of a class. We tested 100 Cuban children aged 6 to 6¾ years. Five experimental series were conducted, with 20 children participating in each.

In the *first series* of experiments the objects of each of the four classes had constantly the same colour: 'bat' were always red, 'dek' — dark blue, etc.; the form was a varying attribute.

---

1. According to this method, the process of assimilation has six stages. Any action, going (passing) from the initial stage to the final ones, changes forms, measures of generalization, measure of automatization, etc. For further details concerning this method, cf. Galperin 1982, 1989; Talyzina 1981.

In the *second series* of experiments, however, each class of objects had a constant form, and the colour was a varying attribute.

In the *third series* of experiments the form of the figures and the colour did not vary inside the class of figures. Thus, in these series either colour, or form, or both colour and form were identification attributes. Based upon these identification attributes, it was possible to relate a figure to a class correctly. But, as orientation basis for the action recognition, these attributes were not included.

In the *fourth series*, each class of figures had its own colour, but all figures in *all four* classes were of the same form (cylinders).

In the *fifth series*, on the contrary, each class of objects had its own form, but the objects of *all* classes were of the same colour (red).

Thus, in the last two series the figures had both those common insignificant attributes, which could objectively serve as identification attributes (colour in the fourth series and form in the fifth), and those, which could not serve as identification attributes (form in the fourth series and colour in the fifth), as they were common for figures of all classes.

The Procedure of Concept Formation

From the very beginning the essential attributes were included into the content of an orientation basis of the action of recognition. On fulfilment of an action in the material form, the subjects used the standards given to them, with which they established the logical scheme of concept identification based on the figures' base and height size, and they defined whether a given figure corresponded to the appropriate class of objects. They also received all necessary instructions on the content of operations which should be carried out, and the order in which they should be performed.

Experimental Training

When performing an action, half of the subjects of each group got additional conditions, facilitating the identification in figures of the general aspect of either colour or form. The identified figures were not removed, they were left in the child's view. The second half of each group did not have these conditions (i.e., identified figures were removed, and each time the subjects saw only the figure with which they worked).

External Oral Description: The children received the descriptions of figures in verbal form. In the figures description both essential attributes (area of the base and height) and insignificant attributes (form and colour) were specified. The whole process of problem solving was done by external oral, verbal description.

Mental Performance: The children *silently* solved a problem by themselves, giving only the answer.

Control Series

After the training the subjects of all series received the same system of control tasks. The basic tasks were recognition tasks: (a) of new figures, at which insignificant attributes, till now common and constant for the objects of a given class, varied either in colour or form, which during the training were characteristic of figures of other classes, or colour (form) not present in training experiments; (b) of figures, having the same colour (form), as figures of a given class, showed in training experiments, but not having the essential (one or two) attributes of the given concept. The tasks were given in two forms: either as direct presentation of new figures and their verbal description by experimenter, or as classifications of objects and description of figures of the given class.

Results and Discussion

The results of the study show that 42% of the children were aware of the presence of a constant colour or form in the objects offered to them, and the majority of them demonstrated that awareness already at the formation of the first concept. However, during the training sessions recognition of objects using these attributes occurred only in 65 tasks out of 7,420 (0.9%). These subjects did not use the attributes directly, but as identification attributes, which indicated the presence of an object with other attributes (i.e., a certain size of base and height). In the control series of tasks the subjects of all experimental training groups had the following results:

Out of one hundred children only three made errors with orientation towards the wrong dimension of attribute — colour or form. It must be noted that the majority of children performed the presented tasks quickly and without the slightest hesitation.

We shall show an example from the first group of children (where colour was a constantly accompanying attribute: red for 'bat', dark blue for 'dek', green for 'roz' and yellow for 'moop').

The first series of tasks in the control series consisted in the classification of figures, on which concept formation took place. The figures were shown previously in a disorganized order. Differences in problem-solving took two directions: (a) the way of composing groups (i.e., some children took figures arbitrary and related each of them to one of the concepts. Other subjects first chose all figures of one class, then of the other, etc.; (b) the form of action: the overwhelming majority of subjects performed the decision in visual form. They used standards (the material form) only in cases where they were uncertain of the perceptual estimation of the figure's size. Ninety per cent of children classified correctly. Two children reported three errors. One figure was ascribed to a class as a result of measurement inaccuracy, and two figures were visually evaluated incorrectly. It is important to note that these errors point to the fact that the realization of the children's classification was not guided by the figures' colour: the colours of the faulty categorized figures did not coincide with colour of the given class.

The second series of control tasks consisted in recognition of figures by their verbal descriptions (6 tasks). In all tasks the essential attributes of the figures of a given class were combined either with colour, which in the training series was characteristic of the figures of the other class, or with new attributes, not taking place in the training series (for example, according to the sizes the figure corresponds to the 'roz' concept, but corresponds to the 'bat' concept on colour). Errors took place in six cases (5%), although the reason was not wrong orientation to colour, but a wrong perception of the information. All errors were corrected by the subjects themselves which can be demonstrated through the following qualitative data:

Euristo: 'This is "moop", because here there is a small bottom and large height.' And here he exclaims: 'Small bottom! But "moop" can't have a small base. It isn't "moop".' 'What is it?' — the experimenter asks. And the boy answers: 'This is "dek".'

Oskar: 'This is "bat", here is the small base, small height.' The experimenter repeats the description and the child notices an error: 'No, the height is large. It's "dek".'

An analysis of the decisions taken in these control problems has allowed us to receive some data which reveals the subjects' attitudes to insignificant attributes. We shall bring a few examples.

1) Huan: Solving a problem correctly, he says: 'This new toy is yellow, but that isn't important, right?'

2) Alina: The experimenter describes a figure: 'I have a round red toy... .' The girl interrupts her and asks: 'It has a small bottom and small height?' The experimenter supplements the description: 'It has a large base and small height.' Then the girl says: 'I thought, that it was "bat", but if the bottom is large, then it's "roz".'

3) Gustavo: Solving a task and reproducing the figure's description, the child changes its colour so it always corresponded to the given base and height. The experimenter corrects, specifying that the colour is different. Despite that, the child has solved the problem correctly.

The two last cases are especially interesting to us. In the first the girl tries to include those essential attributes in the figure's description, which were constantly connected to the appropriate insignificant attribute (red colour) during training. But on hearing the experimenter name the other size of the base, she stopped to take into consideration the figure's colour and was guided only by the essential attributes described by the teacher in her problem solving. Similarly, in the latter case, the subject reproduces colour, which was characteristic of the figures of the given class in the training experiment. When the experimenter corrected him, he did not insist on his former habit of choosing the colour and solves the problem, being guided by the essential attributes described by the teacher. In other words, as soon as the insignificant attribute ceased to accompany the essential one, children did not pay attention to it and their solving of new problems was based only on essential attributes. It means that only the essential attributes of figures have come into the children's content of the concepts.

The third series of control tasks was similar to the second one, but the figures were shown directly, not through the description.

Objectively these problems were more difficult than the previous ones. The child could see all the figures. Each class of figures had a certain colour. The subjects should then attach them with new figures of the same class, but with another colour.

In two tasks out of one hundred and forty, the sizes of the figures, but not the colours, were wrongly estimated. In none of the cases were the children guided by colour. For example, they confidently put the figures of another colour together with a red 'bat', if the figures corresponded in base and height size with the figures of this class.

The control series ended with secondary classification. Now it was necessary to classify anew all figures, which were used both in the experimental as well as in the control series. All subjects solved this task correctly and without use of standards.

After fulfilling the tasks, the experimenter discussed with each child the correctness of the groupings figure arrangements. The purpose of discussion was to emphasize the difference in colour of the figures put into each group, and to provoke possible orientation to this property. It was done in order to check the degree of the child's reliance on the accuracy of his/her decision.

The number of provocative situations depended on how a child behaved. Each subject went through such situations an average of three times. The behaviour of children in these situations was different. Some persistently defended their decision, others defended theirs with less confidence and submitted to some extent to the experimenter's opinion; whilst another recognizing his decision to be faulty agreed to group figures on the basis of colour.

The results show that seventeen children were sure about the correctness of their decisions, two displayed indecision, whilst only one child agreed with the grouping of figures based on colour.

Study 2

The Method of the Study

There were two categories of children: (a) young normal children aged 5-6 years, (b) 6 year old children with intellectual developmental delay.

Choosing these groups of subjects, we have proceeded from data available in the literature, that for normal children younger than 6 years and children with intellectual developmental delay, the visual attributes of objects play a determining role in the generalization process (Bogoyav-lensky & Menchinskaya 1962; Rubinstein 1970; Brushlinsky 1970).

The subjects were divided into three groups: 1) children of 6 years old with normal development (10 children); 2) children of 5 years old with normal development (9 children); 3) children with intellectual develop-mental delay (10 children).

Half of the third group of children tested to a mental age corresponding to early childhood, the second half tested to a mental age of 4-5 years. These children also displayed late development of speech, confused articu-lation, late development of motor function, low efficiency (capacity for work), and high distractibility. All children of this group had the following diagnosis: a neurosis-like syndrome (lack of an inhibitory motor function, emotional lability, delay in mental development). Among these were five children with a breakdown in the operating part of their thinking ability; four of these five children also had a strong infringement on the motive sphere.

Experimental Training

In a training series the same technique, as in the first series of Study 1 was used: essential attributes were the size of figures, while colour was a con-stant accompaniment and a common attribute for all figures of the given class. The difference in the method (procedure) used in Study 1 and Study 2 was that in Study 1 the experimenter formed each of four artificial con-cepts separately, and in Study 2 had entered all concepts simultaneously.

Training Series

The concept formation occurred as a game. The standards were presented as well known objects such as 'stubs' (for measurement of the area of the figure's base) and 'fir-tree' (for measurement of height).

The children received a card, where there were two 'glades' (shaded and pure). On each of the 'glades' there were two 'houses'. The figures represented little gnomes, which should be settled according to their sizes (on the first 'glade' the figures with a small base, and on the second the figures with a large base were placed. The lodging in the 'houses' was in accordance with growth). During the training session it was required from a child that each time, upon identifying a figure, the subject should carry out the following sequence of operations:

1) Identification of the area of the base:
   a) To measure the area of the figure's base;
   b) To put a figure on an appropriate 'glade'.

2) Identification of the figure's height:
   a) To measure figure's height;
   b) To put a figure in the appropriate 'house'.

3) Ascribing of a figure to a class — what is the name of a given figure?

When a child passed all the stages of mastering this process, participating in the game or listening to a fairy tale, a scheme was introduced for the placing of 'gnomes' in houses as an orientation basis for their actions. The material stage was the actual process of placing the gnomes.

After the children had learned to place the 'gnomes' in houses, they were transferred to the verbal expression stage. At this stage the children got the descriptions of the figures as verbal problems (i.e., fairy tales). In the figure descriptions, both essential attributes (area of the base and height) and insignificant attributes (form and colour) were specified. The colour was constant for figures of each class. Here is one of the tasks:

I shall tell you about a little 'gnome', who wants to come here and settle in a 'house'. He asks: 'In which house shall I live?' Let's help him! This 'gnome' is red, he has a small 'bottom', the form of a 'rocket' and is small in size. What is his name?

The children solved these problems by reasoning aloud. But in the final stages the children solved the tasks silently in their heads, using only oral expression for answers.

Process of Concept Formation

The main difficulty of the training series was connected with the children's motivation. Among the normal 6 year old children, half had displayed cognitive motivation (i.e., they worked with pleasure during the whole experiment).

For the other children it had appeared necessary to create special conditions for providing the motivation for actions. Under the cover of other attractive activities (games, dialogue with the experimenter, drawing), the children were invited to perform the action of recognition which they could carry out in breaks between training sessions. This was enough for several five year old and six year old children with normal development; they then performed the action of recognition. An estimation of the fulfilment of the task was introduced, and was used when problems were solved which required a great effort on the part of the children: either due to objective difficulty in the solving of verbal problems, or due to a child's unwillingness to continue to solve these problems.

At the beginning of the training session the children with intellectual developmental delay, and the majority of five year olds, did not understand the purpose of the action of recognition. For these children, the action of recognition was broken into separate micro-actions, which for other children were operations. Originally the connection between the goal and motive was established for them at a micro-action level: the goal of micro-action was for these children connected with the motive that was the attractive activity (game with break between training sessions). Hence, for each of the micro-actions it was necessary to create a motivation component. To create motivation for the whole action of recognition it was necessary to unite the goals of micro-actions with a uniform goal of action and to connect it to the motive. The children could not make it by themselves, as they could not distinguish the goal of action. The experimenter had to unite the intermediate goals of micro-actions for a child and place them in submission to the basic goal of the action, i.e., to become the carrier of the goal hierarchy. It means the participation of the experimenter in the fulfilling of the action (i.e., its realization by the principle 'of shared action') which was a necessary condition for training these children. First, the experimenter completely carried out the function of the carrier of the goal hierarchy. Gradually this function passed to an educational card containing a scheme as an orientation basis for action, where a sequence of fulfilment of micro-actions and rule of recognition was boldly reflected. At the end of the material training stage, a child took possession of goal hierarchy and distinguished the goal of the recognition action. Now the goal of the recognition action was connected with a motive; the motivation, which was earlier formed for each micro-action, covered now the whole action of recognition.

However, this procedure appeared to be insufficient for four children with delayed speech development. They did not accept the play activity as mediation activity between task performance (the game introduced during the breaks). They wanted to play immediately. It was necessary to include the action of recognition (for these children) in play activity, where 'gnomes' who were previously searched for in the 'wood', now were placed in 'houses', and drove in a car.

Thus, in this research training of chosen concepts and actions, studies were conducted of both the operating and motivation components. The results showed a difference in number of tasks necessary for learning, and also in the time spent. The six year old children gave the best results on all parameters, the children with intellectual developmental delay the worst. The five year olds occupied a medium place. All three groups of children have passed then through a series of the control tasks.

Control Series

The first task consisted of presenting the subjects with figures of different colours for recognition, including that colour which was constant for objects of each class. In 235 out of 236 tasks, orientation to the essential attributes concerning the names of the figures took place with the help of the experimenter, but an accurate assessment of size was only found in six cases.

Results

The creation of provocative situations did not actually change the results: only in a few cases did the children agree to be guided by colour. We shall give a few examples from the protocols of children with intellectual developmental delay (group 3).

Misha has correctly referred to a red coloured figure as belonging to the 'moop' group (in the training experiment red was for figures belonging to the 'bat' group). At the experimenter's provocative question — 'maybe the gnome's name is not "moop", you see, it's red?' — he answered: 'The bottom is large, the height is great, it means "moop"!' Andrey from the same group has correctly referred to a yellow figure as belonging to the 'bat' class (in the forming experiment yellow was for figures of the 'moop' class). The experimenter expressed doubt in the correctness of his decision, specifying, that the figures of the 'bat' class were never yellow but were only red. Andrey suggested that the experimenter use the standards to measure a figure, if she does not trust him: 'Measure it! The bottom is small and the growth is small — it's "bat"!' Not the experimenter's opinion, but the standards became the criterion for the correctness of the child's decision.

However, some children with developmental delay were lost when the experimenter posed provocative questions to them.

Serghey correctly referred to a red figure as belonging to 'dek' class (in the training experiment the figures of 'dek' class were dark blue in colour). But he became at once puzzled at the experimenter's question — 'maybe, its name isn't "dek", but another one, you see, it's red in colour!' The boy said — 'I don't know... "roz"... I don't know...' (In the training experiment the figures in the 'roz' class were green).

Then the experimenter once again asked the child to identify a figure and to explain his decision. Thus the experimenter has posed a leading question to him about the size of the base and the height of the figure. By answering these questions, Serghey again came to the correct answer. The experimenter's indications of the figure's colour have not affected his decision, i.e., Serghey had acquired confidence in the correctness of his answer.

The next time Serghey correctly referred a green figure to the 'bat' class (in the training experiment the 'roz' figures were green). The experimenter questioned his decision, specifying that there were no green 'bat'. The child confidently answered: 'It is "bat", because it has a small bottom and a small height!' Serghey further explained confidently the decisions, specifying the essential attributes of the figures.

An aspiration to agree with the experimenter in everything did not appear in the child anymore. Other children who originally were lost at the experimenter's provocative questions behaved similarly.

Because the children with intellectual developmental delay had a restricted long-term memory, we decided to test — over a period of one and a half months after the training — the content of their orientation basis for the recognition action and the quality of fulfilment of this action. Control problems, similar to those which were administered right after the training experiment, were presented. The delayed control showed that one and a half months after the experimental training, all children with intellectual developmental delay continued to be guided only by the essential attributes of the figures. The children had solved correctly and independently 85.5% of the presented problems. The percentage of incorrectly solved problems had, because of measurement errors or forgetting the figures' names, increased from 2% to 12.6%. (However, half of the wrong decisions were corrected independently by the children).

In the delayed second control task, both the figures with new colours and those which were characteristic of the figures of each class at the training sessions were presented. This time they were presented by means of verbal description. The results were guided by the essential attributes of the figures. Only one answer was wrong (orientation to colour), but after the experimenter repeated the figure description the child still made errors, but these were now caused not by colour orientation, but by forgetting the name of a class and inaccurate measurement. The behaviour of the children in provocative situations was similar to that described above.

Results and Discussion

General results are presented in Table 8.1. Comparing decision quality of the different groups, it is clear that children with intellectual developmental delay demonstrated the worst results. There were more faulty decisions, and not one of them was corrected independently. However, it must be mentioned that none of these shortcomings were connected to colour orientation. It is also important to note, that a comparison of the fulfilment of the first and second tasks does not give any reason to believe that direct perception of colour (the first task) provokes children more than verbal information on colour. As shown, there is no difference in the results, although the children had more difficulties with solving the problems presented verbally than with the manual solving of the problems.

In the third and fourth control tasks the subjects should answer which attributes of the figures they considered the 'the most important' to use for classification. The purpose of these tasks was to reveal the level of awareness and reasonability of actions by the children.

It is important to note, that in the fourth control task problems with uncertain conditions were included: here only one of two essential attributes was specified:

1) What's the smallest gnome's name?
2) What is the name of the largest gnome?

3) Is it possible to name the 'roz' gnome as the 'smallest' gnome, when he is not so tall?

4) Is it possible to name the 'dek' gnome as the 'largest' gnome, when he is very tall?

Tested children	Quantity	Generalization of essential attributes	%
6 - 6.9 year old children	100	97	97.0
5 - 6 year old children	19	17	89.5
6 year old children with intellectual development delay	10	9	90.0

Table 8.1. Comparison of children's orientation to the essential attributes.

The third task was carried out correctly by all children: they did not just work practically on the basis of the essential attributes, but were also able to name them. It is characteristic that 44% of the five year olds and 40% of the children with intellectual developmental delay gave generalized decisions, specifying that the most important attributes were the size of the base and height. The other children gave concrete answers (i.e., they specified separately base and height sizes of each class of objects).

Almost all children solved problems correctly, distinguishing the size of the area of the base and height as the set of essential attributes necessary and sufficient for referring a figure to a given class.

The General Discussion of Experimental Data

As we can see from Table 8.1, the results of both investigations coincide completely. Data received on children with intellectual developmental delay are especially remarkable. If it appears possible to introduce the essential attributes into the content of the action's orientation basis for these children, then they successfully generalize objects to these attributes, thus the most visible common attribute (colour) was not included in the generalization content.

All our experimental studies have shown that generalization is not simply applied on the basis of the common aspects of objects. Common aspects are a necessary, but yet insufficient, condition. Generalization was always based on those *properties which have entered into the structure of the orientation basis* for the children's actions, and thereby directing the analysis of these objects. It means that control by way of the generalization of cognitive actions, and the knowledge included in them, should be by means of the construction of trainees' activity, controlling the content of an orientation basis of appropriate actions.

These specific findings allow us to explain also those typical defects in knowledge generalization which appear in the training practice. Thus, let us return to the experiment of training children's geometrical concepts of adjacent angles. In these experiments, the pupils constantly perceived visually the common side of all the adjacent angles, and received instruction by means of concept definition. Nevertheless they could not include this definition in the content of generalization. These facts are explained by the conditions that an attribute 'the common side' was learned by pupils, but did not orient them towards solving problems actually in front of them. We have conducted the analysis of school tasks on application of the 'adjacent angles' concept and have shown that in all these tasks it is the adjoining corners which were always given in the task's condition, i.e., angles which have a common side. Thus, to get an answer the pupils were forced to constantly check only the presence of one attribute: whether these angles made up 180° in a sum. It exhausted the content of the orientation basis of pupils' actions. By virtue of this the content of the 'adjacent angles' concept is limited only by this attribute ('two angles, making 180° in the sum'). 'The common side' did not enter into the contents of the children's orientation basis of actions, and therefore did not enter into the children's content of their concept of adjacent angles.

The widespread cases, where generalization is based on common but insignificant attributes, can also be easily explained. In school training, the best structure of attributes is the content of attributes on which it is necessary to be guided (through definition), but orientation to them in the course of activity is not provided, thereby these attributes do not always enter into the content of the children's orientation basis of action. In these cases, the pupils design for themselves a working orientation basis that first of all includes the surface characteristics of objects. As a result the generalization does not include the attributes of definition, which are common and essential for objects of a given class, but includes casual, insignificant attributes.

Conversely, as soon as the system of necessary and sufficient attributes is entered into the structure of an orientation basis for the action and a systematic orientation to those (and only to those) provided, the generalization takes place on the basis of this system of properties. Other common properties of objects, which are not included in the structure of an orientation basis of children's actions, do not influence the content of generalization. It means in particular, as the results show, that the variations of insignificant properties of objects are not at all necessary for establishing the generalization system of essential attributes. For this purpose it is enough just to include the appropriate system of essential properties in the content of an orientation basis of actions. Thus, the process of generalization is not determined directly by an object of actions, rather it is mediated by the content of the child's orientation basis for her actions.

This finding gives an opportunity to understand also that as the differentiation of only common essential properties occurs, the person does not reflect common properties of the objects as essential, but only those which have come in the content of an orientation basis of his/her actions. The conducted studies have also shown that the opinion existing in child psychology of the leading role of colour and form in children's generalization is correct only under spontaneous conditions. Under conditions of controlled training, from the very beginning the generalization becomes based on a given system of attributes, which can be non-visual attributes. In this case, the presence of common visual properties of the objects does not have any essential impact on the course and content of generalization.

These data coincide completely with results, obtained in research of pre-school and elementary school children by Elkonin & Davydov (1966). The basic meaning of these results is that they change the idea of *when* opportunities are available for children at specific ages. If the process of generalization goes spontaneously (or largely spontaneously), it is typical the generalization of practical (Galperin 1965) or empirical cases (Davydov 1972). If it is a controlled process, then generalization on laws (Galperin 1965), or theoretical generalization (Davydov 1972) can be appropriated by children also at pre-school age.

Finally, it is necessary to reconsider the conception that children are easily influenced by suggestion. Children are only suggestible when acting spontaneously, not being aware of their suggestibility. In cases where the way of actions is trained through awareness, the children become confident of the correctness of their behaviour.

References

Bogouslavskaja, Z.M. (1958). Vydelenie zveta i formy detmi doshkolnogo vozrasta v zavisimosti ot charaktera ich dejatelnosti. [The distinction of colour and form depending on activity type by pre-schoolers]. *Doklady Akademii Pedagogicheskikh Nauk RSFSR*. Report no. 1. Moscow: Academy of Pedagogical Sciences of the RSFSR, 55-58.

Bogoyavlensky, D.N. & Menchinskaya, N.A. (eds.), (1962). *Puti povyshenia kachestva usvoenia znanij v nachalnykh klassakh* [Ways for raising the quality of knowledge in elementary schools]. Moscow: Academy of Pedagogical Sciences of the RSFSR.

Bruner, J.S., Goodnow, J.J. & Austin, G.A. (1956). *A study of thinking*. New York: Wiley.

Brushlinsky, A.V. (1970). *Psichologia myshlenia i kibernetika* (Psychology of thinking and cybernetics). Mowcow: Academy of sciences of the USSR.

Davydov, V.V. (1972). *Widi obobshenia v obuchenii* [Kinds of generalizations in instruction]. Moscow: Pedagogika.

Elkonin, D.B. & Davydov, V.V. (eds.), (1966). *Vozrastnie vozmoznosti usvoenja znanij* [Age abilities of knowledge assimilation]. Moscow: Prosveshchenie.

Fradkina, F.A. (1960). Razvitie obobschenija v doshkolnom vozraste [The development of generalization in pre-school age]. *Doklady Akademii Pedagogicheskikh Nauk RSFSR*. Report no. 2. Moscow: Academy of Pedagogical Sciences of the RSFSR, 37-40.

Galperin, P.Ya. (1965). *Osnovnie resultaty issledovanij po probleme 'Formirovanie umstvennih deistvij i ponyatij'* [Basic results of research of problem 'Formation of mental actions and concepts']. Moscow: Moscow University publishers.

Galperin, P.Ya. (1982). Intellectual capability among older pre-school children: On the problem of training and mental development. In W.W. Hartup (ed.), *Review of child development research*, vol. 6. Chicago: University of Chicago Press, 526-46.

Galperin, P.Ya. (1989). Mental acts as a basis for the formation of thoughts and images. *Soviet Psychology* 27(3), 45-64.

Hunt, E.B. (1962). *Concept learning: An information processing problem*. New York: Wiley.

Levine, M. (1966). Hypothesis behavior by humans during discrimination learning. *Journal of Experimental Psychology* 71, 331-38.

Liublinskaja, A.A. (1954). Rol jazyka v razvitii poznavatelnoi dejatelnosti rebenka [The role of language in the development of a child's cognitive activity]. In *Vsesojuznoe sovechanie. Doklady na sovechanii po voprosam psichologii 3-8 ijula*, 124-37.

Menchinskaya, N.A. (1966). Myslehlenie v processe obuchenija [Thinking in the process of learning]. In E.W. Shorochova (ed.), *Issledovanie myshlenija v soveskoy psichologii* [Investigations of thinking in Soviet psychology]. Moscow: Nauka, 349-87.

Oleron J.P. & Piaget, J. (eds.), (1963). *Traite de Psychologie experimentale* [Aspect of experimental psychology], vol. 6. Paris: Presses Universitaires de France.

Poddiakov, N.N. (1977). *Myshlenie doshkolnika* [Pre-school children's thinking]. Moscow: Pedagogika.

Radford, J. & Burton, A. (1974). *Thinking: its nature and development*. London: Wiley.

Restle, F. (1962). The selection of strategies in cue learning. *Psychological Review* 69, 329-43.

Rozengart-Pupko, G.L. (1948). *Rech i razvitie vosprijatija v rannem detstve* [The speech and the development of perception in early childhood]. Moscow: Akademia Med. Nauk SSSR.

Rubinstein, S.L. (1973). *Problemy obshchej psichologii* (Problems of general psychology). Moscow: Pedagogika.

Shvachkin, N. (1954). Eksperimentalnoje izuchenie rannisch obobscheniji u rebenka [Experimental study of early generalization in children]. *Izvestija Akademia Pedagogicheskikh Nauk RSFSR* 54, 111-35.

Skinner B.F. (1961). *Cumulative record*. New York: Appleton-Century-Crofts.

Talyzina, N.F. (1957). K voprosu ob usvoenii nachalnych geometricheskich poniatiji [To the issue of learning initial geometric concepts]. In B.G. Ananiev & A.N. Leontiev, (eds.), *Materialy sovecshanija po psichologii* [Materials of psychological meeting]. Moscow: Akademia Pedagogicheskikh Nauk RSFSR, 443-51.

Talyzina N.F. (1981). *Psikhologija obuchenjija* [Psychology of Instruction]. Moscow: Progress Publishers.

Wason, P.C. & Johnson-Laird, P.N. (1972). *The psychology of reasoning: Structure and content*. London: Batsford.

Zaporozhets, A.V., Zinchenko, V.P. & Elkonin, D.B. (1964). Razvitie myshlenija [The development of thinking]. In A.V. Zaporozhets & D.B. Elkonin (eds.), *Psichologia detei doshkolnogo vozrasta* [Psychology of pre-school aged children]. Moscow: Prosveshchenie, 183-246.

Zykova, V.I. (1950). Operirovanie ponjatijami pri reshenii geometricheskich zadach [The operation with concepts in solving geometric tasks]. *Izvestija Akademia Pedagogicheskikh Nauk RSFSR* 28, 155-94.

9 Developmental Teaching in Upper-Secondary School

Seth Chaiklin

Introduction

Most research in the developmental teaching tradition has focused primarily on instruction for pupils up to the age of 14 years. In an attempt to develop and expand this tradition further, I conducted several teaching experiments in physics and physical science in the upper-secondary schools in Denmark. There are at least two reasons why such experiments are interesting theoretically within the developmental teaching tradition.

First is the issue of subject matter analysis. An important theme in the developmental teaching tradition is the importance of analyzing the subject matter to be taught. The term *subject matter analysis* may not be used universally, but this kind of process is found in the teaching experiments conducted within the tradition. The goals of subject matter teaching at the upper-secondary level are usually more specific and detailed than in elementary and middle-school education. Is it possible to continue this kind of subject matter analysis at a more advanced level?

Second, using Elkonin's (1972) theoretical sketch about development, we can say that the learning motive is not dominant for most of the participants in these teaching experiments. The dominating motive of upper-secondary school pupils should be oriented to social relations (Elkonin) or socially-useful activity (Davydov, 1988a) or possibly occupational goals, but not learning. What consequences, if any, do these different dominating motives have for the learning of upper-secondary school pupils?

These two themes — subject matter analysis and effects of motives for learning — are examined in this chapter. First, a brief overview of the developmental teaching tradition is presented to set the background against which the research reported in this chapter was conducted. Then, some problems of subject matter analysis are illustrated and discussed for the topic area of atomic physics (at a upper-secondary school level). This is followed by a discussion of the interaction between subject matter and pupil motives, and their implications for developmental teaching. Finally, the chapter moves beyond the conceptual framework of developmental teaching research, to consider the implications and consequences for conceptualizing upper-secondary school teaching in general. The chapter's main point comes forward in this final integrating discussion: To realize teaching that is developmental, then the key is to have a sufficiently good analysis of the subject matter, such that one can create a framework of learning tasks within which variations in pupil motives and motivation can find expression. The simultaneous engagement of subject matter with motives is hypothesized as the heart of developmental teaching.

Historical Overview of Developmental Teaching

The idea of developmental teaching — as an explicit theoretical perspective and empirical praxis — can be traced back to the work of Daniel Elkonin and Vasily Davydov, and Leonid Zankov (1975/1977) in the Soviet Union in the late 1950s. The ideas spread further to Northern Europe, including Germany (Lompscher 1985), Finland (Engeström, Hakkarainen & Seppo 1982), and Denmark (cf. Hedegaard, Chaiklin & Hansen 1991).

These research projects have focused on primary-school education (Davydov 1988a, 55; G. Zuckerman, personal communication, 1995 and 1998). Detailed examples available in the published literature include mother-tongue learning (Aidarova 1982), arithmetic (Davydov 1966/1975; Kravin 1990), social studies (Hedegaard 1988; 1990), and biology (Lompscher 1984, 337-55).

Key Themes in Developmental Teaching

A fundamental assumption in developmental teaching is the importance of subject matter analysis as a foundation for the planning of teaching.[1] The name *developmental teaching* reflects the essential theoretical proposition, formulated by Vygotsky (1960/1978, ch. 6), that teaching takes a leading role in mental development. As Davydov (1988a, 19) wrote:

1. 'In our view, it is essential to base oneself, when elaborating the problems of developmental teaching, on the following proposition: the basis of developmental teaching is its content. From that content stem the methods (of modes) of teaching organization. This proposition typifies the views of Vygotskii and Elkonin.' (Davydov 1988a, 19)

In concretizing this proposition, one should note that the developmental nature of learning activity, which is the leading activity in the younger school-age period, connects with the fact that the content of academic activity is theoretical knowledge.

Davydov's concretization raises the central issues addressed in this chapter — namely the importance of subject matter analysis and its relation to a pupil's motives. The starting assumption here is that the purpose of formal schooling should be 'directed toward the development of their [the pupils'] personalities' (1988a, 17). In the case of primary school teaching, learning activity is the leading activity, and the development of this activity is coextensive with personality development. Moreover, the content of this activity, the development of theoretical knowledge, necessarily presupposes that the content of the teaching activities are related to the conceptual foundations of the subject matter being taught, which in turn are related to the societal traditions within which this knowledge was originally developed. Here the intended relations among developmental teaching, subject matter analysis, and mental or personality development are clear.

However, with the later school-age period, it is assumed that learning activity has been acquired, and is no longer the leading activity for pupils.[2] If teaching for upper-secondary pupils is going to be developmental, then it cannot, at least according to this theoretical formulation, take its starting point in learning activity. There are several different positions that could be taken here. One is that upper-secondary school teaching should (or need) not be developmental; it is sufficient if schools only continue to develop and refine learning activity at a more advanced level. In this case, subject matter analysis would only be needed for identifying and clarifying the content to be used in conducting this teaching.

Another position is to assume or desire that teaching at the upper-secondary level should also be developmental. The theoretical assumption is that development occurs when teaching is formulated in relation to the pupils' leading activity. Now the relationship between subject matter analysis, with its aim at revealing the logic of development

---

2. 'Learning activity ceases to be a leading activity and becomes a component of other kinds of leading reproductive activity — socially useful activity first, then educational and vocational activity...' (Davydov 1988b, 40). Elkonin (1972) has a slightly different analyzis, in which the primary motive is social interactions and professional orientation. But it is clear that learning is no longer the leading motive, so one cannot enjoy the parallel between the leading motive and the main goal of school teaching.

and its use in teaching is more ambiguous, because the leading activity for upper-secondary pupils is not learning activity.[3]

The position developed in this chapter is that subject matter analysis is still necessary and that teaching can be developmental in relation to leading activities. The role and significance of subject matter analysis can be better appreciated against the background of learning activity. Therefore, the next section introduces the idea of learning activity, within the developmental teaching tradition, followed by a discussion of a subject matter analysis for atomic physics.

Learning Activity: A Brief Overview

Although learning activity is not the leading activity for upper-secondary school pupils, this activity is still a major part of a pupil's work in upper-secondary school. Therefore, it is useful to understand the relation of subject matter analysis to learning activity, because the same kind of analysis would be made for upper-secondary school pupils, but different considerations would enter into how one uses the subject matter analysis in relation to the leading activity of the upper-secondary school pupils.

The purpose of learning activity, at least in the developmental teaching tradition, is for persons to acquire theoretical knowledge, that is, to consciously reproduce the theoretical understandings that have been developed in a subject matter area in order to explain the important structural relations that characterize that area. This focus on the theory of knowledge arises out of a more general concern in the cultural-historical tradition with the principle that knowledge is a historical accumulation and formulation of concepts and procedures used to explain phenomenal appearances (Hedegaard, this volume). This knowledge is seen both as a reflection or representation of reality and the process by which this reflection is constructed. So the choice and presentation of school subject matter should, ideally, reflect the goals of schooling, and these goals are formulated in relation to societal traditions.[4]

Theoretical thinking is characterized generally as an ascent from the abstract to the concrete. More specifically, the aim is to develop a general

---

3. 'The true potential of developmental teaching and upbringing is revealed when their content, which is an instrumentality for the organization of the child's reproductive activity, corresponds to his distinctive psychological features as well as to the abilities that shaped on the basis of that activity. The developmental role of teaching and upbringing is reduced to the minimum if it is not in line with those distinctive features or even runs counter to them' (Davydov 1988b, 38).

primary relationship that characterizes a problem area, and discover how this relationship appears in many specific problems. This process of identifying a general relationship (substantive abstraction) and application to analyze particular problems (substantive generalization) produces a number of abstractions that one aims to integrate or synthesize into a concept or 'kernel' for the subject matter. It is important to understand that *concept* here means a set of procedures for deducing particular relationships from the abstract relationship. A fuller discussion of theoretical knowledge can be found in (Davydov 1972/1990, this volume).

The purpose of the learning activity is to help pupils master the relationships, abstractions, generalizations, and syntheses that characterize a subject matter area. This mastery is reflected in their ability to make substantive reflection, analysis, and planning. The basic educational strategy for giving pupils the possibility to reproduce theoretical thinking is to create instructional tasks whose solutions would require the formation of substantive abstractions and generalizations about the central ideas in the subject matter. This approach is grounded in Vygotsky's idea of internalization, that one learns subject matter content by learning the procedures by which one works in the subject matter area.

For example, a typical recommendation is to start with the basic relation, investigate some variations in this relation, attempt a synthesis via a model that captures the essential aspects, apply the model to new, related cases and evaluate the adequacy of the model.[5] The main point, for now, is that the organization of the sequence of tasks in the learning activity is guided by the need to formulate the general relationship and then develop abstractions and syntheses of this relation.

Subject Matter Analysis

With this background about theoretical knowledge and learning activity, it is now possible to see more specifically what is needed in a subject matter analysis. The ideal is that pupils work with the genetically primary, universal, essential relationship. Thus, it should be clear that a

4. Of course there can be and often are conflicts or contradictions between general societal goals and interests on the one hand, and the specific goals and interests in the school classroom, on the other. For present purposes, it is enough to have in view that subject-matter analyzis is motivated in part from the need to be able to explain or justify the content in teaching.
5. More detailed descriptions of these processes can be found in Aidarova (1982), Davydov (1988a, 19), and Hedegaard (1990).

good subject matter analysis will aim to identify the basic relationships that would be used in instructional situations. That is, the subject matter analysis should provide an analysis of the primary relations that organize a subject matter area.

This general idea of identifying the kernel of subject matter areas sounds sensible, but as far as I can tell, it is still a hypothesis whether all subject matter areas can be described in this manner. The existing examples that we have for elementary school subject matter teaching are compelling. I can understand this hypothesis when the focus is on primary school, and specific concepts like *number* or *grammatical tense* are being developed for a period of a year or more. And it seems likely that for many of the topics that are introduced in primary education, it is possible to identify the primary relations that organize these subject matter areas.

But what happens when we are interested in teaching subject matter areas in greater depth, with more relations, and in shorter time periods? In the upper-secondary school, there is a demand for more detail, not only as a mastery of the basic intellectual tools of reading, writing, arithmetic, or some general principle about historical and biological development. Now there is often an interest in, especially in natural-science teaching, that pupils gain control over specific mathematical procedures, and specific empirical results. Of course, one can argue conceptually that these procedures are part of the realization of the basic relationships, but if the analysis is going to be useful for the planning of actual teaching, then these relationships and their implications must be made explicit.

Similarly, what if one is uncertain about whether it is possible to identify a primary relation in a subject matter area? For example, in some areas of social-psychological research, it seems much of the research remains at an empirical level of describing relationships. Although patterns can be identified, a synthesis of their underlying relations is still not achieved (Mackie & Smith 1998). This example suggests that we may not necessarily be able to find the concept for all knowledge areas that are the object of formal instruction.

Even if one wants to assert the ontological validity of the dialectical tradition, we are still faced with the practical problem of actually constructing these kernels for most subject matter areas that are taught in school. And anyone who has tried to construct these kernels has discovered that there is very little help provided in the developmental-teaching literature about how to make the analysis in a new subject matter area.

Until the idea of kernel or concept is tried more explicitly and extensively, I am willing to work with a simpler idea that one can try to identify some basic relationships that need to be explored, and leave undecided whether a kernel has been identified or not.

Summary of Arguments Concerning Subject Matter Analysis

The argument presented here is that regardless of the level at which one is teaching it is necessary and important to make a subject matter analysis — with the idea of trying to identify the basic relations that organize a subject matter area.

At the same time, it has been suggested that the limited extent to which these ideas have been examined in concrete situations makes it difficult to evaluate whether it is really a useful or realizable idea in general. The dialectical theory of knowledge provides an idea for how to address this problem, namely to try to rise from abstract generalizations to a substantive generalization. In the next major section of this chapter, an attempt to make this generalization for atomic physics is presented.

For present purposes, I want to illustrate that it is possible to make some progress in identifying central relations for a more complicated subject matter. While the general or abstract idea of 'identifying the central relationships' is easy enough to understand, it is not a trivial task to work out a possible version. In the present case, four months of weekly meetings, with a university physicist and several upper-secondary school physics teachers (who each had a university degree in physics) was needed to develop the analysis from which some points will be presented here.[6] It is interesting to note that the analysis that results from this work is fairly simple, almost trivial in appearance. I will comment on this issue after presenting the analysis that was used in the teaching experiments.

Subject Matter Analysis for Atomic Physics

The subject matter that was taught in the teaching experiments was the structure and properties of atoms, including the formation of molecules and the structure of the periodic system. The periodic system is important to understand because combinations of chemical elements into molecules depend on understanding their properties, which are summarized therein.

---

6. Gert Hansen, Poul Thomsen, Niels-Henrik Würtz, and Ove Østergaard were the primary participants. Gert and Niels-Henrik were subsequently the teachers in the teaching experiments.

With this knowledge, one can understand that molecular constructions are not arbitrary, and that the limits on specific combinations can be explained by the empirical properties of their atomic structure.

We did not succeed in formulating what could be called a kernel model for atomic physics. But the exercise in trying to construct such a cell had many useful results. From these analyses we were able to formulate the key ideas that would organize the teaching over the six weeks given to this topic.

The main organizing idea was the description of matter at different levels of resolution, which we informally called *zoom*. For example, a coffee cup, can also be described as clay, as a composition of iron, silicon, and other atoms, whose internal structure can be further described. The second main organizing idea was the question of how one could investigate matter. Thus, each time one encounters a material, then the question becomes: How can one investigate the material such that a description can be made? The one general answer to this question is to make transformations (heat, light, mechanical force, contact with other materials) in a material. This general answer reflects the basic strategy that has been used to describe atomic and nuclear properties. The entire enterprise can be described as making transformations and trying to model the resulting effects.

Implications of the Subject Matter Analysis

For present purposes it will be sufficient to illustrate a couple of the implications of this subject matter analysis. The main interest here is to consider the value of an attempt to identify central topics in the subject matter, rather than argue for the specific validity of the current state of our analysis.

The first organizing idea of zoom calls attention to the idea that there are relationships between different levels of description. In principle, each level of resolution can be described in terms of its relation to some of the other levels (skipping over the interesting problems where this may not be possible), and properties at one level are often explained at another level. For example, the description of matter at an atomic level can provide an understanding for macroscopic properties such as hardness, colours when burned, weight, and so forth.

At first glance, these ideas about the relations between different levels of description seem obvious, unworthy of nomination as a central idea for teaching. But when one examines the curriculum plan from the Ministry of Education about what topics should be taught in connection with atomic physics, then there is no indication, not even implicitly, that this was an important idea. And, as we discovered in our teaching experiments, often to our surprise, pupils also had difficulty in considering materials at different levels of resolution.

The idea of zoom combined with the idea of description leads to several interesting ideas about how to develop topics in the teaching. To understand these examples, you have to remember that atoms, at least in the classical model, are conceptualized as having a nucleus surrounded by a number of electrons. Of special interest and importance is that in stable atoms there seem to be a limited number of distances from the nucleus that will accept an orbiting electron. A major part of understanding atomic structure and the construction of the periodic system revolves around knowing about the existence of these so-called shells, why they exist, and what consequences they have for atomic and molecular interactions, as well as observable macroproperties. In the typical didactic approach, one starts by defining these properties, telling about the experiments on atomic spectra that were used to formulate the idea of shells to explain the empirical observations.

In the present approach, these same topics get a different place in the conceptual logic. In starting with everyday materials, and considering their molecular composition, we are forced to introduce this idea of atomic structure, if we are going to explain which atoms are able to form molecules with others. The idea of using transformations to describe materials leads us to use spectra as a phenomenon to be explained by the atomic model, rather than its historical role, in which this was the evidence that was used to build up the atomic model.

The important thing to notice in these illustrations is that the same topics, facts, results may be drawn into the teaching as have always been drawn in, but the relationships between these topics, and the ways in which they are used often seem to become changed from the traditional, didactic instructional forms. In other words, our organizing principles can be understood as a set of procedures that lead us to conceptualize the facts and relations in new ways. If we are able to make substantive generalizations from using these procedures, then we would start to have candidates for a kernel for this subject matter area. For now we were satisfied with having these organizing procedures.

Some Hypotheses About Subject Matter Analysis

Given that we have so few examples of subject matter analyses, especially for upper-secondary education, it is difficult to give any definitive views about how the process should proceed, so for now here are three hypotheses, based on my own experience in making these analyses.

1) It is easy to identify many topics, results, concepts, theories, applications, and illustrations that could be introduced in the teaching situation (and the teaching conducted in many school systems seems to remain at this level of analysis).

When working with subject matter at the upper-secondary school level, there are many empirical results, theoretical concepts, definitions and descriptions that are available. It is easy to make lists of interesting, important, significant, practical results. In the case of the Danish upper-secondary school these lists are given as official regulations from the Ministry of Education. For example, in the area of atomic physics in the upper-secondary school, the required topics are: atomic and nuclear structure, atomic emission and absorption of radiation, radioactive fallout, and ionizing radiation. While the high-level course includes nuclear reactions, equivalence between mass and energy, Q-values, binding energy and nuclear structure, and sub-nuclear particles. These general topics are then further specified in terms of what aspects should be mentioned in teaching, and what topics should have some actions conducted by the pupils. Textbooks that are used typically in the upper-secondary school are written to correspond primarily to the required and optional topics mentioned in these documents. By following these textbooks, teachers can be reasonably certain that they have touched upon the topics that are likely to appear in the ministry-formulated examination questions presented at the end of the school year. At the same time, these textbooks rarely have any sort of coherent structure or logic upon which these topics are developed or related to each other.

What is significant for present purposes is the fact that these lists are given with no indication of how these topics are related to the general goals of physics instruction, and there is no indication of the kinds of relationships that pupils should be acquiring.

This example is probably typical of many subject matter areas and school systems in many different countries. These kinds of lists highlight, by their absence, a lack of any idea of how these ideas are related to each other. If instruction does not develop the relationships between ideas, then how are pupils going to acquire or develop these ideas?

2) It is difficult to formulate a kernel concept, or even just a good model, that relates the multitude of possible topics in a meaningful way. As noted before, it took about four months of weekly meetings to develop the key ideas and the ways that they could be related to the subject matter. The generality of the resulting ideas may reflect the need to have abstractions that cover the different kinds of cases that appear in the instruction. Some of the time is used to simply think through the implications of various models in relation to the many different topics.

3) However, once that model is formulated, it often turns out to be organized by very simple questions. Indeed, the questions appear so simple, that one wonders whether there has been any real accomplishment, because it all appears so trivial. But one important value is that it provides a way to organize the conceptual relations among the different topics, and gives a way to conceptualize the kinds of classroom activities that need to take place in order to give pupils a chance to make these conceptualizations as well.

No one likes to admit that the results of their work are trivial, and the denial of trivial results is not the best starting point for an argument. Nonetheless, I will suggest that it is important to remember that the final models are often a summary of many weeks of reflection about concrete examples that are being summarized by the general relationships. Perhaps the term *kernel* or *central relations* gives the impression that their presentation will result in an enlightening insight ('like a bolt from heaven'). This may be the case in some instances, but it seems worthwhile to consider that the value of subject matter analysis is in the simple, general organizing question or principle. The generality is precisely its strength, in that it gives the teacher, and ultimately the pupils, a chance to hold in view why one is investigating the topics in the subject matter and what relations are being formed.

Interaction Between Subject Matter Content and Pupil Motives

To this point, we have considered some subject matter knowledge that should be acquired from a teaching intervention in the Danish upper-secondary school. The problem to be considered now is the interaction between the content of this teaching and upper-secondary-school pupils' motives. This interest arises in relation to the general interest in teaching that develops personality.

In the developmental-teaching view, (a) subject matter learning and personality development are viewed as a simultaneous accomplishment, (b) subject matter learning alone is necessarily sufficient for personality development (Davydov 1988b, 16), but (c) subject matter learning that is organized in relation to a leading activity is more likely to develop personality. In the present case, the problem becomes: How does one teach atomic physics so that it is developmental?

Before presenting the theoretical analysis and some empirical examples, it is necessary to give some details about the historical setting in which the theoretical analysis is being worked out. In fact, these details should be understood as part of the theoretical analysis, in that when one wants to analyze pupil motives and consider the interaction between subject matter and motives, then it is necessary to consider the concrete, historical facts that organize the actions of the pupils.

A Case Study of Danish Upper-Secondary School Science Teaching

In making an analysis of children's motives, one has to consider the societal demands within which the children function. In the present case, the analysis is developed in relation to the Danish state, where atomic physics is a required part of the upper-secondary school education. Because upper-secondary schooling is not required, this necessarily puts the pupils in a different relation to the instruction, in that they can choose to stop without any direct, institutional hindrance.

Characteristics of Danish Upper-Secondary Schools

In Denmark, there are several kinds of post-comprehensive education. Normally, all children attend the comprehensive school through the 9th grade (about 16 years old), and sometimes a 10th grade. If they want to attend the university or get a professional education, then it is necessary to follow the gymnasium education, a three-year education. In the first six decades of this century only about 10% of the children in Denmark attended gymnasium, but the number has increased regularly so that now almost 50% attend gymnasium. A more detailed analysis would consider the implications of this change in which there is a shift from an 'elite' (mostly upper-class) population, to a more general (or at least middle-class) population.

Within the gymnasium, there are two major lines of education, one oriented to the natural sciences (called mathematical), and the other oriented to the humanities (called language). Normally children go directly from the comprehensive school to the gymnasium. However, some do not. They pursue other goals, including travel, work, and other kinds of technical or business education. At some point they decide that they want or need to get the formal qualifications required for entrance to university or professional education. The Danish state provides a special institution called *HF* (an abbreviation for *Højere Forberedelse* which translates literally to 'higher preparation'). This educational program, normally expected to be completed in two years, is formally equivalent to the three-year gymnasium education. It also has the two major kinds of education lines: mathematical and language.

Pupils enrolled in the HF education are typically somewhat older than gymnasium pupils, and many have had other kinds of life experience, including work. Furthermore, they tend to have more definite goals in terms of a specific further education or training to which their HF education should lead. This goal-directed focus contrasts with most gymnasium pupils who often only have some general educational goals, such as attending university.

Characteristics of Pupils and their Situation in the Teaching Experiments

Classes were selected for the teaching experiments in atomic physics to provide the greatest possible contrast in terms of pupil background. The same subject matter (and teaching plan) was used for two different classes, one in a gymnasium and one in a HF. A third experiment was also conducted with another HF class. Furthermore, the gymnasium class was in the mathematical line, while the HF classes were in the language line. The course was obligatory for both groups of pupils. For the gymnasium pupils, it was only one of several science courses that they will have to follow. For the HF pupils, it is the only science course in their entire program. The general experience of HF teachers is that HF pupils are not interested in taking this course, and it is considered a difficult course to teach because of the lack of pupil interest.

Organization of the Teaching Experiments

Three teaching experiments, each lasting six weeks, were conducted within the regular teaching program of the gymnasium and HF. Two of the experiments were conducted in language line HF classes (22 pupils and 23 pupils), while a third was conducted with a mathematics line gymnasium class (21 pupils). The teachers were the same persons who were teaching prior to and after the experiments, and no other special conditions were made. Pupils were responsible for being examined in the material that was taught. The teachers participated in the process of subject matter analysis. During the teaching experiments, I met regularly with the teachers to plan each day of teaching, and discuss how the previous teaching session went. I attended most of the teaching sessions, making close-to-verbatim field notes of the dialogues, interaction, and activities.

Subject Matter Content and Motives: An Introduction to the Problem

There is an interaction between a person's motives (expressed in their interests or orientations) and that person's way of working with the subject matter content of formal teaching. A simple thought experiment, in which one teaches atomic physics (at the gymnasium level) both to primary-school children and to atomic physicists, should be sufficient to establish the general validity of this point.

Of greater scientific interest is the problem of analyzing the interactions where one expects that the specific subject matter content is chosen (at least *prima facie*) to be at an appropriate level for the participants. Once again several indisputable assumptions appear: (a) within the cohort of people who attend a gymnasium physics course, there will be a diversity of interests with respect to learning this subject matter, and (b) even if one could select a group within this cohort that had more or less similar interests, there would still be a need to adapt or adjust the presentation of the material in a way that would respond to those interests. Furthermore, assumption (b) implies an assumption that (c) the quality and rate of learning is dependent on a pupil's motivation which in turn is dependent on the form and content of the teaching activities. Assumption (c) is the reason for believing that teaching organized in relation to a pupil's motives will be important for personality development.

Now a new set of problems appear. While the general assumptions seem plausible, they give little or no advice about how to realize them in any concrete case. We are left more or less with the principle: 'Start where your pupils start.' In Denmark, it is common to cite Kierkegaard for this advice. But if one is then asked to ascertain where a person is or where they start, then many problems arise.

There are no readily available (psychological or physiological) measuring instruments that can help to identify where 20 pupils are starting with atomic physics. One could, of course, start by giving a test in which the pupils are asked to reproduce facts, and a questionnaire in which they are asked to express their degree of interest in and motivation for learning the topic. But anyone who has tried such things quickly discovers (as we did) that this material is not especially useful for solving this problem. For some reason, it does not seem to grab into the heart of the problem, to make contact with the ongoing interests and motivations of the pupils *while they are participating in the teaching situation*. We need to conceptualize pupils' motives in way that is useful for designing teaching interactions.

Clarifying the Requirements of the Problem

To understand the way in which motives are analyzed, and used in teaching, it is first helpful to consider the idea of personality development. The main interest, in the context of developmental teaching, is to organize subject matter teaching so that it results in development of a pupil's personality.

The meaning of *personality development* used here is inspired by Elkonin's (1972) theoretical sketch of mental development. Personality development is characterized by a qualitative change in a person's orientation to the world. This change is usually marked by changes in what one considers important or meaningful, which in turn is related to changes in one's capabilities for action.

In the context of upper-secondary school science teaching, indications of these kinds of changes would include (a) greater interest in learning about natural-scientific topics, (b) reduced anxiety and self-doubt when working with or reading about natural-scientific topics, (c) greater confidence when working with natural-scientific content, and (d) greater willingness to attempt (and more creatively) to apply one's knowledge to related situations that were not directly addressed in instruction. The demand on teaching specific topics in the natural sciences are that they would contribute to these kinds of changes.

These ideals are not peculiar to the developmental teaching tradition. In the context of upper-secondary school science instruction, similar goals can be seen in the official formulations from the Danish Ministry of Education.[7] Illustrative examples of these official goals include: 'evaluate problems of a mathematical or natural-scientific kind, encountered in other school subjects, in the media, and in daily life'; 'pupils should get an impression of physics as a coherent description of nature'; 'teaching should qualify pupils to participate in cultural and societal life'.

The societal goals, as expressed in the Ministry documents, are built on a legitimating notion of the importance of natural science in contemporary life, and the value of persons acquiring a sufficient understanding of science so that they can participate competently in that societal life.

In the case of language line HF pupils, their science course is possibly the only formal science course they will take for the rest of their lives, and for many of the mathematics line gymnasium pupils it is often the only time they are encountering this particular subject matter in a formal context. So it is not trivial to say that the teaching has the potential to make a significant contribution to a person's orientation to the content, and in this sense, it is meaningfully to talk about this teaching as an opportunity for contributing to personality development.

Many of the indications of personality development listed before for science teaching can be viewed as the development of motives. In all cases, these motives depend on the development of actions. Actions, by definition, are motivated. People engage in actions to achieve goals. School pupils, in a teaching context, are expected to act in a way that will develop specific capabilities. However, the cultural-historical approach notes that actions gain their meaning in relation to societally-organized practices designated as *activity*.[8] In other words, actions get their meaning in part in relation to these societally-organized units.

7. As noted before, there are different kinds of programs for upper-secondary school pupils, and many interesting examples could be given and analyzed from each of these programs.
8. '[I]n society a man finds not simply external conditions to which he must accommodate his activity, but that these same social conditions carry in themselves motives and goals of his activity, his means and methods; in a word, society produces the activity of the individuals forming it (Leontiev 1975/1978, 51).

This perspective shifts a focus from seeking motivation for specific actions to understanding the meaning of the specific actions in relation to activities. In turn, this suggests that actions can be motivated if they can be related to activities. In other words, to get pupils to engage in intended actions, then it will be helpful if these actions can be motivated in relation to the activities.

The idea of motives in relation to actions is the key to understanding the problem of designing instruction in relation to pupil interests, that is concurrently developmental. The logic goes like this: (a) personality development results from acquiring actions that enable qualitative shifts in a person's relation to the world (e.g., development of new motives); (b) persons are oriented to acquiring actions that are related to their motives; (c) therefore, developmental teaching should create opportunities for pupils to engage in actions that are related to their motives, while being simultaneously oriented toward the acquisition of the intended subject matter knowledge. Thus, the problem is how to identify pupil motives such that these motives can be integrated into classroom teaching in a way that supports personality development.

Analyzing Pupils' Motives

One step in the process of analyzing a pupil's motives in relation to specific subject matter teaching is to have a more general analysis of the pupil's activity. An analysis of the societal demands for upper-secondary school pupils in Denmark led to the formulation of four central motives that were hypothesized to organize their activity. These are: institutional qualification, intellectual qualification, general development, and social development. Institutional qualification concerns acquiring institutionally-defined achievements (in this case, usually course grades) that are necessary for further study. Intellectual qualification is focused on learning subject matter that is relevant to one's projected future activity. For example, a person who intends to attend dental school will be interested in obtaining capabilities that are perceived as being relevant to that schooling. General development is concerned with being an all-round person.[9] Social interaction refers to nonscholastic practices such as going to parties, doing sports with friends, and so forth.

This analysis was explored in a pilot study of 17 Danish first-year

---

9. In Danish, there is a special concept (*almen dannelse*) that is known and discussed in society. Similar concepts are found in Germany (*Bildung*), and France (*formation*).

gymnasium pupils (Kjeldsen & Harrit 1995). A questionnaire formulated to explore the four hypothesized motives was used. One question was designed to explore the institutional qualification motive, and 14 of the 17 pupils answered that they would not have attended the gymnasium if it did not qualify them for further education. This result is interpreted to reflect the importance of institutional qualification as a motive for attending gymnasium. Similar results were obtained in answers to questions about the other hypothesized motives.

The general analysis of upper-secondary pupil motives does not include learning activity as an important motive. Learning activity has not disappeared, but its place in the motive hierarchy has taken a subordinate role, compared to other motives such as intellectual and institutional qualification. Upper-secondary school pupils still engage in learning activity, but it is rarely the leading activity that organizes the pupil's actions and interests.

An important part of learning activity is the perceived need for acquiring knowledge. This need cannot be assumed to be a dominating motive among upper-secondary school pupils. Because learning activity per se is not likely to be motivating, this suggests that upper-secondary school pupils will not be motivated to learn topics in physical sciences simply from an interest in getting to know more about these topics. Learning activity is a means for realizing other motives — such as intellectual qualification and general development — that are more important in the hierarchy of motives for upper-secondary school pupils.

Learning activity is manifest in a propensity for study, a perceived need for study, and the ability to study. Upper-secondary school teaching is not to help the pupils acquire diverse actions within this activity, such as reading assignments at home, thinking about the questions being posed in class and so forth, and teaching that is oriented in this direction will not be developmental in the upper-secondary school.

This analysis of the motive hierarchy suggests that it will be especially difficult for pupils who are in the language line of the upper-secondary school to see the relevance of science teaching to their dominating motive of professional preparation. If there are no genuine, motivated reasons to instruct pupils in the physical sciences, then it will be difficult to make developmental teaching.

Subject Matter Teaching and Personality Development

The main hypothesis is that subject matter teaching which is aimed at the leading activity is more likely to be developmental. But so far we have only made an analysis of the general motives that organize a pupil's activity. We are still faced with the problem of how to relate to these general motives in the context of a specific teaching intervention, such as about atomic physics. We need a strategy for how to relate the development of motives for specific subject matter in relation to the dominant motives that organize an activity.

Moreover, in the present case, there are pupils with different historical and societal relations. Not only must we consider the subject matter teaching in relation to the general, central characteristics of the age period, but we must also consider that within this age period there can be different relations to the subject matter.

The thesis is that teaching should start with the subject matter goals that have been formulated in the subject matter analysis, regardless of the pupil's background. It is important to see that (a) the subject matter goals do not necessarily get modified or changed because of differences among pupils, and (b) the differences among pupils should be allowed to grow out of the pupils' meeting with the material in which the teacher is posing questions and problems that reflect the scientific tradition's way of asking questions and posing problems.

If pupils do not meet the tradition's way of working with problems, even if they are opposed to it, then how can they come to develop some feeling for this approach. This is important in relation to the developmental goals for instruction. If language line pupils are more likely to raise questions about the approach, than mathematics line pupils, then it should be possible to respond to these interests in the classroom tasks and interactions.

Similarly, a subject matter analysis, which identifies the central, organizing ideas of a problem area, makes it easier for a teacher to organize teaching problems that contribute to both intellectual qualification and general development, because the teacher can honestly work with the pupils to understand the significance of the subject matter.

Opportunities for discovering and responding to pupil differences is enabled by the general form of developmental teaching. There are periods of reflection and discussion about the goals of the work. It is during these periods that differences in pupil interest are likely to appear, and it is here that it will be possible for a teacher to help formulate and articulate these interests, drawing them back into the specific subject matter goals that have been formulated.

In the teaching experiments we started with the same learning task for both the gymnasium mathematics line and the HF language line. The first task was based on a homework assignment in which pupils should come to class with examples of materials about which they were interested in obtaining more information. This was then used to make a transition to the problem of describing a single material (along the lines of the zoom discussed before). In the gymnasium class, the pupils came with their examples and eventually started to work on making descriptions of materials, showing their relatively sophisticated knowledge about materials.

In contrast, in the HF class, some pupils raised the question about what physics is and the relation between mathematics and physics. As one pupil said 'Calculation is not so important, that is mathematics, not physics'.

This question carried over to the next class session as they also started to describe materials (wood, clay, metal). Many questions were raised about 'what is physics', and its relation to biology and chemistry. For example, some said that analyzing a piece of wood was not physics, but biology. (This is an example, as previously mentioned, that pupils have problems with different levels of resolution in description of materials.) At the end of the class, the teacher said that people would probably like to have a proper answer about the relation between chemistry and physics. One of the girls in the class said in response (in a genuine way), 'I am going to die. I am curious'. This response is interpreted as a sign of the development of an interest in learning the subject matter, which in and of itself is considered as contributing to motive development. These kinds of reflective, critical questions about the nature of the sciences did not appear in the mathematics line gymnasium class.

These brief descriptions from the classroom observations illustrate many of the general points that have been discussed here. We have started with the same subject matter analysis and the same tasks for two different groups of pupils. The organization of the classroom interactions in developmental teaching gives the possibility for different groups of pupils to find their own relation to the tasks. In both cases, it is possible to develop a better understanding of the relationships between atomic and macrolevels of description, but through very different paths of classroom work. The language line HF pupils raised many more philosophical questions about what they were doing, while the mathematics line gymnasium pupils spent more time constructing examples based on their prior knowledge.

In one of these instances, the question was raised in a HF class about why one had to learn about the periodic system. One of the arguments used by some of the pupils was that it was part of one's general development. The use of this argument is consistent with the general motive analysis, and is consistent with the idea that specific motives in learning the subject matter are developed in relation to general motives.

The typical expectation is that language line pupils are simply trying to survive their science course. The field observations, however, indicate that if given suitable conditions, there is considerably more interest than might be apparent in the traditional teaching forms. There is a general impression that as the language line pupils get the opportunity to confront these 'big' questions (in relation to this limited situation), they are able to find an interest and motivation to work with the subject matter that grows more from genuine interest, rather than externally imposed requirement.

For example, one pupil in the HF language line class made the following spontaneous comment at the end of the second day of the teaching experiment:

This is exciting, because we have to think about what we are doing. Instead of having everything written up on the blackboard or read in a book, we have to think ourselves about how to come forward. I really like that.

In this particular case, the pupils were working on the problem of trying to find out how many atoms were in a metal cup.

Conclusion

The present analysis suggests that the general form of the developmental-teaching approach could be adapted at the secondary level as well.

My suggestion is that one starts teaching with the same orientation and goals, regardless of whether it is language line or mathematics line pupils, because the teaching goal is to help pupils acquire some understanding of the subject matter content, both in its substantive terms, and in terms of learning to understand the scientific traditions' values for asking and investigating questions. One expects that some differences between groups of pupils will arise along the way. In each case, we should (a) take the pupils' motives and their interests seriously, and (b) do it in a way that builds within the spirit of the original starting point of developing a scientific approach to the subject matter.

Contextualizing These Research Goals

This chapter has been formulated within current concerns in the developmental teaching tradition. The interest, from the researcher's point of view, is how to make a teaching that is developmental for the pupils. But it is important to recognize that this interest can also be said to exist, at least to some extent, in official policies from the Ministry.

The interest in personality development changes the research focus from identifying classroom tasks that support subject matter learning or interest the pupils. At the level of classroom teaching, it is always possible to come with some activities that will engage the pupils, or at the very minimum to maintain some semblance of order and discipline in the classroom. Where the interesting research (and difficult practical) problems appear is in organizing classroom activities that simultaneously develop pupils' knowledge of the subject matter while contributing to their general personality development. It is this concurrent realization of these multiple interests that can be difficult to achieve. The main assumption here is that the subject matter analysis can be used as the bridge between the specific content of the teaching and the more general developmental interests.

The key insight is that by identifying the organizing assumptions for a subject matter area, one is simultaneously discovering the concrete reasons why the subject matter area has developed in importance in the first place. By providing pupils with an opportunity to discover (through participation in structured classroom teaching activities) these relations, then there is a greater chance of developing personality, through developing their motives for the content and its relation to the general motives of their leading activity.

References

Aidarova, L. (1982). *Child development and education*. Moscow: Progress. (Original work published 1982)

Davydov, V.V. (1975). The psychological characteristics of the 'prenumerical' period of mathematics instruction. In L. Steffe (ed.), *Soviet studies in the psychology of learning and teaching mathematics: Vol. 5. Children's capacity for learning mathematics.* Stanford, Calif.: School Mathematics Study Group, 109-205. (Original work published 1966)

Davydov, V.V. (1990). Types of generalization in instruction: Logical and psychological problems in the structuring of school curricula. In J. Kilpatrick (ed.), *Soviet studies in mathematics education: Vol. 2.* Reston, Va: National Council of Teachers of Mathematics. (Original work published 1972)

Davydov, V.V. (1988a). Problems of developmental teaching. *Soviet Education* 30 (9), 3-83.

Davydov, V.V. (1988b). Problems of developmental teaching. *Soviet Education* 30 (10), 3-41.

Elkonin, D. (1972). Toward the problem of stages in the mental development of the child. *Soviet Psychology* 10, 225-51.

Engeström, Y., Hakkarainen, P. & Seppo, S. (1982). The necessity of a new approach in the study of instruction. In Komulainen (ed.), *Research on teaching and the theory and practice in teacher training* (Research Report 4). Helsinki: Department of Teacher Education, University of Helsinki.

Hedegaard, M. (1988). *Skolebørns personlighedsudvikling set gennem orienteringsfagene* [The development of schoolchildren's personality viewed through the social science subjects]. Aarhus: Aarhus University Press.

Hedegaard, M. (1990). The zone of proximal development as basis for instruction. In L.C. Moll (ed.), *Vygotsky and education: Instructional implications and applications of sociohistorical psychology.* Cambridge: Cambridge University Press, 349-71.

Hedegaard, M., Chaiklin, S. & Hansen, V.R. (1991). The influence of the cultural-historical tradition on Danish educational research: A survey. *Multidisciplinary Newsletter for Activity Theory* 9/10, 55-56.

Kjeldsen, A. & Harrit, L. (1995). Gymnasieelevers livsverden [Upper-Secondary school pupils' lifeworld]. Unpublished manuscript, University of Aarhus.

Kravin, D. (1990, May). Algebra in the elementary grades: An instructional process based on Davydov's concept of generalization. Paper presented at the meeting of the 2nd International Congress for Research on Activity Theory, Lahti, Finland.

Leontiev, A.N. (1978). *Activity, consciousness, and personality.* Englewood Cliffs, N.J.: Prentice-Hall. (Original work published 1975)

Lompscher, J. (1985). *Persönlichkeitsentwicklung in der Lerntätigkeit* [The development of personality in learning activity]. Berlin: Volk und Wissen.

Lompscher, J. (1984). Problems and results of experimental research on the formation of theoretical thinking through instruction. In M. Hedegaard, P. Hakkarainen & Y. Engeström (eds.), *Learning and teaching on a scientific basis: Methodological and epistemological aspects of the activity theory of learning and teaching.* Aarhus: University of Aarhus, Department of Psychology, 293-357.

Mackie, D.M. & Smith, E.R. (1998). Intergroup relations: Insights from a theoretically integrative approach. *Psychological Review* 105, 499-529.

Vygotsky, L. (1978). *Mind in society*. M. Cole, V. John-Steiner, S. Scribner & E. Souberman (eds.). Cambridge, Mass.: Harvard University Press. (Original work published 1960)

Zankov, L.V. and others (1977). *Teaching and development: A Soviet investigation*, B.B. Szekely, (ed.). White Plains, N.Y.: M.E. Sharpe. (Original work published 1975)

10 From Piaget and Vygotsky to Learning Activities: A Long Journey and an Inescapable Issue[1]

Felice Carugati

Introduction

At the end of this century the complex interplay between grand theories becomes apparent. The claims and limits of the scholars' empirical evidence, and the utility of casting these grand theories as an orchestra of 'multiple voices' has been playing over the century. Evolutionism, functionalism, structuralism, contructionism, constructivism, social interactionism and artificial intelligence metaphors, could be seen as grand ideatory systems which have been providing general orientations for developing more specific dynamics of research methods and procedures in human and social sciences. But as suggested by Lévy-Brühl since the 1920s, general theories can encourage contempt for specific and detailed studies since everything is explained in such general terms as matter and form, means and end, structure and content and, for the present discussion, adaptation and cultural transmission. But even more dangerous seems the dogmatism often aroused by grand theories which result in a condemnation or contempt of research efforts not directly linked to those theories. Furthermore, competition between scientific teams could provide supplementary sources of influence with non-trivial perverse effects as dynamics of propaganda, which seem to be at work during scientific activity itself.

In this chapter some crucial issues of the theories of Vygotsky and Piaget will be considered from the point of view of social psychology: social sciences at the beginning of this century (Baldwin, Levy-Brühl), considered logical processes as products of historical development. This recommendation had a great influence on the psychologists of the 1920s who tried to go beyond simplistic notions about the mind as a by-product

---

1. A preliminary version of this chapter has been presented during the symposium 'Constructivism and social interactionism', Second Conference for Socio-Cultural Research, Geneva, September 11-15, 1996.

of natural selection and to understand human consciousness as a product of sociocultural development. The experimental social psychological approach to development which has developed particularly in European countries since the 1970s will be presented, in order to illustrate the possibility to go from the abstract of grand theories, which postulate social-historical dynamics as constitutive of cognitive functioning, to the concrete experiments and empirical illustration of the heuristic value of the 'postulate of the social construction of cognition'. Recent ethnographic studies of the everyday life of children will be presented as well, and discussed for a complementary understanding of how social practices are important in building up both socialization and meaning of social reality. A final discussion of the theoretical implications for both learning methods and for a possible dialogue with activity theory will be presented.

Vygotsky, Piaget and the Search for a Social-Psychological Perspective

As Moscovici (1990) suggests, there are at least two ways of approaching the interplay between 'the social' and 'the cognitive' (i.e., between social and cognitive or developmental psychology) or, in other terms, how deeply social relations and social changes are accompanied by profound transformations of thought, with regard to the appropriation of cognitive instruments both in children and in adults.

The 'Bartlett way' recommends comparison of representations and beliefs of groups situated at different levels of evolution. In particular, Bartlett (1928) reminds us that the best introduction to the understanding of the social dynamics of cognitive constructions is to compare the novices and the experts within their own field or culture and not to compare the primitive with the ordinary member of a modern social group. Thus the main aim of cognitive social psychology must be carefully to describe the modern and normal persons in their milieu and in relation to topics which are significant for their common life. A complementary contribution to this way is to be found in Cattaneo's work (1864) about the crucial role that interpersonal and group conflicts play in producing mental phenomena and mental organization.

The 'Piagetian-Vygotskian way', describes the child as the equivalent to a person of a simpler or more primitive and younger culture, that follows its own development. This way therefore postulates that the social nature of human cognition appears in the individual's appropriation of social experiences. Appropriation is used here as a way of keeping the notion of adaptation (accommodation and assimilation) and the notion of transmission (externalization and internalization) as the two different and grand ways by which Piaget and Vygotsky tried to understand how human beings negotiate between the physical world and society.

Reading Piaget from the perspective of social psychology is often a very frustrating experience. Few authors have been as attentive as he was to the microgenetic aspects of the research process itself in his description of his clinical interviews. Yet despite this, microgenesis has only a limited role to play in his theoretical account of the developmental processes. On reading his accounts of the child's development, one often has the impression of listening to only one partner in a triangular conversation (I use explicitly *partner* and not social actor), the two missing (others) are (1) those representations of cultural objects (number, time, space, etc.) which circulate around the child and constitute the instruments of his/her everyday experience with adults and their peers, and (2) the adult as a genuine social actor.

On the other hand, the Vygotskian formula which suggests that all development proceeds from the interpsychological level to the intrapsychological level seems to offer a very general solution to the question of how children become social actors; this formula may however, be too general, it may, as Serge Moscovici put it recently, be too good to be true. But there is a strange feature of Vygotsky's work which I don't think has received sufficient attention. This is that it lacks any real social psychology, or said in other words, the Vygotskian approach needs to be integrated with a social psychological theorization. The main point here is that in Vygotsky's contribution there is no clear notion of social groups nor social identity. Culture is conceptualized as more or less homogeneous, comprising a single social group and a single social identity. The child who develops along strictly Vygotskian lines internalizes this more or less homogeneous culture and will, in turn, be instrumental in transmitting it to successive generations. How then is it possible to conceptualize social change, or again, what becomes of the Vygotskian formula when there is more than one conversation circulating in society, when the child is exposed to multiple and possibly contradictory discourses or voices?

Similar arguments could be addressed to Piaget's theory, though we should recognize that there are at least two (or even more) versions of Piaget's theory which need to be confronted. There is the less familiar sociologist version concerned with constraint as a principle theme in the constitution of society, and which, like many other sociological theories depict the significance of the psychological internalization of constraint and describe childhood as the major period of this process of internalization: the child who develops is in this sense, always the well-socialized child. But there is also the version of Piaget's theory which asserts the radical autonomy of the constructive aspects of cognition.

Piaget stresses the inner logic of the coordination of actions which always tends towards the equilibration of universal cognitive structures; the emphasis on developmental logic leads to that extraordinary equation which asserts that forms of social interaction are isomorphic with cognitive structures. To cooperate, as he put it, is to operate in common: a radical cognitive autonomy thus leads inevitably to a universal system of co-ordinations. This is an extremely fragile argument which can be sustained only as long as it remains at the level of Piaget's global metapsychological formula. Whenever it is subject to a closer scrutiny it seems to fracture into two unconnected lines of argument as the sociologist becomes unravelled from the psychologist.

Curiously enough, Piaget's grasp of the dialectic fails him at this crucial point, or perhaps we should say that he failed to assimilate the finer details of the lessons in the dialectics he received from Goldmann.

In fact, some of Piaget's work embodies insightful investigations of the ontogenesis of representations of social reality, i.e., accounts of how the child becomes a participant in collective semiotic systems. But there is also the version of Piaget's work that insists that the development of cognitive structures is an endogenous biological process. It is this version that is the most troublesome, since, despite Piaget's recognition of social interaction as a factor in development, this argument seems to reserve what is essential about cognitive development to a sphere removed from social life. From this point of view the development of representations of social reality consists of no more than a generic assimilation of the adult world at successive stages of cognitive development; a corollary of this line of argument is that a logical thinker should be a well socialized adult and, with some irony, logical thought and social conformism should go hand in hand!

In more general terms, how is the issue of the social addressed by Piaget and Vygotsky? It is reasonable to assert that both Vygotsky and Piaget share a common reference to the French tradition in sociology and anthropology, thus both claim and share a sort of collective psychology or a psychology of crowd, foule or masses; a tradition which is in line with the 'Zeitgeist' during the 1920s in Europe. More specifically we refer to the French sociologist Durkheim and the anthropologist Lévy-Brühl, with a specific reference to Blondel and Halbwachs which Vygotsky acknowledges (Kozulin 1990, 122ff.). The collective psychology of Piaget and Vygotsky holds the dualism between collective representations and individual human cognition, (culture for Vygotsky, adults' representational world and their constraints upon children for Piaget) a dualism which is well expressed by Durkheim:

There are [in man] two classes of states of consciousness that differ from each other in origin and nature, and in the end toward which they aim. One class merely expresses our organism and the object to which they are most directly related. Strictly individual, the states of consciousness of this class connect us only with ourselves, and we can no more detach them from us than we can detach ourselves from our bodies. The states of consciousness of the other class, on the contrary, come to us from society; they transfer society into us and connect us with something that surpasses us. Being collective, they are impersonal; they turn us toward ends that we hold in common with other men; it is through them and them alone that we can communicate with others. In brief, this duality corresponds to the double existence that we lead concurrently: the one purely individual and rooted in our organism, the other social and nothing but an extension of the society. (From *Essays on sociology and philosophy*, quoted in Kozulin 1990, 126).

This dualism is resolved by Piaget by means of a radical autonomy of cognitive functioning (the social being isomorphic with and derivative from the cognitive) whilst Vygotsky sees the social as being logically, causally, and temporarily antecedent, transmitted/internalized to/by the individual. Thus in Piaget's terms the social becomes individual on the conditions that the cognitive structures can assimilate the social contents, the child thereby becomes socialized by society.

For Vygotsky the transformation of the social into the individual is seen as a matter by which society individualizes itself in different persons; or in other words, society expresses itself continuously through each singular individual. Moreover the way of transformation of the social world into the individual's mind constitutes the main issue of Vygotsky's research program, i.e., the development of higher forms of behaviour: the mastering of the external means of cultural development and cognition (language, writing, counting, drawing); the development of the higher mental functions (selective attention, logical memory, concept formation, etc.). The generative function of meaningful human activities becomes a major concern in his theoretical approach; the function of mediating systems of symbols through joint activities with material tools, symbolic tools, and other human beings becomes apparent. Vygotsky, echoing one of the major theoretical points of agreement during the 1920s, comes very close to Janet and Mead when he states that children begin to use the same form of behaviour in relation to themselves that others initially used in relation to them (Kozulin 1990, 115), though in his theory individuation remains a problem. The problem of a theory of socialization founded *not* in the dualistic formula of society vs. the individual, was neither resolved by Piaget nor by Vygotsky.

The main issue here is less the issue of what is internalized than how society could be successful in making people internalize. In other terms, what is lacking in both Vygotsky's and Piaget's theories is a conceptualization of socialization which implements the Self as the third partner between Mind and Society. The concept of Self implies a theoretical articulation of society and culture (or adults in Piagetian words) into small groups, significant others, peer groups and peer culture; which means a conceptualization which is founded in the processes of communication and use of semiotic tools.

Both Vygotsky and Piaget had to cope with the corollary issue of individuation i.e., the paths of individual development and the dynamic of socialization. The theoretical contribution of the French school at the beginning of this century seems indispensable in the understanding of how Piaget and Vygotsky approached this problem within their theories of human cognition. But the majority in the French tradition was dominated by an interpretation of human behaviour as induced by imitation and impressionability (suggestibilité). Another view on behaviour and cognitive functioning was held by the Italian philosopher Carlo Cattaneo who in 1854 asserted that cognitive activities are better realized through conflicts between different view points and conflicts that arise between groups as well as between individuals. Cattaneo is the only voice which claims that intergroup and interindividual conflicts could be useful for cognitive functioning and problem solving.

The reference to Cattaneo and to the issue of conflict allows us to consider another major problem in Vygotsky's and Piaget's contributions from the point of view of social psychology: the lack of a dialectical interpretation of the relationships between society and the individual. This dialectic is in Piaget's theory reduced to an individual level through the dynamics of conflict between schemes and observations or between schemes and the general model of 'equilibration'. In Vygotsky's theory we do not find any real dialectic function, but instead the central role of cultural transmission is stressed. The Vygotskian approach is concerned with an overwhelming emphasis on the transmission from adult-expert to child-novice in the way of thinking, with no reference to the possible role played by peers. In this sense, interaction between expert and novice is reduced to cultural transmission within the field of ZOPED (zone of proximal development).

One may ask why Vygotsky did not take into account the dialectic interaction, but anchored his theorization in Durkheim's and Lévy-Brühl's approach? The issue is of great interest both at the historical and cultural level, but since I am not an expert in these domains I will only propose a tentative way of understanding this issue by a insightful remark put forward by Berger and Luckmann 30 years ago. According to Berger and Luckmann (1966, 15-17) Marx extensively discusses the issue of social determination of human knowledge and the role of dialectics in understanding the relationships between human and nature, in the *Economic and Philosophical Manuscripts* written in 1844 (but fallen into oblivion for decades and rediscovered and adequately studied only since 1932). Moreover, the classical dominant sociological thought interpreted by Durkheim, Weber and Pareto in a sense misinterprets the power of dialectics in building the sociology of knowledge.

At this point an integration of Durkheim, Mead, and the dialectical approach to knowledge could be useful. Once more a possible way of coming out of the dualism between society and the individual and to avoid the shortcomings of a model of socialization based on imitation, internalization, impressionability and constraints, is to work conceptually with the notions of interpersonal communication, interpersonal conflict, Self, and identity as social-psychological useful tools for studying cognitive functioning. This general program of research was recommended by Moscovici decades ago when he suggested that social psychology could, or should be the anthropology of the modern world and that social psychology should conceptually hold a triangular perspective for studying cognition: where cognition is by no means a matter of the relationships between the Self and the object or the relation between the Other (the society) and the Self, but the Other being an integral part of the triangulation between the three partners.

Towards a Social Psychology of Cognitive Functioning and Learning: European Perspectives

At this point one might ask which key notions there are upon which a social developmental line of research could be founded. Several notions assume a crucial role. We shall only map them and make a few remarks, as a way to build a conceptual framework for understanding a specific European approach to the social construction of cognitive functioning.

The first pair of notions is cooperation vs. competition. The well-known tradition in social psychology, from Sherif's classical studies (1967) to the more recent ones (cf. for a review, Grzelak 1988) underlines that every act of decision-making is both affected, and affects, various social dimensions like value orientations, superordinated goals. Very important for our argument here, is the general claim that cooperation and competition are neither abstract, universal qualities of social interaction, nor individual traits of individuals; on the contrary, both these social situations are highly affected by concrete variables and do affect partners' cognitive performances.

The second pair is imitation vs. conflict. We have already discussed these two notions as being the core of both social and developmental psychology since their first introduction into psychology. Cattaneo's contribution (1864) about the foundation of social psychology as a new discipline, autonomous from both philosophy and sociology, emphasizes mental phenomena not as a result of internal contradictions within individual minds but as a concrete and overt disagreement between concrete individuals and groups. On the other hand, at the beginning of the 1920s hypnosis, suggestion, and the more general notion of imitation was widely shared as an explanatory principle of psychic life by scholars like Tarde (1890, 1898), Binet (1900) and Baldwin (1895).

If we carefully look at the amount of research that has been done in the Anglo-Saxon tradition on cooperative learning and conflict in classroom (e.g., Feldman 1990; Slavin 1990;) evidence of success of different co-operative learning methods becomes apparent. On the other hand, if teachers wish to maximize achievement, creativity and motivation to learn, they will be well advised to structure controversies among students. Controversies are constitutive episodes of the classroom's everyday life and they manifest themselves when one student's ideas, information, conclusions, theories, and opinions are incompatible with those of another, and they then seek to reach an agreement. Controversies spark conceptual conflict within students, create epistemic curiosity, promote active representations and elaborations of students' positions and rationales, and result in students' reorganizing and reconceptualizing what they know about the issue being studied. Teachers can encourage constructive controversies by structuring learning activities cooperatively, ensuring that the cooperative learning groups be heterogeneous, structuring and conducting the controversies, teaching students collaborative skills about productive disagreement, and ensuring that the rules of rational argumentation are followed.

Summing up, nearly all methods are successful, though *it depends!*. Sometimes they are *not* successful, and therefore cooperation and conflict are inextricable in the students' everyday life. Still lacking is an interpretation or explanation of the fine dynamics of the different conditions and methods that lead to success. In other words, the large amount of research in social psychology of cooperation and conflicts on methods of education should be understood as phenomena and facts that are in search of an adequate theoretical framework.

The 'First Generation' Studies

A specific European program has been worked out since the mid 1970s, first of all in Geneva, and soon disseminated in several European research groups, through experimental studies of the influence of social interaction in building cognitive structures (with Piagetian-like tasks). A first sketch of a sociogenetic model of cognitive functioning was presented by Doise and Mugny (1981) where the role of cooperation was claimed as a tool for eliciting the coordination of concrete actions and different points of view (or schemes, in the Piagetian sense) concerning a concrete operational task (i.e., motor coordination; conservation of length, liquids, number, spatial relations). The coordination during an interaction between two children was found more beneficial for a better common solution than either child would be capable of individually.

Three important results must be underlined: first, children are able to solve a similar task in an individual post-test situation, which implies that they have transformed their previous pre-operational schemes. Secondly, children in the post-test situation show the ability to generalize a better solution in a different conservation task. Third, the children might benefit from the partner's answer even when it is inferior to their own: meaning that it is not necessary for one partner to be more expert than the other — a result which is of major importance for a reformulation of the understanding of what the ZOPED might be, with an adequate acknowledgement of the efficacy of the negotiation of different solutions and of joint solution of the conflict. Even if it is not theoretically inevitable, it is apparent that an interpretation and operationalization of ZOPED mainstream research in cognitive development and education over-emphasizes the role of experts in scaffolding new cognitive abilities.

These kinds of 'first generation' studies sought an explanation not in terms of imitation nor in terms of internalization of a response mastered by a partner, but in terms of *socio-cognitive conflict* between partners. Recovering the importance of the notion of conflict both in social (cf. Lewin's contribution) and in developmental psychology, this notion (Doise and Mugny 1981; see also Mugny, De Paolis & Carugati 1984; Carugati, De Paolis & Mugny 1985; Carugati & Gilly 1993) stresses the effect of the simultaneous comparison of different individual perspectives or points of view during social interaction that necessitates and gives rise to their mutual integration within a new cognitive organization, with no specific prior necessity for one of the partners to be more expert than the other.

A further evidence of the dynamics of diverging and conflicting solutions in communication between children is offered by deaf children who are requested to work with deaf or normal hearing classmates in a cooperative game. The task is to draw a course with a pen guided by two children at the same time, one in front of the other. As from the 7th year, there are no differences in the performances among dyads (hearing-hearing; hearing-deaf; deaf-deaf), but for all of them the initial phases of the co-operative game show the difficulty of progressive coordination between subjects, the way in which the children are able to solve the conflict also without talking (Allegri, Carugati, Montanini, Selleri 1995).

A final evidence of the efficacy of socio/cognitive conflict situations is offered by research in learning scientific concepts, like speed (Druyan & Levin 1989), in pupils aged from 11-14. Comparing individual versus dyadic conditions, children working together do not only perform better, but they reach the correct solution and the correct argumentation, by referring to everyday routines and events at school and in the family, using the concrete interaction as a zone of proximal development where the two partners build up the dyad as an activity system: their initial (often divergent) meaning and representations of the task are made explicit, as well as ambiguities; provisional solutions are defended, controversies could arise, analogies with other tasks which look like the actual task are dis-cussed, until a final solution is reached as well as the appropriate argumentation. What is worth noting in the course of interaction is the rich activity of gesture which parallel the verbal communication between partners, as evidence of the role concrete activity plays for the construction of cognitive tools, be these tools, concrete operation, academic concepts, and last but not least, reasoning (like 'if ... then' inductive reasoning: cf. Carugati & Gilly 1993).

Socio-cognitive conflict may be a source of cognitive progress for several reasons. First, the plasticity often found in immature thought allows the young child to make successive changes in response without experiencing any contradiction. Then only the simultaneous and more or less consistent opposition of another can bring the child to question his/her own system of responses and help the child to elaborate more advanced cognitive instruments allowing a more complete integration of contrasting points of view. Thus the other by introducing a difference in response may render the child conscious of other points of view. To resolve this social disequilibrium, the child may be provided with points of anchoring for his construction. Thus the other's disagreement gives the child information which can be relevant to such an elaboration, though it should be stressed that this elaboration is often collective (and therefore more a matter of co-elaboration). It is not necessary, however, to provide the correct response (Carugati, De Paolis and Mugny 1979, 1985), cognitive progress being the result not of the straightforward imitation or acquisition of a social heritage but of a collective construction. This derives from a social coordination of points of view, from their integration within a more general cognitive system which gives them a unity, while accounting for the diversity of the viewpoints of different individuals (the elaboration of projective space is an obvious example here). Finally, socio-cognitive conflict may lead the child to be especially involved in the situation, primarily because the apparently cognitive problem the child faces in fact entails a social regulation of some kind or other. A search for inter-individual consensus constitutes such a regulation, as does the acknowledgement — transposed to the cognitive level — of an asymmetrical (or symmetrical) relationship between two or more participants. Cognitive development may result therefore from the social necessity of regulating a social situation characterized by an opposition of responses.

A further result of these studies is that the social regulations that govern a given interaction are constitutive for the building of a new cognitive coordination. Thus the articulation between the level of representations of norms (made salient through a specific device in the task) and individual cognitive functioning is apparent. The case in point is the task of the conservation of spatial transformations, where two different representations are used: a village vs. a classroom. The latter version of the task is thought to be more effective for a non-conserving child than the former, insofar as the reproduction of a classroom (through the position of pupils and teachers) necessitates the respect of a social norm governing the reciprocal position in space and the asymmetrical status of both pupils and teachers. This is an example of *social marking* (Doise & Mugny 1981) a notion which reminds us of the normative interplay of relations of cognitive order (topological) with those of a social order (status asymmetry), relations which can be activated in children even in the absence of direct interaction with a partner. Here the importance of social relations and norms as a symbolic order giving meaning to the everyday practices at school is apparent, and operationalized in order to study how symbolic order mastered by children might be effective in building cognitive tools.

A nice example of social marking in terms of the meaning of the rules which govern the solution of a spatial task is offered by Mugny et al. (1988). These authors used the general paradigm of the classroom, manipulating the rule underlying the placement of the pupils' and the teacher's desks. The explicitation of the rule (pupils' desks must be placed according to their status in classroom as 'good pupils') governing the topology of the classroom does improve the acquisition of the conservation of spatial relations, in particular when pupils are first allowed to construct the model and subsequently to reproduce it from a different more difficult topological position (transformation of 270°). In general terms, it seems that social marking is more effective when children recognize it as a meaningful set of social rules governing the solution of a cognitive task.

The 'Second Generation' Studies

As suggested by Cattaneo even scientific work shows a thesis — antithesis pendulum represented by concrete research groups. It is the case of the 'second generation' studies, which switched the pendulum both from Piagetian to procedural perspective and from the notion of socio-cognitive conflict and social marking to the destabilization and control of procedures. For the authors of these sets of studies, the beneficial effects of interaction depend on the destabilization of the procedures of problem-solving as far as it triggers the questioning of and the change in procedures and representations concerning a given task (for instance, reasoning by recurrence, the notions of left and right, hypothetical-deductive reasoning in a fictitious weighing task: cf. for a review, Gilly, 1988; Gilly, Blaye & Roux, 1988; Gilly, 1989). To be effective, the partner's action must disrupt the other's problem-solving modes at the very beginning when they are being implemented. In this case, explicit and argued opposition expressed in a conflictual mode has indeed been shown to be highly effective. But the authors have also found that interaction does not necessarily have to take place in a social conflict mode in order to bring about beneficial destabilization. The control function takes on various forms, which might be more extensively studied. For instance, control can be exerted by triggering a verification of a statement or solution proposed by the partner, or by simply agreeing with or reformulating the partner's proposal.

Another characteristic of these studies is that they stress the role of initial cognitive functioning of the subjects, not just their initial levels of development. In fact, several studies have shown that the definition of the problem situation does influence both the individual problem-solving procedures initially triggered, and the ways in which the subjects interact. Hence the claim of an explanation of sociocognitive mechanisms that must be based on the analysis of the interdependency between the cognitive functioning of the individual and the socio-cognitive functioning of the dyad in the type of problem to be solved.

Social Meaning, Social Practices and Cognitive Constructions

The problems of meaning of a cognitive task and the expectations activated in the subjects questioned both in experimental and in more concrete scholastic situations are well-known in developmental psychology. Rose & Blank's studies (1974) on the role of double questioning in Piagetian tasks (cf. conservation of length); Light, Buckingham & Robbins' (1979) contribution about conservation tasks as interactional settings; Donaldson's (1978) notion of tasks which 'make human sense' for young children are only several examples of a well-established, though theoretically hetero-geneous, tradition which underlines the inextricability of meaning and expectations in every cognitive activity. More recently, a series of studies whose common ground is the notion of 'contract' (communication, experi-mental-contract, didactic contract) have renewed the general claim (Schu-bauer-Leoni 1986; Elbers 1986) that experimental and learning situations are interactional settings governed by specific contracts made up of explicit and implicit rules upon whose basis social actors adjust their behaviour.

Grossen's analysis of test situations (1988) and Schubauer-Leoni's work on teaching relationships (1986) have provided some interesting examples of the role played by the meaning attributed to the situation, in terms of both children's and adult's reciprocal expectations and meta-expectations concerning the task and the final solution.

A further perspective of the inextricability of meaning and cognitive performances has been developed in an explicit social psychological framework. The case in point is the effect of social positions attributed in a learning situation to boys and girls in conditions of social comparison (Monteil 1988). Here small groups of young students (14 to 16 year olds) are given a task by a teacher under classroom conditions. In the basic form of this paradigm, students first perform a lure task whose content is similar to that of their own class. During the experimental phase (the class), the first variable manipulated is the students' status: according to the results of the lure task, 50% of the students in each class-like group are publicly assigned to the 'success' status, while 50% to the 'failure' status. The second variable is the social insertion mode, which is used to define two social positions: anonymity vs. visibility. In the anonymity position, students are told that none will be questioned during the class; whereas in the visibility position, students are told that each of them will be questioned.

The effects of being assigned to success vs. failure status clearly interact with the effect of being assigned to a visibility vs. anonymity position: in fact, students in failure status show better performance in an anonymous position than in a visible one. Conversely, students in the success status succeed in visible (or individualized) position more than in the anonymous one. When the class subject is manipulated (maths vs. biology, vs. technical training) the same pattern of results are the strongest in the case of maths, whereas in technical training condition they are very weak. The overall pattern of findings in this section clearly shows the systematic influence of the pupils' attribution of meaning to the experimental situation : meaning concerning the task, the expectations of partner, the representation of self as student and of school subjects.

The Contribution of the Ethnographical Approach

A further complementary approach to everyday cognition is offered by ethnographical research of everyday life (e.g., Corsaro 1993) which has shown that children are capable of original interpretation of the adult's world, and of building a genuine peer culture, which can be characterized by a interpretive reproduction of the adult world and not as a simple transmission of societal meaning to each single child, working separated from others. Everyday social interaction between children and between adults and children, and everyday routines, are what matters in building the relationships between the societal world interpreted and mediated by adults (*Significant Others* in Mead's terms) in concrete and everyday activities. Children's everyday world should first become meaningful and signified, for later to become transformed into concepts, and activities. What first seems to be strange, mysterious, troublesome, meaningless for children in isolation, could become familiar, and meaningful through children's participation in their peer culture (both in nursery and in elementary school), where discussion, play, provisional interpretations of the bizarre adults' world are mediational tools built up for interpreting and reproducing the adults' world.

The ethnographical approach also stresses the importance of collective processes (which are documented here as active processes at the everyday level) and argues that children, through participation in everyday routines, creatively appropriate information from the adult world to produce their own unique peer cultures. Suggesting a theoretical model inspired by the 'spider web' metaphor, individual development is seen as embedded in the collective production through everyday routines of a series of local cultures which in turn contribute to the reproduction of the culture of the society in general. This medium-level interpretation of where and how society is influencing does not prevent us from studying and theorizing the interplay between societal ideas and world views and their everyday counterparts, mediated by significant others and peers. In other terms, the claim here is the usefulness of the social-psychological approach of social representations (Mugny & Carugati 1985) of the ideas that circulate in society and become the contents (the objects) of the everyday discourses between adults and children and between children about 'how, and why things go on as they do'.

It has been illustrated that routines of peer culture play a specific role in engendering new cognitive tools by the notion of social marking, which is central in socio-cognitive conflict theory (cf. *supra*). In several encounters a relationship or a correspondence could be followed between a social norm of equality or inequality and the cognitive rule governing a correct solution of a task. It is in these specific encounters that we see the presence and the influence of peer culture, as far as peer culture is rule-governed by some basic rules as the equality/inequality of social relations, the distribution of rights/duties and permission/obligation of activities. We may think of routines of everyday life in the classroom where specific rules govern the arrangement both of teacher's and pupils' desks. If we transform the village tasks into classroom tasks (with the instruction of placing pupils' desks so that 'the two classrooms became the same') we have two types of tasks with the same topological organization but they are staged so that the classroom tasks are marked by the social necessity to respect the social norms which govern the authoritative teacher-pupils relationships in the classroom environment. The results of this line of research (which has been done since mid 1970s and onwards) with children from their fourth year, give evidence of better performance and stability of topological organization, in socially marked classroom tasks versus village tasks. Pairs of children who work on classroom tasks are performing better than children with the village task; and what is worth noting is that socially marked tasks are more beneficial for children than village tasks, when children are requested individually to solve a similar task. This latter result gives evidence of the reorganization of knowledge that children produce and not of a mere imitation: imitation of task solutions which is impossible to be claimed, because no child was able to solve this task individually in a pre-test session (cf. Carugati, De Paolis & Mugny 1979; Mugny, De Paolis & Carugati 1984).

The Interplay of Cognitive Development, Learning and Teaching

Vygotsky stressed both externalization and internalization in his theory of children's appropriation of culture. He argued that children through their acquisition and use of language come to reconstruct a social world that contains within it the experience and knowledge of prior generations. Thus children's socialization must be understood as a social and collective process, whereby children do not construct their knowledge 'in solitude' but they do it as a 'multiple voices' endeavour, in multiple communities of practices with adults and peers who share their sense of belonging to a culture: more specifically, children make sense of the world as far as they are allowed to enter a microculture of peers which enables them to produce collectively the social order of society. Thus the Vygotskian, external phase of 'between people' or 'interpsychological activity', in the construction of cognition, must not be taken for granted. Instead its occurrence could be illustrated by an accurate ethnography of the everyday life of children, where they collectively produced and shared peer culture, as interaction between mates, as stable sets of activities or routines, with artifacts, values and concerns. The focus is therefore on routines, which are recurrent and predictable activities that are basic to day-to-day social life; moreover routines that through socialization practices become familiar. It is this aspect of familiarity of routines that enables children to use them as cultural arenas for transforming the unfamiliar events of everyday life into familiar ones. Routines serve as anchors that allow children to deal with ambiguities, the unexpected, the problematic events, the particularities of adults' society and their requests, to deal with adults' rules and norms while comfortably within the friendliness of everyday peer life. It is for this reason that it can be argued that peer culture is crucial for children in producing successful conditions for learning insofar as participation in peer culture is a matter neither of simple imitation nor of direct 'inoculation' of the adult world. Children creatively appropriate information from the adult world, such appropriation is creative insofar as it both extends or transforms information from the adult world to meet the concerns of the peer world and simultaneously contributes to the reproduction of adult culture.

A cluster of specific dynamics has been described: sharing, friendships negotiations, discussions, conflicts, and conflict resolution. Several central themes consistently appear in peer culture research: the importance of sharing and social participation (examples: sharing toys, plays, simply enjoying doing things together; friendship); children attempt to deal with confusion, concerns, fears, ambiguities, rules, norms, demands, and conflicts in daily life; children try to resist and challenge adult rules and authority. A central feature is the role of conflict in children's friendships and peer culture. Evidence illustrated in previous sections challenges the assumption that such behaviour is inherently disruptive and disorderly, demonstrating that conflicts and disputes provide children with a rich arena for the development of language, social skills and knowledge.

This brief sketch of interpretive approaches to understanding children's (social and cognitive) development extends the emphasis on children's activities in constructivistic theory (like Piaget's), stressing that such activities are always embedded in social context and always involve children's use of communicative tools and interpretive abilities. Within these general premises, every social encounter which researchers build up for studying and describing cognitive activities, like problem solving, must be seen as a specific case of a more general activity, when children meet adults who propose situations and tasks that from the children's eyes, appear strange and inexplicable. Cognitive problems actually should appear to the children as strange and inexplicable, this should be the case within both experimental learning and school scenarios. Therefore the first and primary aim for children in these encounters is to grasp what meaning the encounter should be given, which kind of expectations or answers adults have in mind, which kind of legitimity this encounter allows. For instance, the first step in any encounter between child and adult, or between children, invited by an adult to participate in experimental problem solving or to be engaged in a learning situation, is to answer the following questions 'Is this situation a free play or classroom-like situation where I am asked to perform according to some school standards? Am I at risk of being questioned and assessed, and what kind of marks will be distributed? What kind of previous experience, play, or task, does this situation and this task look like?'

In more general terms, the first phase of any encounter should be devoted to the construction of both the intersubjectivity between partners and of the common object of their encounter. In the same line of thought, a general assumption of activity theory and particularly Engeström's (1990), claims that the crucial characteristic of a team and network-based work organization is not the external form of interconnection between people but the way these partners conceive of and construct the very object of their work. Moreover, a crucial question in any research on dyads or teams is how to integrate the subject/object and the subject/subject, or the instrumental and the communicative aspects of the activity. Engeström suggests that beside coordination and cooperation, reflective communication could be seen as an available way whereby actors focus on reconceptualizing their own organization and interaction in relation to their shared objects. Both the object and the scripted routines are reconceptualized as is the interaction between partners. Engeström describes a general model of team work, underlying that reflective communication are rare situations in the ongoing flow of daily work activities, and he stresses that transition to communication include disturbances, ruptures, innovations, expansions, conflicts between partners' different voices, representing different social positions, (ideo)logical viewpoints and cultural traditions.

Summing up, it could be said that working together is not enough for automatically ensuring a better solution to a cognitive task, neither is it enough for learning. For this a certain number of requirements have to be fulfilled. A central condition is that the interaction entails opposition of divergent cognitive responses. In this respect we could speak about socio-cognitive conflict insofar as two partners are presented with a task for which they dispose of divergent initial solutions, and then have to communicate in order to reach a final unique solution. It is actually a conflict of communication between partners. This definition is quite similar to Engeström's (1990) definition of 'reflective communication' and to his more recent claim about development as 'breaking away and opening up' (Engeström, 1996).

Concluding Remarks

From a radical constructivist perspective, cognition is mainly an individual construction; from a radical socio-interactionist perspective, cognition is essentially a socio-cultural construction. From the perspective of social psychology, both Piaget's and Vygotsky's contributions are in search for a theorization of the social-cognitive dynamics which could overcome the classical dualism between individual and society. The contribution of Mead's approach, which triangulate Mind, Self and Society seems useful, with a special attention to a dialectical formulation of the relationships between the three poles.

A European socio-constructivist approach has been summarized, complemented by the ethnographic approach to the understanding of everyday life; both these approaches give special attention to experimental and qualitative field research into ways of children and adult negotiation, discussion, and entering into interpersonal conflicts, in order to make sense of everyday and experimental activities. In these activities, children and adults build up specific micro-cultures in which the cultural tools, the shared representations of our complex societies as embedded in specific communities of practices are interpreted and reconstructed, and neither simply transmitted, nor merely constructed in solitude. Moreover, as scholars in activity theory unceasingly claim (i.e., Hedegard 1996) societal knowledge, personal aspects of pupils' life, cultural identity and social practices are of crucial importance both for teaching experiments and the planning of educational projects, particularly for minority children. Meaningful learning and the acquisition of positive social identities are of major importance for teachers, pupils and for scholars, as well as for education architects.

The experimental social psychological approach to development and learning and its 'tool-box' of empirical evidence and conceptual framework (e.g., socio-cognitive conflict, and social marking) could be understood as a plausible set of dynamics which is at work in concrete teaching-learning in everyday activities.

When evidence is offered that social identity at school (e.g., a good/mediocre pupil), and practices in the classroom (e.g., questioning and evaluation) are crucial for a different appropriation of science concepts, this evidence could be of some interest for a better understanding of different results offered by the 'cooperative learning' methods (cf. Slavin 1990). This evidence could also be interpreted in the light of the insightful (but fairly ignored) results offered decades ago by Rutter (Rutter et al. 1979) that schools do 'make a difference' — in general for pupils' results, and specifically for pupils' cognitive, social and moral progress.

When evidence is offered that specific shared representations of social norms and representations of school micro-culture could positively match cognitive problem solving (as in the case of social marking), this evidence seems to be compatible with a major claim of activity theory which emphasizes 'going from the abstract to the concrete'.

When evidence is offered that peer culture is of crucial importance for the construction of shared meaning of school demands and for learning in everyday life, we are at the core of the (possibly conflictual) dialogue between scientific and everyday knowledge. It is plausible to work out the general hypothesis that the peer culture of classrooms is the everyday laboratory within which specific interpretations of science selected by teachers and taught as school subjects, are interpreted and given sense by pupils through a common work.

In more general terms, a future dialogue between scholars in education, learning, and development could be improved, concerning, particularly two general issues. First a more articulated conceptualization of ZOPED, which include the role played by peer culture at school and in everyday life, and its interplay with teachers' role, is requested.

Second, a re-examination of the role of children's construction of representations of school system, roles, norms, and values in concrete teaching-learning dynamics, should be carefully proposed. As far as Leontiev (1981) suggests the study of (and the analytic distinction between) 'meaning' and 'sense' as a way for a more adequate understanding of human subjectivity, we could (at least provisionally) interpret his claim with reference to teaching-learning dynamics. Teachers have to present school subjects not merely as subjects as such, but, as relation-to-self, and this would imply a pointing out of its significance to the self. Thus the teachers have to scaffold the transformation of societal meaning of science subjects into the individual sense for the pupils. But in this tremendous transformation a major role is played by school peer culture and its specific dynamics:

cooperation, conflicts, previous representations of topics, a search for or protection of positive social identity, and negotiation of different points of view. Within the everyday laboratory of school peer culture, societal meaning could be negotiated and transformed into a shared interindividual and intraindividual sense.

At that point we join the three major challenges to most developmental and learning theories and education methods (cf. Engeström 1996):

1) Instead of just benign and automatic information, and mechanical-like achievement in mastering new (taken for granted) empirical knowledge, learning may be viewed as a partially destructive rejection of old ways and old organizations of knowledge and a matter of normative influence of the majority.

2) Instead of just individual transformation, learning may be viewed as (at least partially) collective transformation;

3) Instead of just vertical movement across levels, learning may be viewed as horizontal movement across borders.

Future empirical research and conceptualization should articulate these challenges both for a deeper understanding of what learning in modern societies is, and for planning more efficient educational methods. Thus the major Piaget's and Vygotsky's legacy and their long-lasting dialogue should be extended and refined. Contributions from both activity theory and experimental social psychology of development could be interpreted as concrete cultural tools in this endeavour.

References

Allegri, A., Carugati, F., Montanini, M. & Selleri, P. (1995). Interazioni sociali fra coetanei e operazioni logiche: il caso di soggetti sordi e udenti [Peer interaction and cognitive functioning: The case of deaf and hearing children]. *Giornale Italiano di Psicologia* 12(5), 1-12.

Baldwin, J.M. (1895). *Mental development in the child and the race*. New York: Macmillan.

Baldwin, J.M. (1913). *History of psychology: Vol. 2. From John Locke to the present time*. London: Watts.

Bartlett, F. (1928). *Psychology and primitive culture*. New York: Macmillan.

Berger, P.L., Luckmann, T. (1966). *The social construction of reality*. Garden City, New York: Doubleday.

Binet, A. (1900). *La suggestibilité* [The impressionability]. Paris: Schleicher Frères.

Carugati, F. (1983). Dalle variabili extralogiche al conflitto socio-cognitivo nello studio del pensiero [From extralogical variables to socio-cognitive conflict in the studies of thinking]. *Studi Urbinati* 56, 135-50.

Carugati, F. (1988). Dinamiche sociali, divergenze, conflitti: il modello del conflitto socio-cognitivo nella comprensione dello sviluppo del pensiero [Social dynamics, divergences, and conflicts: The theory of socio-cognitive conflict and the development of thought]. In Ugazio (ed.), *La costruzione della conoscenza. L'approccio europeo alla cognizione del sociale*. Milano: Angeli.

Carugati, F. (1989). Facilitazione sociale dello sviluppo cognitivo [Social facilitation in cognitive development]. In M.W. Battacchi (ed.), *Trattato enciclopedico dell'età evolutiva*, vol. 2. Padova: Piccin editore, 459-90.

Carugati, F. (1988). Interactions, destabilizations, conflits [Social interaction, destabilization, and conflicts]. In A.N. Perret-Clermont & M. Nicolet (eds.), *Interagir et connaître*. Cousset: DelVal.

Carugati, F. (1991). Interazioni, conflitti, conoscenze [Social interaction, conflicts and knowledge]. In G. Gilli & A. Marchetti (eds.), *Prospetive sociogenetiche e sviluppo cognitivo*. Milano: Raffaello Cortina Editore.

Carugati, F., De Paolis, P. & Mugny, G. (1979). A paradigm for the study of social interactions in cognitive development. *Italian Journal of Psychology* 6, 147-55.

Carugati, F. & Gilly, M. (1993) Everyday life, social meaning, and cognitive functioning. *European Journal of Psychology of Education* 8(4) (special issue).

Carugati, F. & Selleri. P. (1996). *Psicologia sociale dell'educazione* [The social psychology of education]. Bologna: Il Mulino.

Carugati, F., De Paolis, P. & Mugny, G. (1985). La théorie du conflit socio-cognitif [The theory of socio-cognitive conflict]. In G. Mugny (ed.), *La psychologie sociale du développement cognitif*. Bern: Peter Lang.

Cattaneo, C. (1864). Dell'antitesi come metodo in psicologia sociale [On antithesis as a method in social psychology]. *Il Politecnico* 20, 262-70.

Corsaro, W.A. (1993) Interpretive reproduction in the 'scuola materna'. *European Journal of Psychology of Education* 7(4), 375-90.

Doise, W. & Mugny, G. (1981). *Le développement social de l'intelligence*. (The social development of intellect.) Oxford: Pergamon Press.

Doise, W. (1982). *L'explication en psychologie sociale* [Explanations in social psychology]. Paris: Presses Universitaires de France.

Doise, W. (1989). Constructivism in social psychology. *European Journal of Social Psychology*, *19*, 5, 389-400.

Donaldson, M. (1978). *Children's minds*. Glasgow: Fontana.

Druyan, S. & Levin, I. (1992). Socio-cognitive transactions as learning environments of everyday and curriculum-based concepts. In S. Strauss (ed.),
Learning environments and cognitive development. Norwood, N.J.: Ablex.

Dunn, J. (1988). *The beginnings of social understanding.* Cambridge, Mass.: Harvard
University Press.

Elbers, E. (1986). Interaction and instruction in the conservation experiment.
European Journal of Psychology of Education 1(1), 77-99.

Engeström, Y. (1990). *Learning, working, imagining: Twelve studies in activity theory.*
Helsinki: Orienta-Konsult.

Engeström, Y. (1996). Development as breaking away and opening up: A
challenge to Vygotsky and Piaget. *Swiss Journal of Psychology* 55(2/3), 126-
32.

Feldman, C. (1990). Stage, transfer and academic achievement in dialect-
speaking Hawaiian adolescents. *Child Development* 61, 472-84.

Garfinkel, H. (1984). *Studies in ethnomethodology.* Oxford: Blackwell.

Gilly. M. (1988). Interaction entre pairs et constructions cognitives: modèles
explicatifs [Interaction within pairs and construction of cognition: Explanatory models]. In A.N. Perret-Clermont & M. Nicolet (eds.), *Interagir et
connaître.* Cousset: DelVal.

Gilly, M. (1989) The psycho-social mechanisms of cognitive constructions.
Experimental research and teaching perspectives. *International Journal of
Educational Research* 13(6), 607-21.

Gilly, M., Blaye, A. & Roux, J.-P. (1988). Elaboración de contrucciones cognitivas
individuales en situaciones sociocognitivas de resolución de problemas
[Socio-cognitive construction of problem solving situations]. In G. Mugny
& J. Pérez (eds.), *Psicologia social del desarollo cognitivo.* Barcelona: Anthropos.

Grossen, M. (1988). *La construction sociale de l'intersubjectivité entre adulte et enfant
en situation de test* [The social construction of intersubjectivity in adult —
child testing situation]. Cousset: DelVal.

Grzelak, J. (1988). Conflict and cooperation. In M. Hewstone, W. Stroebe, J.-P.
Codol & G.M. Stephenson (eds.), *Introduction to social psychology.* Oxford:
Blackwell.

Hedegaard, M. (1996). History education, cultural identity, and practice. Department of Psychology, University of Aarhus: Unpublished manuscript.

Kozulin, A. (1990). *Vygotsky's psychology.* London: Harvester Wheatsheaf.

Leontiev, A.N. (1981). *Problems of the development of the mind.* Moscow: Progress.

Light, P., Buckingham, N. & Robbins, A.H. (1979). The conservation task as an
interactional setting. *British Journal of Educational Psychology* 49, 304-10.

Light, P., Blaye, A., Gilly, M. & Girotto, V. (1989). Pragmatic schemas and logical
reasoning of 6 to 8 year-old children. *Cognitive Development* 4, 49-64.

Luria, A. (1976). *Cognitive development*. Cambridge, Mass.: Harvard University Press.

Mead, G.H. (1934). *Mind, self and society*. Chicago: University of Chicago Press.

Monteil, J.-M. (1989). *Eduquer et former. Perspectives psycho-sociales* [Teaching and education: Social-psychological perspectives]. Grenoble: Presses Universitaires de Grenoble.

Moscovici, S. (1990). Social psychology and developmental psychology: Extending the conversation. In G. Duveen & B. Lloyd (eds.), *Social representations and the development of knowledge*. Cambridge: Cambridge University Press.

Mugny, G. & Carugati, F. (1985). *L'intelligence au pluriel*. Cousset: DelVal. (*Social representations of intelligence*. Cambridge: Cambridge University Press, 1989).

Mugny, G., De Paolis, P. & Carugati, F. (1984). Social regulations in cognitive development. In W. Doise & A. Palmonari (eds.), *Social interaction in individual development*. Cambridge: Cambridge University Press, Editions de la Maison des Sciences de l'Homme.

Mugny, G., De Paolis, P., Renzetti, P., Bortoluzzi, S. & Carugati, F. (1988). Saillance du marquage social et progrès cognitif: Influence de l'explicitation des règles sociales [Social marking and cognitive progress: The influence of meaningful social rules]. *Revue Suisse de Psychologie* 47(4), 261-66.

Rose, A. & Blank, M. (1974). The potency of context in children's cognition. An illustration through conservation. *Child Development* 45, 499-502.

Rutter, M., Maughan, B., Mortimore, P. & Justow, J. (1979). *Fifteen thousand hours*. London: Open Books Publishing.

Schubauer-Leoni, M.L. (1986). Le contrat didactique: Un cadre interprétatif pour comprendre les savoirs manifestés par les élèves en mathématiques [Didactic contract: A theoretical interpretation of pupils' mathematical knowledge]. *European Journal of Psychology of Education* 1(2), 139-53.

Schütz, A. (1960). *Der sinnhafte Aufbau der sozialen Welt* [The meaningful construction of social world]. Wien: Springer.

Sherif, M. (1967). *Social interaction, processes, and products*. Chicago: Aldine.

Slavin, R.E (1990). *Cooperative learning: Theory, research and practice*. London: Allyn and Bacon.

Tarde, G. (1890). *Les lois de l'imitation* [Laws of imitation]. Paris: Félix Alcan, 1898.

Tarde, G. (1898). *Etudes de psychologie sociale* [Studies on social psychology]. Paris: Giard et Brière.

Wilkins, M.C. (1928). The effect of changed material on the ability to do formal reasoning. *Archives of Psychology* 16, 102-112.

11   Diagnosing Learning Initiative[*]

Galina A. Zuckerman

Introduction

The goal of this paper is to find a criterion for learning cooperation and to define the factors promoting its development. The notion of learning cooperation, as used herein, does not apply to all the joint classroom activities of students during a lesson. It should be applied only to the particular cases when children face a new problem and must independently find a way of solving it — assisted by their teacher, but never prompted to a ready-made decision or model of a new action.

My experimental research is based on the following theoretical premises:

1) Initially, all abilities of a child exist only in an interpsychological form, in the form of a joint action with an adult and/or peer (Vygotsky 1978). The child's competence in entering this joint action marks the beginning of an overt phase in the development of this ability.

2) The child upon entering school for the first time is by no means a novice in regard to joint actions. Though quite inexperienced in learning cooperation, the child is an expert in building personal communication, imitation, play, etc. (Elkonin 1972).

3) When a teacher invites the first-graders into a new, learning activity, which requires a search for new ways of solving problems (Davydov 1988), many students misinterpret this invitation and transform a learning task into a game, or communication, or — most often — into performer's task, calling for the reproduction of the teacher's models (Venger and Polivanova 1990).

[*]   Acknowledgment: Preparation of this paper was generously supported by the Competitive Program 'Cultural Initiative' (Open Society Institute, Russia). I express my profound gratitude to Elena Sushkova, a graduate student of the Department of Psychology, Moscow State University, and all the students of the first 'levy' of the International Psychological College, The Psychological Institute, Russian Academy of Education, who helped me collect the experimental data.

4) How can one discern the type of activity in which the student is involved? We suggest that in the situation of joint action with an adult the presence of initiative is the basic behavioural criterion of a child's subjective action. If there is no initiative, there is no way to discriminate between the children who are acting on their own, and the children that are manifesting a substitute activity.

5) The nature of initiative can serve as a behavioural criterion to classify the particular action the children go into on their own initiative: learning, playing, communicating, following instructions, etc.

6) The formula of learning initiative, i.e., the evidence that the child is engaged in learning activity is as follows: 'I'll be able to solve this problem if...' Then the child requests missing information and formulates a hypothesis on the essence of the unknown. Thus the child shows the adult that she or he has already set the goal of the forthcoming action. It is quite evident that this setting of goals is the key issue of subjective behaviour. Setting the learning goal is strong proof that the child is the subject of specific learning activity.

7) The formula of the performing, and not learning, way of drawing the adult into joint action is as follows: 'I can't work it out, won't you tell me what to do...'. Thus the students attract the adult's attention to the difficulties they come up against and ask for a model of further action. It is the adult who is given the privilege to set the goal of further action. The child shows the preparedness to carry out any action designated by the adult, i.e., to be the subject of performing reproductive action.

Previous attempts to disclose and measure children's initiative in separating the known from unknown and searching for the unknown were based on the material familiar to the students from their Russian language studies (Zuckerman 1991). Any diagnosis made on the basis of educational material has one fundamental drawback: the impossibility to discriminate the effects of instruction from those of development concurrently arising in the course of education but not identical to direct outcome of instruction. Below, I shall describe the results of diagnosing learning initiative on so-called non-educational material that removes the factor of training.

At the stage of interpsychological action, when children cannot as yet act on their own, without the adult's assistance, it is practically impossible for an external observer to decide whether or not children are the subject of their own actions. The emergence of initiative is the first and the crucial behavioural criterion of their acting as a subject in the situation of joint child-adult action. The content of the initiative is the criterion of what particular kind of action children undertake on their own accord: whether they are learning, playing, communicating, obeying instructions, etc. We suggest the criteria to discern the case of learning initiative, per se, from other types of situations when the child involves the adult in joint activities, and describe a method of diagnosing the learning initiative. Different models of elementary school instruction are compared to define the educational and interactional factors that most effectively develop the learning initiative in 7 to 10-year-old students.

Children's Ability to Ask the Adult for the Missing Conditions of a Problem

The method of 'Mittens' worked out on the non-educational material of spatial problems permits us to diagnose the qualitative characters of a learning and a non-learning request of a student for an adult's help. The experimental situation is built up in such a way as to deprive beforehand the student of any chance of solving the problem without turning to the partner for assistance. How the child asks an adult for missing information is the issue under direct observation in the first series of the 'Mitten' experiment. How the same child addresses his/her peer-partner with a request for missing information is the character under observation in the second series.

The First Series: Cooperation with an Adult when Solving an Insufficiently Defined Problem

Instruction

Two children sit opposite each other, with a tall, nontransparent screen between them. The adult places him/herself so that the actions of both children can be observed. In front of each child are three paper 'patterns' of white mittens of different sizes. The adult explains the conditions of the problem: 'Make-believe you are artists working at a mitten-making factory. Your duty is to make these white mittens as attractive as possible. To speed up the job, all three of us will work on every mitten. This is how we will do it. You two artists each paint your half of the mitten (puts a sample of the simplest ornament before them), while I will sew the two painted halves together and make a whole mitten (shows the children how that is done). We must work swiftly, neatly and — most important of all —

silently. You must not say a word to each other. But if you have any questions, I'll answer them willingly — that is, if you ask them in turn, whisper them right into my ear.'

Each child sees only his/her own 'workplace' and does not know how the mittens are arranged over with his/her partner, i.e., in which direction the thumb points. The adult deliberately lays the halves of the mittens in disorder, so that without a preliminary agreement on the size and orientation of the halves already painted by the children, they cannot be joined together. The natural way of acting unerringly in this situation is to ask the adult to suggest a concrete plan of action to the other child or to simply ask what the partner is doing. In any other case, the child is acting at random and is doomed to fail: the two painted halves will not make a whole mitten as they will most likely be of different sizes, with the thumb pointing in different directions.

The First Attempt to Solve the Task

Most of the children begin acting at random. Right after the teacher's instructions, they fall to work: pull up any half a mitten and start painting it. Some do not begin painting at once but first ask the adult: 'Which mitten should I paint?' or 'What should I start off with?' That is a typical global request for assistance, characteristic of a person engaged in performing activity but in no way involved in learning activity directed at independent searching for the missing conditions of the new problem being solved. These infantile questions the adult answers with invariable goodwill: 'whichever or whatever you like'. It is a rare child that is not satisfied with such an answer and keeps on asking: 'did Dan take a big or a little mitten half?' or 'please tell Ira to take a big one, too'. Only to the child who comes up with such a concrete question or request does the adult describe the actions of his/her partner.

Thus, we can divide the children into three distinct groups according to their behaviour in the very first attempt to solve the experimental problem:

- pure performers, formalists, those who do not ask about anything at all, who accept and carry out merely the superficial part of adult's requirements: to paint the mittens and to work silently;

- children who realized the impossibility of achieving the necessary result and ask the adult for global assistance ('I can't do it myself, tell me what to do and I'll do it gladly');

- students who realized that they could not solve the problem independently and also apprehended, if only partially, <u>why</u> they could not do it; pointing this reason out to the adult, these children ask him or her for the missing terms of the problem (in this particular case, for information on the partner's actions).

It is quite clear that 7 to 10-year-olds cannot practically plan their actions in a thorough manner all at once. Therefore, the child's behaviour can best be diagnosed after his/her first unsuccessful attempt and a detailed analysis of the reasons for the failure.

Learning from the First Failure

When both children have completed painting the first ornament on their halves of a mitten, the adult proclaims: 'OK, one mitten is ready', takes the two halves together and, with the children closely watching, joins them. The errors are self-evident: all eyes immediately catch the difference in size, the fact that the thumbs point in different directions. 'Do we have a mitten?' the adult asks. 'No, we don't,' and the two children themselves name the reasons for the failure. 'Never mind, the second one will be a real one. But you must think hard what you should do, so as not to make a mistake again. If you need my help, I'll be glad to answer any question.' The whole process is repeated again and again (usually the children are given from three to five chances). And once more the adult comes to the assistance of only those students who can define what particular help they need. If a child asks, for instance, 'Which way does Tom's mitten point?', the adult helps the student to point his/her half the right way, thus removing the purely technical and non-essential obstacle (in this particular experiment) to solving the spatial problem. But if the child asks which way to point the thumb, the adult helps him or her only in this specific aspect, never mentioning the size (and *vice versa*).

Qualitative Differences in the Ways to Solve an Insufficiently Defined Problem, which were Observed in the First Series

On the basis of the experimental design described above, we can earmark three levels of children's initiative in building up learning cooperation with an adult.

–   At the *highest level* are those children who at the very first attempt to solve the problem turn at once to the adult for meaningful assistance, irrespective of whether they ask about *both* obstacles (size of the mitten and direction of thumb) or only *one*. When estimating the children's initiative in learning cooperation, we are not interested in their ability to solve spatial problems and in the thoroughness of their planning capacity.

–   At the *medium level* are those children who, after analyzing the first failure, change the strategy of their action, reject the independent method of trial and error and pass on to a meaningful cooperation with the adult.

–   At the *lowest level* are those children who, after three or four unsuccessful attempts, still fail to perceive that the adult is their sole chance of solving the problem and, despite the permanent offers of cooperation, do not establish any meaningful relationship with the adult.

The fact that there are many ways to involve an adult into joint work permits us to expose more emphatically the distinction between the learning and performing positions of the child in the course of joint activity with the adult. The student who knows how to learn with the help of the adult (*the subject of joint learning activity*) turns to the grown-up for assistance in order to solve the problem and employs the grown-up as one of the most effective means of doing it. The pure performer solves the problem to please the adult. The latter remains the universal condition for every sort of well-being, including a correct solution of the problem. However, the performer is unable to benefit from this condition, which means that such a student does not know how to learn from the adult, expects an adult to teach, and stays *an object of instruction*.

The Second Series: Cooperation with a Peer when Solving an Insufficiently Defined Problem

It has been experimentally established that the key condition for the appearance of learning forms of child-adult cooperation is the organization of learning cooperation among peers (Rubtsov and Guzman 1984/85; Zuckerman 1994). The 'Mittens' method permits us to diagnose the ability of children to establish a meaningful relationship with each other, to ask peers for missing information when jointly solving an insufficiently defined problem.

The Experimental Procedure

No matter what were the results of the children's attempts to jointly produce a mitten in the first series, the adult sums up their work in the following way: 'You have shown that you can work quickly, neatly and — which is most important of all — without unnecessary chatter. Now I shall allow you to discuss everything you need in the course of your work. However, you must cope with your assignment completely alone and not ask even a single additional question.'

The children make several more mittens (3-5). The adult notes the form of their addressing one another and, whenever children try to agree on the thumb direction, silently helps them find the right one. Thus, eliminated are the differences between the children who solve spatial problems and the differences in the level of verbal interaction during the solution of a common problem (which just cannot be solved without meaningful interaction).

Qualitative Differences in the Ways to Solve an Insufficiently Defined Problem, which are Observed in the Second Series

In order to remove any personal biases, only those children who express the desire to work together, i.e., those who are beforehand prepared to interact, are invited to participate in the experiment. Against this background of cooperation, an inability to interact meaningfully is diagnosed (especially manifestly).

In this series of experiments, just as in the first one, we can earmark three levels of development of the children's ability to establish meaningful relations with each other for the solution of a common problem: (a) the children establish these relations 'at first go', without any preliminary trial and error; (b) after an unsuccessful attempt, the children pass on from acting at random to meaningful cooperation; (c) the children do not display any capacity (inclination) to enter into meaningful interaction.

Sources of Learning Initiative in Elementary School Children

Table 11.1 shows the results of a 'Mitten' test on 304 junior school children of Schools #91 and #944 in Moscow. The experiments were conducted at the end of the academic year. The data given in Table 1 permit us to compare three hypothetically possible sources of a child's initiative and independence in building up learning relations with an adult and with peers: (1) the age of the children, (2) the content of their education, and (3) the principal form of cooperation practiced in the classroom. School #944 is a regular state school with a traditional, i.e., teacher-centred, pattern of schooling. Children are trained to follow teacher's instructions and to copy the teacher's models of action. Davydov (1990) identified the content of traditional education as empirical one vs. theoretical content of learning activity, which is practiced in school #91. Theoretical in this concept is not synonymous to verbal or abstract. Students are confronted by real problems and helped to discover the most general ways of solving them. The search for general ways of solving a wide range of similar problems typify the theoretical approach to the task, as opposed to the empirical approach, focused on the practical solution of an isolated problem.

The theoretical content of learning activity can be brought in: (1) in the form of a whole class discussion, when the teacher helps 25-30 students to formulate their opinions on how to solve a new task, (2) in the form of small group discussions, when 3-7 students are given a new task and have to find its solution independent of the teacher, who enters the group discussion only when asked for help.

The Age Factor as a Possible Source of Learning Initiative by a Student

To pinpoint the effect of the age factor as such, we compared groups of children who differed only by age. Under the system of traditional education, first-, second-, and third-graders do not differ at all in

Grade (the number of students tested)	The first series: Organization of learning cooperation with an adult		The second series: Organization of learning cooperation with peers	
	solved the task after 1-5 attempts	solved the task from the first attempt	solved the task after 1-5 attempts	solved the task from the first attempt
Traditional cooperation directed by the teacher				
1 (30)	7	0	0	0
2 (30)	0	0	15	15
3 (30)	0	0	26	7
Whole classroom discussion				
1 (34)	29	0	47	6
2 (32)	19	0	56	31
3 (44)	46	9	96	91
Learning cooperation in small groups of students				
1 (42)	38	10	95	81
2 (32)	63	13	94	69
3 (30)	64	29	100	100

Table 11.1. Effect of the predominant form of cooperation in the classroom on the capacity of elementary school children to solve the task for organization of learning cooperation with an adult (the first series) and peers (the second series), when facing insufficiently defined problems. The percentage of dyads in which the task was solved is shown.

their ability (or rather complete inability) to ask an adult for missing information. An interesting fact is that though traditional education tends to involve manifold 'child-adult' interactions, within this relationship we observe only performing interactions between the adult, who sets models, and children, who follow them uncritically. There is nothing resembling the learning interaction, when children learn from the adult on their own initiative, asking questions and expecting the adult to answer them.

Likewise, instruction in the form of whole-class discussion, where interrelations between children during a general discussion in class may take the shape of direct argument, does not produce any substantial development in the ability of children of different age groups to receive missing information from the adult by merely asking questions. The difference between first- and third-graders in the first series of experiments is not statistically significant. It is only the joint form of teaching, when the children's interaction is purposefully and systematically built up that shows a manifest, age-dependent, progress of the students' ability to make use of the adult as the source of new information.

These data show the absence of any 'spontaneous' age-dependent enhancement or 'maturation' of the ability of the elementary school children to independently build up learning relations with the adult. What we do see is more or less manifestly expressed with regularity: the more consistently and systematically the children are taught to interact with each other in the solution of learning problems, the more effectively their ability develops to establish learning relations with the adult and to obtain from the latter, on their own initiative, the missing information essential for solving the problem.

As to the children's ability to establish relations with each other, we note a certain progress as they grow older: in the course of traditional education, the tendency towards cooperating with peers is reinforced from the first to the third grade, without any influence of external teaching factors. Most likely, the non-learning habits of cooperation with peers are picked up from everyday life and employed in learning situations. This spontaneously amplified tendency, however, is not manifestly expressed: even towards the end of the third grade, the majority of students in the traditional school (74%) do not establish cooperation with one another, even if they cannot act successfully without it.

The Content of Education as a Possible Source of Learning Initiative of a Student

In order to determine how the content of education affects the development of learning initiative in elementary school children, we wanted to compare the grades that differed only in this parameter, but, unfortunately, we were unable to do this since the teacher-centred interaction most characteristic of the traditional content of education is counter-indicative to the content of learning activity. Yet the data provided by the frontally-taught grades are manifest enough in themselves, without any comparison: traditional education *does not* develop the children's ability to display learning initiative, *does not* create the subjects of learning activity, whereas the learning activity with its specific content *does* provide for the development of its subjects.

The Form of Cooperation in the Classroom as a Possible Source of Learning Initiative of a Student

We compared the grades in which the content of learning activity was the same, but the form of introducing this content differed. We found that to guarantee the development of learning independence, of the ability to actively learn from the adult and each other, in elementary school children, it was not sufficient to merely introduce theoretical content that redirects the children towards the ways and means of their own actions. By their level of development of learning initiative (that is, of subjectivity), the children who had three-year experience in the whole-class discussion can be compared to those who had one-year experience of cooperation in small groups. The manifest and statistically significant differences in the way the children addressed an adult and each other, stipulated by the form in which learning cooperation is organized, allowed us to conclude that it was precisely this educational factor which most substantially affected the development of children's initiative in learning relations. And the greater the children's experience in co-operating with each other, the higher the learning independence when building up these learning relations. In the traditional school, in the absence of such experience, the indices of children's learning independence were almost naught.

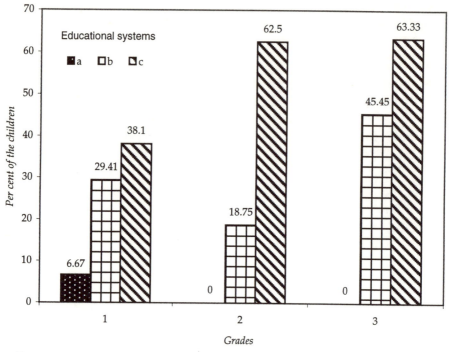

Fig. 11.1. The level of reflective initiative in school children (1st to 3rd grades) taught under the different educational systems (per cent of children who required missing data from the adult).

To understand why the joint work of a group of children gives rise to more meaningful, less infantile forms of addressing an adult, let us observe the cases in which the students working together at a lesson are obliged to request the teacher's help (Fig. 11.1). This happens mainly in cases of disagreement, of a conflict of positions, when the children are unable to come to a shared opinion. The point, however, is that before the disagreement becomes evident, there is always an argument in which the opinions are formulated explicitly. Therefore, the typical way to address the teacher by such a group of children is: 'We can't come to an agreement — he thinks that... and I think that... Which of us is right?' In this case the children have already done the job of discovering their own logic, their own viewpoints, and now present the latter to the teacher for appraisal and correction. Let's compare this situation with the classical request for help in the case of frontal education: 'I can't do it... will you tell me what to do?...' Here the teacher is required to discover the child's logic, and it is the adult who has to do the major reflective work. The students find it unnecessary to share this reflective burden of the teacher and reconstruct their own logic in solving the problem; children do not grasp the situation and continue to address their teacher with infantile requests for help, every time receiving it.

Conclusions

Let us sum up our evidence and assumptions on the sources of learning initiative in elementary school children. Children's initiative in establishing learning relations with an adult is, most certainly, not the function of their age, it depends essentially on the content and forms of elementary education. Under traditional education, the children's learning initiative is virtually absent throughout the entire elementary school age. The theoretical content of learning activity boosts the development of reflective capacities in students and thereby to some extent gives them the ability to perceive what they cannot as yet do alone, and to turn to an adult for meaningful assistance. The experience of learning cooperation with peers amplifies the children's initiative in their cooperation with grownups, but does not guarantee it: at least one-third of the students, who practiced learning cooperation with peers during three years of elementary school education, did not display learning initiative in the described experiment. This fact means that there are missing conditions for the development of learning initiative. Hypothetically (Slobodchikov and Tsukerman 1992), such a missing factor could be the student's experience of discovering and realizing their own changes in the course of education (the experience of learning cooperation with oneself) — that, most likely, is as yet untapped reserve of learning initiative which is the interpsychic form of the future learning independence, of the capacity to learn.

References

Davydov, V.V. (1990). *Types of generalization in instruction: Logical and psychological problems in the structuring of school curricula.* Reston, Va.: National Council of Teachers of Mathematics.

Elkonin, D.B. (1972). Toward the problem of stages of the mental development of the child. *Soviet Psychology* 10, 225-51.

Rubtsov, V.V. & Guzman, R.Ya. (1984-1985). Psychological characteristics of the methods pupils use to organize joint activity in dealing with a school task. *Soviet Psychology* 23, 65-84.

Slobodchikov, V.I. & Tsukerman, G.A. (1992). The genesis of reflective consciousness at early school age. *Journal of Russian and East European Psychology*
30, 6-27.

Venger, A.L. & Polivanova, K.N. (1990). Distinctive features of six-year-olds'
relation to adult-assigned tasks. *Soviet Psychology* 28, 42-53.

Vygotsky, L.S. (1978). *Mind in society: The development of higher psychological
processes*. M. Cole, V. John-Steiner, S. Scribner & E. Souberman (eds.).
Cambridge, Mass.: Harvard University Press.

Zuckerman, G.A. (1991). Invariants of cognitive development and educational
patterns. *Gestalt Theory* 13, 86-97.

Zuckerman, G.A. (1994). A pilot study of a ten-day course in cooperative
learning for Russian first-graders. *Elementary School Journal* 94, 405-20.

12 Development of Evaluation at the Initial Stage of Learning Activities

Yuri A. Poluyanov & Tatyana A. Matiss

Introduction

We present the results of an experimental study on the conditions of the organization of learning under which the teacher's evaluating actions and judgments might have a productive impact on the development of the learners' ability to independently evaluate his own actions and their results. For the child, such an evaluation serves as the basis of the formation of being able to learn. We start with a short theoretical analysis of the evaluation problem in pedagogy and psychology. Then we introduce the method of the interventional experiment which we use in our research. We then describe the phases of the formation of evaluation as a learning action and analyze our experimental data. Finally, we formulate some consequences and hypotheses based on our study.

The Problem of Evaluation in Pedagogy and Psychology

From ancient times till today evaluation remains perhaps the most steady pedagogical instrument. It has taken various forms ranging from verbal designations and marks (in five-point, and wider scales) to indices and coefficients that are received in tests, etc.

In any form, evaluation serves as a measure that shows how students' knowledge is related to the socially determined norms in order to define the age-related, teaching-upbringing stages through which culture is appropriated by students. Evaluation has several functions. For society it indicates how ready each student is to go on to the next educational grade or any particular kind of practical activity. For young people, evaluation serves as a means of achieving their social self-affirmation among others of the same age and in relation to the expectations of adults. For students, evaluation indicates their advancement in learning activities (i.e., it serves as a measure of perfecting their capabilities and aptitudes). Students psychologically need evaluation as a measure and incentive for learning at every educational stage, and society needs evaluation as an indicator of the student's readiness for independent activities.

At the same time, in real pedagogical practice, many evaluation forms tend to play an ambiguous role (especially at the first stage of learning). Often, they do not stimulate, but rather inhibit the process of a child's development. To a great extent this is due to the fact that school-marks in their structure, criteria, and functioning originated from adults, not from children. As a rule, students are not familiar with evaluation norms. They just accept evaluation from their teacher. The criteria on which the evaluation is based are mostly obscure, hidden from students and are revealed to them in rather negative forms — for example, a teacher's claim that a particular student 'does not know' anything. In such a context the student, through the teacher's positive or negative attitude, perceives evaluation either as an approval or as a disapproval of his personality.

In all didactic theories and in many psychological conceptual frameworks, traditionally the teacher does the grading, and the grade the teacher gives a child is regarded as a reflection of the child's activity. Even Jerome Bruner, when discussing conspicuous characteristics of the evaluating actions which teacher and students perform during teaching/learning acts, allocates the leading role to the teacher (Bruner 1977). Amonashvili (1984) points to the problem of grading as one of the most critical aspects of education. He showed convincingly that the school grade system is, in fact, groundless and non-objective. He argues for the advantages of 'gradeless teaching' for primary schools. Grades given according to test results, without including the teacher's personal evaluation, are perceived as objective by pupils (Anastazi 1982), but the very situation of 'tests' is unnatural and perceived psychologically different for different children (Neisser 1981). Moreover, testing results often become a 'label' on children, thereby preventing some opportunities of development (Stones 1984).

Vygotsky put forward the idea that to promote the child's psychological development, child and adult should collaborate in making evaluations. He stated the hypothesis that during the 'crisis' of the seven year old child, a kind of general, non-situated, and stable self-attitude is formed in children which integrates children's experience acquired through activities and communication and, thus, allows children to control their behaviour in accordance with social norms (see Vygotsky 1984). Traditionally, age-related aspects of such 'self-evaluation' were studied in the context of the 'ego-concept' and related to the moments where self-consciousness develops (Vygotsky 1984; Rubinstein 1940; Burns 1986; and others). These moments have, however, not been considered as something directly related to the issue of school grading.

To resolve, on the one hand, the conflict between the fact that evaluation is obviously necessary for the learning-teaching process and, on the other, its negative psychological effects upon the child's development, we need to transform evaluation into an instrument which students could use themselves in their learning activities and learning initiatives and, in doing so, they could demonstrate themselves as true subjects of the teaching-learning process. Such an approach underlies the concept of teaching-learning activity suggested by D.B. Elkonin (1974) and V.V. Davydov (1972) in which assessment is regarded as a necessary component for 'learning to learn' — together with modeling of knowledge and appropriation control.

However, this concept does not address the very process of how a child becomes the subject of learning, though its theoretical formulations repeatedly state that learning activity is the student's activity. In pedagogical practice, this leads to the situation in which there is only a small space left for students' initiatives and independent activities, and so students only have to perform or execute operations. This also occurs because at its primary stages learning is always a process that is jointly performed by teacher and student and in this process the child learns not so much from the teacher as with the teacher and this situation requires a more clear and definite distribution of activities between the two subjects.

Experimentation as an Interventional Method — A Teaching Experiment

Empirical studies, in which the effects of dynamic assessment on children were examined, have been conducted in several schools in Moscow during 'Art' lessons. These lessons followed the program that was directed mainly towards developing the children's ability to form mental images based on principles of beauty. These principles are related mainly to the aesthetical, basic structures such as proportions, rhythm, symmetry, contrast, compositional and structural balance, and other historically developed directions for beauty-building. These principles were introduced into the curriculum not through verbal explanations of concepts, but instead by means of explorative activities performed by the students themselves in order to provide them with a sense of proportion, rhythm, etc. Lessons were constructed according to the idea that the child's learning and creative efforts should be united. In particular, these lessons had three sections:

1) discussing paintings, where the pupils evaluated the results of previous lessons together with the teacher;

2) teaching-learning work in which general methods of artistic activity were appropriated through joint solving of learning tasks; and

3) children's self-directed activity through which they creatively expressed themselves, using already tested methods in accordance with their individual ideas. In this last case the teacher collaborated not with the whole class or a group of pupils, but with every child separately.

In our experiment, the content, methods and organization of teaching art were based on the consideration that fine arts activity in childhood (between 2 and 12 years of age) is, for the child himself, not so much a special but a general developing activity. Early school age represents the final and most salient period for expressing the artistic talents of almost all children. However, these potentials do not appear spontaneously, but only under certain conditions, the main one being the organic unity of children's learning which is created under instruction. The principle of 'free creative self-expression' was elaborated rather completely and productively in theory and educational practice. More complicated is the situation with instruction. It is either organized after the model of a simplified professional instruction where creativity is interpreted as the final result of instruction, or it is prohibited as destroying the child's creative self-expression. Between these extreme positions stand the people who unite teaching and creativity in different relations, but in these cases both processes remain parallel, caused by the fact that one of these processes is organized only as a process where adults teach children and not as a process where children learn together with the adult. The contradiction of the positions mentioned lies in the fact that in creative self-expression the child is seen only as a subject of activity, and under instruction only as an object.

In order to overcome this contradiction, we based the teaching on the subject's needs. Thus we had to determine which needs evoke and sustain children's general passion for pictorial activity. It is meaningless to seek these needs in the sphere of professional fine art, because at this early age

(1½ to 3 years of age), a child's activity cannot be specialized, and because the real pictorial component itself does not play a substantial role in children's drawings. By his drawing the child seems to satisfy some kind of need, stimulating all kinds of artistic activity not being developed by any other factor. This need must be something necessary for all people leading to the development of an ability universal to any human activity. These are needs concerning beauty and imagination.

Therefore, in early school age, the content of instruction is directed towards the development of the 'ability to construct images based on principles of beauty'. Doubtlessly, such an ability might be developed by lessons in other arts as well. But fine art has unquestionable advantages compared to other kinds of art:

– Visual modality dominates others (motor, auditive, etc.) in the development of imagination.

– With few exceptions, all children enthusiastically engage in drawing, which is not the case with other kinds of art (literature, music, dance, etc.).

– At the beginning of school age, or even earlier, many children are able to express their personal relation to life by means of drawings or other fine art forms. Creativity in pictorial activity is accessible to them earlier and fuller than in other kinds of activity. Therefore, occupation with pictorial art presents the child with the possibility of becoming a full subject of artistic activity.

Principles of beauty to be acquired by children concern the construction of images. These are, particularly, principles of measure, rhythm, symmetry, proportion, compositional and constructive balance and others belonging to structural characteristics of harmony or disharmony of artistic form. These principles are universal to creators of all kinds of art, of all eras, styles, genres, from ancient, classic times until modern time where avant-gardists were also guided by them. These principles were in their original form determined in a sufficiently simple manner by the ancient aestetics and accessible to children of early school age.

In its developed form, the principle of measure is the most general aestetic category characterizing quantitative and qualitative aspects of the construction of any artistic whole. Rhythm, symmetry, proportions, and grace are nothing but methods of organizing measure: adequacy, correspondence, balance, etc., the best relationships between the whole and its parts expressed in any features and substances *including emotional and sensuous* ones. All artistic standards known in the history of art — the most complicated constructions of the 'Golden Section' among them — are based on principles of measure. The task of a curriculum of fine art in elementary school is, of course, not the information about all these things. The curriculum has to create such conditions of activity to ensure self-development of the ability called 'feeling of measure'.

This feeling of measure generates the ability to include into own-activity *measurability* concerning different features — but not in the sense of units of measuring (meters, litres, etc.), but as the relationship between whole and parts. This is thoroughly accessible for first graders, e.g., concerning the size of a graphic representation and spots as its parts — big, medium, small ones. In the case of such measurability, children establish relations to the whole and between the parts independently of their actual sizes. Small spots on a big piece of paper become big ones, if transferred onto a small piece, and smaller spots in relation to them appear to be medium-sized, etc. It is not difficult to introduce measurability concerning brightness of any colour (bright, dark, medium) or form (round, cornered, mixed, etc.). At the beginning, this way of understanding measurability is introduced into all aspects of the children's pictorial activity: Concerning size and form of paint-brushes (broad, medium, narrow or plain, round), the placing of colours in a box, their mixture, etc. Measurablity is not introduced via the teacher's explanations, but by means of tasks constructed in a certain way. Solving these tasks, the children create criteria of such measurability through their own actions. They determine themselves some intended wholeness of their drawing.

Later on, based on the example of interaction of colours, the ability of visually recognizing not only measures of the singular features of a drawing, but also their interactions creating expressive relations (emotions, senses) is formed. Further, the ability of organizing these relations in such a way that they express the intention of a drawing is formed. In this sequence, the principle of measure is acquired by the learners as the general method of constructing images and applied as the criterion for the appraisal of process and product of their drawing.

Children do not study and repeat all the methods of constructing beauty mentioned here, but try them out by solving learning tasks and through their creative work. The main reason is, on the one hand, that young school children have a sharp artistic *perception* of the world, but, on the other hand, children with highly developed true artistic abilities are very seldom found and, as a rule, these abilities develop later in early youth. The principle of using the student's actions as the basics of instructional content allows each learner to acquire methods of artistic activity that correspond to his/her potentiality. But in order to ensure this learning activity, a special organization of instruction is needed.

A Teaching Experiment: Based on the Interventional Experimental Method

The research techniques were aimed at revealing how pupils themselves became evaluators of subject matter in various situations (i.e., how they became able to evaluate their actions and respective results independently, being directed by their own initiatives in accordance with criteria and ways of evaluation learned during the lessons). Thus, the research techniques went in three directions which were then juxtaposed in the conclusions: a) fixation and analysis of evaluative judgments made by the children while discussing pictures; b) fixation and analysis of ways of actions performed through collectively solved learning tasks; c) analyzing the results of the lessons (i.e., children's pictures) according to an index of creative activity and an index of appropriation of general methods introduced in each lesson. The results were analyzed by the experimenters together with the teachers; for the teachers such analysis served as a means of efficiency evaluation with regard to each lesson.

For our research, this kind of analysis provided the most definite data about the subjective aspects of evaluation, because when the child analyzes his artistic ideas (i.e., in creativity) he/she could either use or not use the general method of performing artistic tasks that were appropriated during the 'teaching' part of the lesson. When analyzing pictures the rate of 'creative activity' and 'general methods of appropriateness' turned out to be almost equal (except for the lowest rates). This shows that in making independent evaluations of pictures (both of the intermediate stages and of the completed work) the child oriented himself toward the general methods as a tool for evaluating the choices (according to own ideas) of the activity in the creative tasks. Conversely, when the rate was different as when the creative activity was lower than the general methods of appropriateness, this showed that the child lacked independence. The same could be concluded when the child lacked evaluation initiative and was not oriented toward general methods (i.e., lacked learning effect in cases when the idea was good but its implementation was poor). In all three applications of this technique we evaluated the qualitative characteristics of pupils' independence and their initiative at various learning stages.

Stages of the Formation of Evaluation as a Learning Action

As a result of this experiment the following stages have been found at which the learning-directed effect of evaluation was formed.

Before starting to learn, despite their long experience in painting, the children were not in the habit of evaluating their work. They waited for their teacher to make evaluations using terms like 'right' or 'wrong', and regarded such an evaluation as a general indicator of, for example, good behaviour (whether or not a particular pupil soiled clothes and/or table with paint) and/or the painting quality itself (i.e., whether or not the people, trees, and houses in their painting were depicted correctly).

The first stage of formation of evaluation activity was aimed at including evaluation into the children's painting activity in the form of a special step that finished each lesson. Only completed paintings were evaluated, using any criteria that were clear and comprehensible to the children. As before, the children accepted the teacher's evaluations in a non-differentiated way, as an indicator that affirms them in the game of teacher-pupil. Each child, while copying the teacher's way of evaluation, readily used the teacher's criteria, but this did not count for their own work, but only for evaluating other children's paintings.

On the basis of this feature, the teacher organized mutual evaluation of pictures (as a kind of 'playing school') during which the teacher would control how the children followed their roles and rules and was active in resolving difficult evaluations.

The experiment revealed one characteristic feature of the artist's evaluation of his pictures which is important for the subsequent learning stage. The children especially valued drawing as a means of implementing an idea and rarely took into account what could really be seen on the picture. The children often forgot their own artistic ideas, even wonderfully bright ones. Sometimes, though, these ideas were recognized by other classmates with expressions such as 'I like it' ('it was good', 'well done'). However, pupils' evaluations nearly always contained biting criticism with regard to many 'wrong' elements present in the picture. Often this led to more or less formulated conflicts between the children.

At the *second stage* of formation of evaluation activity, the teacher, in order to decrease mutual evaluational conflicts in discussing pictures, changed roles in the same game of 'teacher-pupil'. Here the 'teacher' found and evaluated only advantages of a picture, whereas the 'pupil' found and evaluated only shortcomings. In this condition the teacher also performed the role of a 'judge' who controlled that the rules of the game were strictly followed. Also, by means of particular criteria for selecting pictures for exhibition in the classroom, the teacher directed the children's attention to their search for artistic qualities in paintings, especially for those expressive elements of pictures that most often conveyed their personal intonations.

The second stage differed from the first one by its goal, content, and relation to evaluation. The pupils perceived the evaluations made by the teacher and — to a certain extent — by their classmates, as tokens indicating attention to themselves, as a way of being noticed among other children. This kind of evaluation, however, was conjuncted to the rest of the learning-teaching process as a necessary component which is performed together with the teacher so that a particular artist participated in it as 'pretending'. At this stage, though evaluation had its permanent function, it was still no part of the child's independent action. In this place the teacher's evaluations, even the most unflattering ones, were accepted without discussion. As to the classmates' judgments, the pupils often readily accepted the evaluations that pleased them and argued and claimed for arguments about the ones that did not. At the same time the pupils often believed that they were very critical about their own works.

The *third stage* of formation of evaluation activity was aimed at forming in children the ability to separate those components, while making evaluation, that were directly visible in a picture from the ones that were within the author's intentions, but not visible without additional explanation. With this goal the children have been given the roles of either a) 'artists', or b) 'spectators'. We have to emphasize that this was still a game that required the 'spectators' to search for what they liked in the pictures, make an evaluation, and make suggestions to the 'artists' concerning which pictures should be chosen for exhibition, while the 'artists' should accept or reject the choices through argumentation. At this point, if suggestions come from other 'artists', the 'artist' in question must argue his own case. As in the previous stage, the teacher played the roles of judge, producer, and organizer.

As a result, evaluation of the child's artistic-creative product had a special learning-related and personal value for the child. Even long after the evaluation the children wanted to take home those of their pictures that received positive responses. At the same time they threw out pictures that received negative or no evaluation.

The *fourth stage* of the formation of evaluation activity coincided time-wise with the period in which the general method of colour harmony was appropriated.

To characterize this stage we should note those changes that occurred, and how the children psychologically perceived the results of their learning and creative work. Previously, when the children evaluated these results they mainly oriented themselves to the successive process of depicting and its verbal accompaniment. The children did not so much see the acting relationships presented in the artistically expressed idea as their own intentions, including the ones that were not realized in the picture. *When* we introduced into the teaching-learning process the techniques of 'moving backwards', in which by means of enlarging distance to the picture the children could get a concentration of various colours and see relations between them and, also, change their viewpoint to a new unaccustomed one. Of course, in this condition intentions underlying the child's basic idea did not disappear, but instead this gave a new possibility to the child to see his own picture with another person's eyes in addition to the 'position of his own artistic view'; that is, the children could see their work from the positions of 'artist' and 'spectator' at the same time. Here the children found opportunity to include in their own evaluation not only all the things that others (classmates and teacher) could see and tell, but also those aspects that have been defined in 'the general appropriation method.'

Thus, this stage was aimed at forming in the children the ability to evaluate the process and result of their actions as viewed from the position of others. This goal was achieved by means of *distributing* the *positions* (not roles!) of 'artist' and 'spectator' between the children, between teacher and the entire class, and between the teacher and pupil.

Unlike a *role* where the child performs social, professional, as well as other functions with which he/she is not associated in everyday life, a *position* represents a child's actual standpoint either from the angle of the 'artist' who performed the picture and who sees the picture as if from within (i.e., the way in which the child wished to express something — even if this had not actually been implemented), or from the position of 'spectator' who does not know anything about the artist's idea and thus does not perceive the most expressive qualities of the picture, but instead only sees what is actually depicted. When the two positions are success-fully combined into the single position of 'artist-spectator' this allows children to evaluate their paintings according to the 'general method' criteria, and to make evaluations for themselves in order to express their ideas more perfectly.

Analysis of Experimental Materials

As can be seen from the analysis of actions and judgments made by children at this stage and at the earlier stages, learning evaluation is not formed as a new autonomous entity, but instead it is formed on the basis of the children's already existing self-attitudes through reforming their attitudes to their activities.

The phenomenon of children's paintings results from a joint effect made by psychologically conflicting processes, of which some occur consciously and some happen involuntarily. Each separate display is a unit of the child's picture which not so much depicts as designates, for example, a man, an animal, a house, etc. With this purpose it is sufficient for the first-grade pupil to draw body, head, two hands, two legs, and features showing whether this would be a boy or a girl. All other things can merely be named.

Children depict, not in the way in which they can actually see anything, but rather in the way in which they can imagine something. They construct a picture by means of sequentially attaching one display to another and demonstrating with words, gesture, and mimics what are the relations between the displays. Children draw for themselves, they do not take into account what others, i.e., the spectators, would see on their picture. Thus, even though the children evaluate each separate display, they do not necessarily separate what can be seen on their picture from what they imagine (Goodnow 1977).

It may seem that in doing so one cannot create any integral artistic image, yet it is the impressionistic qualities of images that are naive and sometimes funny which help to make the most valued pictures. This reflects another process that cannot always be met within school lessons, because it strongly depends on how a particular child captured an imagined content in his picture and how he experiences his own relation to what is being depicted. This process arises and occurs involuntarily and is manifested in the child's creative playing with lines, dashes, and colours, for which the child sees some reason, though he does not recognize what these lines, dashes, and colours express in conjunction, and so he cannot evaluate this expressive component (Poluyanov 1982).

Each of these processes is reflected in the children's evaluations: The first process — in verbal judgments about pictures and in the evaluation of independent activity; the second process — in evaluating actions performed together with teacher and classmates.

Now we will describe how all this revealed itself during the first three stages through an experiment of putting paper pieces together. At the lesson, the children first tried to join the pieces together in order to create a picture of something which they found interesting. This research involved twelve pieces of black paper of different shapes and sizes. Each child had the same set of pieces. During the teaching part of the lesson, the teacher and all the pupils used six such pieces in order to find a figure, and then explored various combinations on the magnetic board (conjunctions, replacements, rearrangement, etc.), transforming them into silhouettes of various 'creatures' that had been invented beforehand by the teacher (see Fig. 12.1).

The teacher showed many possible combinations and initiated the forming of each silhouette. After that the pupils continued themselves to construct without oral instruction. On the first silhouette, the teacher combined three pieces and only then stimulated pupils with such questions as: 'What does it do?' 'Is it cheerful or sad?' 'What and how should we rearrange to make this better?', and so on. The second silhouette included only two pieces, the third silhouette had only one piece, the biggest one, that is placed diagonally. The teacher's questions gave the pupils the criteria for evaluating what was seen on the magnetic board and what would result from the rearrangement of the pieces. Almost all the pupils participated in the search for combinations. They successively complemented and corrected one another and not only successfully built on all the three silhouettes, but also found combinations that showed dynamics and state for each 'creature'. Consequently, in their joint search with teacher and classmates each child mainly evaluated the expressive factor of the pictures.

The children were not allowed to repeat silhouettes composed on the board. Therefore, each child chose from the overall set five or six pieces with a shape that met his/her individual idea. Several pupils made original and expressive silhouettes, but with the same qualities as in other children's works, the individual silhouettes were more or less similar to those found collectively. In other words, for most pupils an evaluation of the ex-

Fig. 12.1. Samples of search for combinations of paper pieces on the magnetic board.

pressive aspect took place, but it was mediated by compositions found together with the teacher.

While evaluating these pictures, the children spoke primarily of the creature depicted. Therefore, critical judgments were directed mostly at the completeness or non-completeness of the pictures. Silhouettes similar to the one shown in Fig. 12.1.1 were evaluated positively. Silhouettes evaluated negatively were similar to those shown in Fig. 12.1.2 (two paws, not four) and 12.1.3 (no forepaws, and backpaws 'had fallen off') and, also, similar to those composed collectively. Thereafter, and only if they provided a silhouette which was recognizable, the children evaluated the expressive aspect of movements if these were depicted (but their absence was not evaluated as a shortcoming). Having discussed the pictures, the children chose the best pictures to be continually exhibited in the classroom, thereby providing no judgments of expressiveness (but evaluative actions had already taken place). These actions of evaluating completeness or non-completeness strongly differed from the previously expressed judgments where the most expressive silhouettes were selected and, despite negative judgment, pictures similar to the ones composed collectively were among them.

Thus, evaluating actions came to be formed by the condition of joint learning activity with the teacher. The possibility for such evaluative actions was already formed involuntarily in the process of artistic-creative work. During the fourth stage such evaluative actions successively transformed into evaluative judgments. It is important to note that the basis of this transformation was the way most children perceived colour coordination, because children of this age are especially sensitive to the emotional meaning of colours while relations between different colours were not localized on separate displays and could only be observed when the entire picture (i.e., combinations of colours and depicted object at the same time) was perceived integrally. Therefore, the emotional-meaning aspect of the contents of pictures (expressive aspect) is perceived and evaluated first of all, thus influencing subsequent evaluations made with relation to separate parts and details of the picture.

Discussion

In the evaluation of the first stage of learning activity of a subject matter, the factor to be evaluated was if a child, led by his own initiative, could perform independent learning actions directed towards general methods accepted in the culture, and which could in general be appro-priated during studies of a particular subject matter in school. In our case this involved general methods for constructing artistic forms in arts.

Judging on the basis of the factors at the end of first year of learning, we observed how evaluation as a kind of learning-related action became (after passing certain formation stages) a subject matter related action for most children. 'Controlling action' as subject matter related action was formed later to a small degree by the first-grade pupils. This occurs on the basis of evaluation both in the form of controlling-evaluative action performed for intermediate results and in the form of step-by-step oper-ational control. Our experimental data let us assume that 'control actions' originate as an effect of the 'pupil's doubt'. This facilitates the pupil's action and promotes the stage of evaluation formation where the learning result is juxtaposed to the 'general appropriated method'. First-grade pupils are only prepared for 'modeling action' through the appropriation of substitution types, such as the *selection of relations and actions related to them*. While appropriating these 'preparatory' actions, teacher and pupils get the opportunity to include general methods into the list of evaluation criteria. Thus, by means of evaluation, pupils who solve tasks and still cannot be considered completely 'learning-directed' become able to participate together with the teacher in constructing models of general methods of solving tasks, where signs of the initial relations are still not completely abstracted. At this stage, however, the pupils' initiative and independence in putting forward similar 'learning tasks' are limited to the direct episodical participation which is part of the condition for joint work between teacher and pupils and between classmates.

During the first year of learning we cannot unconditionally state that 'evaluation' has a teaching effect. At the first stage it is not so much evaluation, but rather the judgment which does not have any defined criteria and which teacher and pupils connect to the lesson as a kind of summary. In the second year, evaluation of learning result is divided into what was personal and desirable, on the one hand, and what has actually been realized in the picture construction (the drawing), on the other (i.e., evaluation becomes an action that is performed by the pupils themselves). The quality of 'teachability,' however, if judged through concrete results on the basis of the criteria of the general method, is only acquired at the last stage, when together with his own position the child takes into con-sideration other persons' (teacher's, classmates', etc.) positions. This new position, being two-fold and thus conflicting, allows the child to see his painting 'from the perspective of other persons' (general method criteria) and, furthermore, allows the child to keep his own internal point of view (ideal goal). Due to this, *he will be able* to evaluate the process of depicting how good or poorly his idea is expressed — and during discussing the pictures to agree with argumented opinions about the spectators' opinions, or argue in favor of his own evaluation when other opinions and arguments are not relevant or significant, etc. In other words, formation of the 'artist-spectator' position in children becomes a condition for forming in them the ability to behave as a subject responsible for evaluations of own actions and their result. But at the initial stage of learning activity, such appearances in children are rather rare and incomplete, and so their responsibility for evaluation of self (understood as indicator of its subject matter orientation) takes the form of potential ability for its subsequent formation.

Conclusion and a Hypothesis

In conclusion we would like to state that in our research we have accepted as the indicator of subject matter learning activity such factors as the pupil being an active source in relation to the learning object (activities that in general are appropriated at school). On his own initiative, the pupil should also be able to independently perform learning-related actions oriented toward the general methods of the solving of tasks (first of all learning tasks). It should be noted also that subject matter orientation of evaluation particularly requires the pupil's responsibility for proper use of criteria and requires that his own evaluation is adequate in relation to the general method. The pupil must demonstrate the full range of these criteria through his subject matter actions.

In the frame of our studies, such factors are not often observed in the pupils' evaluation of his own creative work at the first stage of learning. Perhaps this could be explained by the fact that in young school children a *sharing* and *distributing* in the learning activity always occurs between the pupil and teacher. Under these conditions the subject matter orientation of a child's evaluation is therefore always dependent on other persons (i.e., teacher and classmates) particularly in the learning activity.

The main role in the learning activity is played by evaluation of the various types and forms of 'exploration actions'. The purpose in the first grade is that the explorative activity of any pupil must receive positive evaluation even if this activity leads to an erroneous result or is expressed in non-goal-directed actions — sooner or later the child arrives at the question of 'how to explore?' In this first period (and also later) such evaluation originates from the teacher and is always personal and concrete in its directness as to the content of the subject matter being appropriated. Any type of encouragement is suitable (from oral praise to emphasis of exploration result during 'discussion' at the exhibition), except those forms that restrain the confidence of other pupils. This kind of evaluation is more often than other kinds of evaluation, transferred by the child into an independent activity, becoming an internal stimulus of the child's learning.

In our observations, the teacher's use of this type of evaluation activity significantly affects learning motivation. It is well known that seven year old children, before coming to school, form a strong wish to become a good pupil (see Elkonin 1974). But this wish is exclusively based on social motives such as aspiration to become strong in the new quality of being a school pupil. Thus, the teacher's evaluations expressed in any form (marks, grades, oral remarks and statements to child and parents, etc.) are perceived by the first-grade pupil as affirmation and a way of distinguishing themselves from other children. There is little or no 'proper teaching' of motivation in school. As we have shown, orientation to subject matter effectively re-orientates the children's motivation from social to a predominantly learning- and knowledge-oriented position because 'exploration action' involves both 'playing' and 'learning' components. Any kind of game (role game, rule game, with either cognitive or creative demands) makes children feel satisfied by the very process of exploration and testing various ways of problem solving due to which they actively participate in a specially organized learning-teaching process. During lessons this can be judged, first of all, on enthusiastic independent work, trials, and the desire to test own capabilities in those special (in our case artistic) kinds of activity that are appropriated. The exploration component is especially important in the first year of learning, though it is also significant later during the studying of subjects that are closely related to 'mental production'. Apparently, motivation for learning activity in first-grade pupils starts to be formed internally in relation to evaluation of 'exploration acts,' and this motivation contributes more and more to how these pupils become the source of own activity — the subject of own learning.

In this connection we would like to note, on the one hand, an essential difference between evaluations made by the teacher, other adults, and classmates, and on the other, the learning effect of evaluation made by the pupils themselves. Evaluations made by other persons are always directed toward a particular person as an object to be evaluated, whereas a person's own evaluations with regard to own activity are made for own purposes, not for those of others. The process of formation of evaluation arises in pupils in an arbitrary way. This arbitrariness originates in joint learning actions with all persons involved in lessons. They draw the child's attention to criteria and how they are related to learning material, norms and levels of evaluation. Having been formed (whether completely or in some parts), the learning-related effect of evaluation may be realized involuntarily and have no external incentive. Thus, if we need to know to what extent a particular child has appropriated and individualized evaluation as an action and how the child is involved in the learning-teaching process and where his actions continuously are being transformed because of new criteria, norms, and requirements of evaluation that are introduced at each new stage of learning, researchers should continuously analyze pupils' results in solving learning tasks that allow multiple correct decisions (i.e., such research should reveal how reflective pupils' evaluations are during the learning process).

References

Amonashvili, Sh. A. (1984). *Vospitatel'naya i obrazovatel'naya funkcia ocenki uchenia shol'nikov* [Educational function of marks for students' learning]. Moscow: Pedagogika.

Anastazi, A. (1982). *Psichologicheskoe testirovanie, tom 1* [Psychological testing, vol. 1]. Moscow: Pedagogika.

Bruner, J. (1977). *Psikhologia poznania* [Psychology of cognition]. Moscow: Progress.

Burns, R. (1986). *Razvitie ya-koncepcii i vospitanie* [Development of I-conception and education]. Moscow: Progress.

Davydov, V.V. (1972). *Vidy obobshchenia v obuchenii* [Kinds of generalization in instruction]. Moscow: Pedagogika.

Elkonin, D.B. (1974). *Psikhologia obuchenia mladshikh shkol'nikov* [Psychology of teaching younger school children]. Moscow: Znanie.

Goodnow, J. (1977). *Children's Drawing*. Cambridge, Mass.: Harvard University Press.

Neisser, U. (1981). *Poznanie i real'nost'* [Cognition and reality]. Moscow: Progress.

Poluyanov, Yu. A. (1982). *Voobrazhenie i sposobnosti* [Imagination and abilities]. Moscow: Znanie.

Rubinstein, S.L. (1940). *Osnovy obshchey psikohologii* [Fundamentals of general psychology]. Moscow: Uchepedgiz.

Stones, E. (1984). *Psikho-pedagogika* [Psychopedagogics]. Moscow: Pedagogika.

Vygotsky, L.S. (1984). *Sobranie sochineniy, tom 4* [Collected works, vol. 4]. Moscow: Pedagogika.

13 Teaching Opportunities in Play

Bert van Oers

Culture arises in the form of play...
Johan Huizinga, Homo ludens (1939)

Introduction

This chapter deals with the play activities of children ranging in age from 4 to 7 (8) years, in the context of a school setting. Starting from Elkonin's developmental theory (Elkonin 1980; see also Oerter 1993), we assumed that play activity is a leading activity for these children preparing for the next leading activity (learning activity). However, the transition from play to learning activity is probably not a simple change, but a complex process that contains elements of both play and learning. Hence we focused on the problem of learning in the context of play and — consequently — on how a teacher could use various moments of play as opportunities for teaching without disturbing the play itself. Considering the socio-semiotic character of learning activity, we furthermore assumed that it would be important for the teacher to assist young children in the performance of semiotic activities during play. More particularly, we studied young children's abilities to use schematic representations (diagrams) meaningfully and reflectively in their play activities, and tried to discover some of the main conditions for this activity to occur during play.

Development and Play

The importance of play in young children's development is generally recognized nowadays. The arguments, however, underpinning this recognition are diverse, as are the opinions about how play should be related to the educational process. According to Piaget (e.g., 1962), play should be conceived of as an activity in which assimilation has primacy over accommodation. It is mere functional or reproductive assimilation of environmental aspects. As such it is the counterpart of imitation that essentially involves accommodation to situational characteristics. In combination, play and imitation are the essential components of representational and symbolic behaviour. In play, according to Piaget, the child is autistically constructing a private reality. It makes no sense to communicate cultural meanings into this child's private reality, let alone to negotiate about a variety of meanings that can be attributed to this reality. By experiencing reality, the child assimilates objective parts of its physical world and builds up its first impressions about that world. These impressions are essential, indeed, for further development (with the help of imitation) towards genuine symbolic behaviour. From a developmental perspective, play is for Piaget a necessary stage in the development of symbolic activity, but a stage where educational intervention is pointless. Consequentially, teaching in play is considered to be a contradiction. The Piagetian point of view on play underscored the widespread maxim about play: *let them play, but don't interfere.* It is still very influential in western educational practices for the younger child (until about five years old).

The Piagetian approach to play has been criticized by Vygotsky and his followers. The idea of play as essentially egocentric and non-social is rejected (Vygotsky 1978). Instead, a strong intrinsic relationship between play, learning and development is assumed. Play — especially role play — is seen as the outstanding context of the young child's process of cultural learning. It is the medium where the child's way of dealing with the world is meeting cultural forms embodied in the actions of adults and more capable peers. As Vygotsky (1978, 103) once pointed out, 'the child moves forward essentially through play activity'. Play should be seen as a leading activity, that is, a driving force behind the child's cultural development.

Although in the Vygotskian point of view, there is no inherent contradiction between play and adult intervention, there are still a lot of problems to be solved as to the role of play in development, as to the role of peers in the development of play, and as to the integration of play and adult intervention, by all means when educational intentions are involved. Following Vygotsky, we can define play as a voluntary activity characterized by public rules and by (to some degree) a freedom of choice for the actors involved.[1] From this definition it can easily be seen that the more educational interventions define rules and actions externally, the more they restrict the degrees of freedom of the child, and the less this activity is play in the proper sense of the word. Strongly directing forms of instruction are

---

1. Consider for example Vygotsky's words: 'In one sense a child at play is free to determine his own actions. But in another sense this is an illusory freedom, for his actions are in fact subordinated to the meanings of things and he acts accordingly', (1978, 103).

a real threat for play activities of the child. An important question, then, obviously is: can we ever teach young children without impairing the quality of their play activities?

A variety of controversies remain as to the dynamic inter-relationships between playing, learning and development. We still need an adequate explanation of the role of play in development. We can agree with Vygotsky, writing: 'only a profound internal analysis makes it possible to determine play's course of change and its role in development' (Vygotsky 1978, 104). In this article I want to discuss the interrelationships of leading activities during school age, and I want to argue for a view on teaching within the context of play that promotes both the development of play, and supports the transition from play to learning activity. Actually, we are discussing the possibilities for developmental teaching of young children.

Play as a Context for Learning

Basically all learning is founded on a subject's actions. Hence, young children also learn a lot during their play activities. Most of the time this learning is contingent on the order of events during play, or depends on the structure of the play material. This learning is, as already pointed out and substantiated by the Dutch psychologist van Parreren, incidental and spontaneous (van Parreren 1988). According to van Parreren, in young children (until seven years old), this learning cannot be strictly planned, nor promoted by way of special learning tasks, because these children do not master the strategies of self-regulation and planning abilities. These occasional learning processes contribute mainly to the child's ability to participate in the play activity itself. They learn new words or rules that are functional in the play, or they master new abilities (like discriminating colours, identifying forms, or counting).

But there is yet another kind of learning within play activities. In his seminal study of human psychic development Leontiev (1981) already pointed out that every episode in the child's development is characterized by some kind of leading activity and a special relationship of that child to the world. An activity is called 'leading', because the child is especially eager to perform this activity, and above all because it contributes in a decisive way to the development of the child by promoting new actions and psychological processes that anticipate a new episode of development (Leontiev 1981, 485). In a leading activity new forms of actions and motivation are emerging. Consequentially, we can assume that play as a leading activity is also a context for the learning of these new qualities. As these learning processes actually run ahead, preparing new future activities, we can call them 'proleptic'.[2] By inference, the developmental potential of leading activities is essentially dependent on the occurrence of this kind of proleptic learning processes. The next question now is: what is the nature and the content of these learning processes, and can these learning processes be intentionally promoted without at the same time impairing the quality of play?

Leontiev was not very explicit in characterizing these kinds of learning processes. Neither was Elkonin in his elaboration of the theory of leading activities. Both descriptions suggest a strict successive order between play and systematic learning. A similar view seems to be adopted by many educational psychologists (like Davydov and Van Parreren) They did not give much attention to the issue of intentional promotion by a teacher of the proleptic forms of systematic learning within the context of play in early education. In a very interesting article Davydov (1995) recently outlined his view on developmental teaching in comparison with other approaches (e.g., Zankov, Bibler). Again he argued for an interpretation of developmental teaching as an educational system that stimulates the development of learning activity in pupils. However, he confines his analyses to processes within the developmental period of learning activity (with primary school children), thus suggesting that the potentials of this developmental period can be studied reliably, apart from the earlier play activities.

Without doubt, Davydov's investigations into these problems are very important. However, he gives no attention whatsoever to the problem of transition to this stage of learning activity. In our opinion, it is necessary to study how the transition to this stage of learning activity can (or perhaps even: should) be optimized in an earlier developmental stage, and how learning activity can be prepared in the educational activities of young children. This necessarily leads to the question of the potentials of developmental teaching in young children's play.

Another very interesting, encompassing view on developmental education from a longitudinal perspective was recently outlined by Rubtsov et al. (1994). They argued for a school curriculum with different stages, based on different kinds of communities (defined by typical teacher-pupil

---

2. As compared to the original, narrowly linguistic meaning of this term, I used this word here in a more generalized way, referring to any process bringing the future into the present. This term was not used by Leontiev himself!

relationships and characteristic activities). For the younger child (5-6 years) the authors proposed a 'Mythical school' (in which the children are engaged in, for instance, activities like dealing with perceptual qualities of objects, symbols and symbolic means of expression). This 'mythical school' is followed by a 'Master school' (7-9 years old) in which learning activity as meant by Davydov (including model making, abstract thinking with culturally developed symbol systems, theoretical generalization) is the fundamental activity. Eventually, this school is to be followed by a 'Laboratory School' and a 'Project school'.

The longitudinal perspective on the curriculum of Rubtsov et al. is a very interesting and thought provoking contribution to the discussion on developmental teaching. However, this system still turns out to be strictly linear (successive), with apparently separated compartments ('schools'). It does not give a satisfactory answer to the problems of transitions.

The Complexity of the Transition from Play to Learning Activity

The transition from play to learning activity still needs an adequate explanation. In his critical article Petrovsky (1987) already pointed out that there is no empirical basis for the thesis that young children should be exclusively engaged in play activity. He argued that the age characteristics of a child's activity are probably strongly related to the social situation of the child's development. Hence, the characteristics of young children's activity are also a matter of social choice. Considering the importance of the many-sided development of a child's personality, Petrovsky argued for a complex interpretation of the developmental process, stating that different activity forms (e.g., play, learning activity, social activity, work) should get a proper place in every stage of development.

I agree with Petrovsky that for pedagogical reasons we should choose a definition of the young child's activity as a complex of playing, learning, and social interaction. However, we stick to the assumption that play activity is fundamental for young children as a context for learning and development. Therefore we will maintain that play activity dominates in the early ages of the child, but it essentially integrates elements of learning activity and social interactive activity. One of the educational tasks, then, is to improve all of these activities in an appropriate way within the context of play. The developmental process during primary school age (say 4-14 years of age) should not be conceived of as a linear succession of play-learning activity- social activity, but rather as a process in which new activities are fostered by educators within the context of the child's actual life. New activities emerge out of prior activities and eventually may become independent new leading activities. This is in accordance with what Werner called the orthogenetic principle (see Werner & Kaplan 1963, 7ff). This provides for the psychological continuity in the developmental process of the child's personality. Vygotsky largely endorsed Werner's explanation of the orthogenetic principle (see Vygotsky 1983, 118).

In general, consecutive stages of development are related, basically, in two ways. The transition from play activity to learning activity in this complex interpretation of development, then, draws our attention to two different aspects in particular:

1) *Identification of precursive components.* Elements of the later learning activity must be traced, fostered and improved within the context of play; put in Vygotskian terminology, we can call these precursors the buds of future development, waiting to be roused by cultural inter-actions; by improving the development of these components the developmental potentials of play are maximally employed, and the future transition to genuine learning activity is prepared;

2) *Expansion of play activity into learning activity.* Hence, learning activity must be fostered as a new special form of play activity. As a new quality emerging from play activity, it can be argued that learning activity has to be conceived of as *a language game* in which negotiation about meanings in a community of learners is the basic strategy for the acquisition of knowledge and abilities (Carpay & van Oers 1993). However, in order to maintain the character of play, it is essential that children participate in this activity on a voluntary basis. Moreover, there must be some degree of freedom for the participants' choice and performance of actions. However, it is not purely free play: some social conventions with respect to the learning strategies must be observed as well. In this connection reference can be made for example to the promising investigations of Ellice Forman (Pittsburgh) into the Gricean conversational maxims as constituents of genuine learning activity (e.g., Forman 1992).

In this article I confine myself to an elaboration of the first mentioned issue. The first question that must be answered, then, is which elements of the child's play activity can be conceived of as precursive components of learning activity that can be evoked within play without impairing the quality of the young child's play, and that consequently might pave the way into learning activity?

On the basis of ample research literature, several important psychological qualities can be identified as emerging from play. These qualities contribute to laying a foundation for the full development of learning activity. For example (and more specifically), references can be made to the development of the *learning motive* (see Elkonin 1972; Hakkarainen 1985) or an *achievement motive* (Holodynski 1992), the development of *communication* (Lisina 1976; Lisina & Kapčelja 1987; Poddyakov & Michailenko 1987), including the conversational rules that have to be abided by in the process of negotiation of meaning (Forman).

In our own research we set up an argument for the importance of children's *semiotic activity* as an integral element of play that might be one important precursor of an essential element of the later learning activity (see van Oers 1994a), especially with regard to the development of literacy and numeracy (see van Oers 1996; 1999). We will turn to the issue of children's semiotic activity in the following section.

Main Characteristics of Children's Semiotic Activity

Studies of several researchers (Salmina 1988; Glotova 1990; Sapogova 1993) have supported the idea of children's semiotic activity. Our own research focused on semiotic activity of young children (aged 4 -7 years of age). As a working definition we conceive of semiotic activity as the cognitive activity of reflecting on the relationships between sign and meaning, or more particularly, *reflecting on the mutual relationship between the change of signs and the change of meanings*. Many studies of the early development of language show that children from a very early age are engaged in a problem solving activity of figuring out the meaning of words of their everyday language (see for example Bates 1979). Characteristically, children try to assimilate words with objects, events, or actions, and they experience how the meaning of words changes with alterations of the word form. Young children often even experiment in a playful but intentional way with word forms and meaning (see Bruner et al. 1976, 596-618).

Apparently, it is not only language that young children use in order to represent meaning. Also, children's drawings often have the intention to communicate (private) meanings (see van Oers 1994b; Athey 1990). Analyses of children's drawings and their conversations about their drawings reveal that children sometimes try to improve their drawings in order to make sure that these indeed communicate the meanings they have in their minds. Sometimes they change the drawings and make graphic or even verbal (both oral and written) additions to their drawings. These facts seem to suggest that the *form* of the sign (in this case: the drawing) is an important aspect in semiotic activity; adjusting the sign in order to improve its adequacy to convey an intended meaning seems to be an essential part of semiotic activity. However, until now most attention has been given to the *meaning component* of semiotic activity (for example, Wertsch 1987, 1990). Sinha quite appropriately argued for a 'theory of the materiality of representation' (1989, 65), pointing out that the adequacy of the sign form depends on socio-pragmatic conditions, like success in the expression of intentions and circulation of meaning. The educational implications of this is, however, greatly undervalued.

In our conception of semiotic activity both the modifications of the sign, and the modifications of the meanings, in order to improve their inter-dependency and psychological functioning, are essential constituents of semiotic activity. Specialization of this semiotic activity into different directions (with different objects and different bodies of conventions) leads to further developments in the domains of (e.g.,) literacy and numeracy (compare Munn 1994). This is the process of 'hierarchic differentiation' as elaborated by Werner & Kaplan (1963).

We suppose it is appropriate to say that some activities of the very young child have some of the characteristics of semiotic activity. During the early school years (Kindergarten), however, no systematic attempts are being made to improve the child's ability of meaning making (semiotic activity)

In our observational studies of young children in play, we witnessed several moments of semiotic activity in children, often fragmentary, incomplete, unsystematic, and unreflected. We have reason to assume that encouraging young children to take part in socially organized semiotic activity, assisting them in accomplishing that activity, and even improving this activity is one form of developmental teaching in early education. The opportunities for such teaching emerge easily during young children's play.

Assisting Children in Semiotic Activity Requirements for Early Developmental Teaching

Some Preliminary Remarks about Research Conditions

During the past eight years we have been able to collect evidence of young children's semiotic activity in a variety of cases of child play.[3] The teachers involved in our studies are acquainted with what we called developmental teaching. They participated in the play activities of children.

One of our basic methodological assumptions was that any educational setting is a cultural construction. When an educational setting is used as a research setting, it should be conceived of as a joint and consensual product of teachers and researchers/educationalists. However, the teachers may differ as to the extent they have appropriated the strategy of developmental teaching. The researcher/educationalist actively contributes to the classroom activities to the extent that is required by the abilities of the teacher. The researcher sometimes acts as an assistant of the teacher in order to construct an optimal educational situation (van Oers, et al. 1996).

In all the cases referred to here, we worked from the above mentioned assumptions. Children were playing together in small groups within a context that was suggested and partially organized by the teacher. The children participated voluntarily in this activity setting and they were allowed to collaboratively arrange the situation further according to their own choice. In all the cases the teacher somehow participated in the activity, although the role she took could vary from one situation (or moment) to the other. The nature of the activity setting varied, however, in the cases discussed here. In one situation children (of about 5 years old) were playing in small groups (2 or 3 children) with a *toy train set*; after they had constructed a railway, the children were invited to make a drawing of their railway track. In another situation different groups of children (4 to 7 years old) were engaged in a social role play in the context of a shoe shop established in one area of the school; within the course of this play

---

3. I am very grateful to my colleague Bea Pompert for her comments on these cases and for reporting to me the case of constructive activity that she described and documented in great detail; moreover I would like to express my gratefulness to colleagues who were willing to discuss these cases with me, as well as providing help in collecting the data: Frea Janssen-Vos, Peter Maaskant, Trudy Pas, Trudy Schiferli, Jenny Vlamink.

different problems arose that encouraged the children to invent symbolic representations or notational systems. In a third situation three boys (ages ranging from 4½ to 6) were involved in a constructive activity (building a 'nintendo'-racetrack with blocks and toy cars); again the boys were invited to draw their track as precise as possible so that it could be rebuilt some other time.

The cases referred to are unrelated; they took place at different schools at different times. Methodologically, all studies conform to the case study strategies, as elaborated by Yin (1994).

Basic Requirements for the Promotion of Semiotic Activity

In all these cases a representional activity regarding some aspects of the activity setting was somehow introduced as a part of the shared activity. The teacher encouraged and (when necessary) assisted the children in reflecting on the relationship between their representations (sign) and meaning. Close analysis of the three cases revealed a few communalities that seem to shed light on what might be necessary conditions for accomplishing shared semiotic activity with children in the context of their play activity. Two of them will be discussed here: Functional embeddedness and including a semiotician's role in shared activity.

Functional embeddedness

In order to be acceptable for the children the semiotic activity must be embedded in their play activity in a functional and meaningful way. In the 'train play' the children were initially asked to make a diagram of their railway track, in order to be able to rebuild the track at a later moment. The children however, to a large extent tended to rely on their private memories and, consequently, were not motivated to make a very precise drawing. This first attempt for creating a starting point for a shared semiotic activity was not very successful. For the children, the drawing of the diagram was not meaningfully integrated in their play. When we suggested another group of children (that played with the same train set) to make a drawing of their railway for children at another school (who wanted to know what kind of interesting tracks could be made), then the children started drawing diagrams of their railway tracks and were prepared to reflect on the adequacy of the drawing as to the real track; the drawings were really sent to another school where children also got deeply involved in interpreting the drawings and what they could mean (in terms of possible railway tracks). The communicative goal could easily be assimilated in the play activity. According to the teachers, this actually added a new dimension to the railway play for the children. This made reflection on the interrelationship between drawing and the actual situation a functional and meaningful activity, integrated in play. No signs whatsoever were found, that signalled disturbance of the children's play (see van Oers 1994a).

In the constructive play activity (Pompert 1995) the boys made a racetrack with multifunctional rectangular and oblique blocks and chocks. The semiotic activity was initiated within this constructive activity by encouraging the boys to draw their track in order to 'save' it, and to be able to rebuild it at a later moment (or have it rebuild by other kids). Remarkably, these boys did not want to rely on their memory (in contrast to the children in the train play). They found their track very exciting and wanted to be certain that it could be rebuilt exactly as it was (see Fig. 13.1). We should realize, however, that the number of possible outcomes when the children have to rebuild the race-track with these types of blocks, is much bigger than in the case of the railway track (where there are far less variations). It is clear then that precise drawing is a much safer strategy than just to rely on your memory. Drawing in this case was a sensible thing to do. So drawing was indeed functional for the kind of play the children were engaged in.

The children made drawings of the racetrack, each choosing his own perspective. The teacher also made a few photographs of the track. In a conversation with the teacher the boys gave comments on their drawings indicating what it meant. With additional symbols (figures, arrows) the teacher indicated on the drawing where to start and how to proceed (see Fig. 13.2).

After 10 days the teacher showed the boys the drawings again in order to find out how they would 'read' them, and see if they could rebuild the racetrack on the basis of the various drawings. Again it was clear that the boys could see this as a meaningful activity, related to the play in which they wanted to be involved. An intensive reflection occurred on the interrelationship between situation and possible situated actions on the one hand, and the drawing on the other. This switching between sign and meaning and vice versa, as well as reflecting on the constraining force from the one (sign) onto the other (meaning) is a basic form of semiotic activity.

Fig. 13.1. Drawing by a boy representing the collaboratively constructed race-track.

Fig. 13.2. Boys building a race-track.

Again the meaningful embeddedness of this semiotic activity in the play activity turned out to be a necessary condition for the semiotic activity totake place (even after 10 days).

In the shoe-shop role play we found similar events. When the children had to tally which kind of shoes and how many were in stock, they had to invent notations for different classes of shoes, as well as for the amount of shoes. By drawing the different piles of sorted out shoeboxes (daddy shoes, mama shoes, children shoes) they kind of reinvented histograms. The reflection on the relationship between these drawings and reality was obviously supported by the embeddedness in the shoe-shop role play.

Including a Semiotician's Role in the Shared Activity

Recent descriptions of the sociocultural approach to the development of human cognition emphasize the distributed character of human knowledge and ability. When participating in a sociocultural activity, actors always make use of cultural resources that are embodied in other persons or mediational means. Actually, their personal knowledge and abilities essentially depend on assistance by external cultural resources (see Salomon 1993). Depending on the situational circumstances and the participants, the precise organization of the activity (i.e., the distribution of the resources over participants and means) may be different (see, for example, Cole & Engeström 1993).

From a developmental perspective this is an important idea: if we want to promote the development of the semiotic function in the young child, we will have to take care that this function is somehow represented in a sociocultural activity. As the child cannot yet perform this semiotic activity (independently), someone participating in the activity must take care of the semiotic aspects of that activity. To put it more straightforward: in the cast of the role play activity there must be someone with expertise at semiotic activity who plays the role of a participating semiotician.

This actor is especially in charge of performing publicly the actions related to the semiotic activity, and of trying to get the children involved in this new activity. So if we want the semiotic function to emerge from the shared activity, someone within the activity setting should be the public performer of this role and thus demonstrate the actions in which semiotic activity can be embodied. One of the tasks of the public performer of such a role is to explicitly demonstrate the structure of the semiotic actions.[4] In line with this kind of reasoning, we assume that the public performance of the semiotic activity by the teacher or more capable peer within the play activity will be one of the favourable conditions for the promotion of the development semiotic activity in young children. By encouraging the children to get involved in this activity, we put them in the position to adopt the role of 'legitimate peripheral participant' (to use an expression of Lave & Wenger 1991). By helping children to improve their ability of performing this semiotic activity, we might gradually initiate them in a culturally developed form of learning activity (academic learning; scientific thinking).

In the three studies mentioned above, the explicit and public reflection on the interrelationship between representations and situation, and above all, on the mutual dependence of changes in representation and changes in situation, was an important part of the play activities. In all these cases the teacher (or sometimes an experienced child) questioned the relation between representation (drawing, diagram, symbol) and the situation to be represented. In the case of the Nintendo racetrack, the teacher queried the meaning of the drawings, and tried to encourage the kids to improve the 'readability' of the drawings at a later moment. Constantly checking the drawing against reality and vice versa, actually drew the children into a form of intense semiotic activity. By her questioning, suggesting considerations, problems and answers, the teacher was an important motor and model for the shared semiotic activity. In the initial situation (when the kids were making drawings of the race-track) the teacher had made photographs of the track. These pictures were used as checking aids ten days later, when they tried to rebuild the track with the help of the drawings. Again it was the teacher who took the lead in the semiotic activity. By questioning, and suggesting possibilities she demonstrated this kind of semiotic reasoning about representations and situations. By reflecting together on the drawings/pictures and using them as mediational means for the reconstruction of the track, the teacher and the pupils together came to the conclusion that the drawings and pictures still did not unambiguously represent the track. It turned out, that some questions about details of the first construction had to be left open.

---

4. In his famous study on the possibility of boosting children's intelligence level, Selz (1935) already pointed out the cognitive importance of such action-demonstrating procedures (which he then called 'Sichtbarmachung der Verhaltensweisen').

A similar story could be told about the teachers in railway play (see van Oers 1994a). The teacher was constantly asking about the adequacy of the representation: 'Did you see that curve in your track?' 'Where is it in your drawing?' Or: 'Do you really have to draw all those sleepers in order to be able to rebuild the track?' Or: 'This thing on the drawing, what could it be?' Again the teachers performed the semiotic activity concerning the relation between diagram and situation in an openly and explicit way. By doing so, they got the children involved in semiotic activity, that they could not do independently (or wouldn't have thought of doing on their own).

Many instances of the teacher in the semiotician's role were also found in the shoe shop play (compare van Oers 1996). At one moment during their play, the children encountered the problem of how to mark shoe-boxes in order to be able to know immediately what was inside. The conversation went as follows (T=teacher; P=pupil):

T: (...) 'Maybe it is a good idea to make something for
   the outside of the box so that you can recognize what's
   inside ?'
P: 'Yes, I know!' (one pupil starts looking for a pencil or
   something to write with), 'I know!'
T: 'Tell me what you are looking for'
P: 'We are gonna put letters on them'
T: 'Which letters?'

The teacher suggests a possible solution, which implies finding out a notational system. However, she also indicates that letters alone will not be helpful. We have to find out which letters are functional for solving the problem. The teacher then also suggests:

T: 'Maybe we can make a drawing of the shoe in the box,
   to be sure we recognize them'
P's. Start making labels, to stick them on the boxes
T: (asking children) 'Which shoe are you drawing?'
   'And you?'
P: One pupil shows his sticker with a drawing of a shoe on it
   'Look, miss, this is for that shoe'
T: 'Ah, you also put letters on it? Which shoe does it
   match to?'
P: Roy shows a sticker he made
T: 'What did you write on it?'

P: ??
T: 'You cannot read it yourself? Do you think that you
     can find again which shoe is in which box? (Teacher again
     prompting for certainty!)
P: 'Yes'
T: 'Well, then stick it onto your box'

By her questioning the teacher shows the relevant semiotic actions and she suggests that not just any symbol would do. The idea of putting letters on the label is adopted by other children, but the teacher is constantly asking about the meaning of the letters, and whether the letters chosen will be adequate as an indication of the kind of shoe in the box.

The pupils are very busy making stickers and show them to the teacher. Some children show the following labels:

R D T I   or   R A I D

P's: 'What does it say, miss?'
T: 'Raid'   (T. reads: [raid])

Then one child comes and shows her a label with the letters MAAR.

T: 'It says 'Maar'
P: (repeats) 'Mmmaar ...these are mmmama-shoes'
T: 'What a good idea of you to put an 'M' on it for mama-
     shoes! Do you think we could do that for all the mama-shoes?'
     'Do you think you could do that too (to another pupil)?'
P: 'No'
T: 'Well, if you cannot write the letter, you may stamp it'
     (teachers offers a box with stamp materials)

Then the children started putting 'M' on the boxes for mama-shoes, 'P' for papa-shoes, and 'K' for children shoes. Now, the teacher suggests that they can put the marked shoe-boxes in piles (one for mama-shoes, one for papa-shoes, one for children-shoes). And a few moments later she suggests whether it would be possible to draw the piles precisely, so that we can read from this drawing how many shoes of each kind they have in stock. The results are represented as a kind of histogram of the amounts of shoe boxes. By counting the real piles and the drawn boxes the children made a precise representation of the piles of boxes. The children have been busy reflecting on the notations on the boxes, as well as on the adequacy of the histogram-like drawings for the representation of classified quantities.

By asking all these questions about notations (representations, diagrams, symbols) the teacher performed the role of the semiotician within the context of the children's play. As this embedded activity was a functional part of the role play, the children were eager to get involved in this semiotic activity. The starting point for learning about semiotic activity was laid.

Conclusion

On a theoretical basis we assumed that play as a leading activity might entail forms of semiotic activity that can be seen as precursors of the learning activity in a later developmental stage. When semiotic actions occur, these might be employed as opportunities to assist children in improving their ability for semiotic activity. These *teaching opportunities for the promotion and development of semiotic activity* are considered to be crucial for developmental teaching in early education. Until now, however, we only focused on semiotic activity itself (its dynamic qualities, its conditions). Longitudinal studies, unequivocally showing the developmental outcomes on the long run are still to be waited for.

However, in order to be able to teach semiotic activity meaningfully within the context of play, we should, first of all, be able to promote the relevant actions meaningfully within children's play activity. In detailed analyses of a few case studies of children's role play, we found that children can be involved in semiotic activity without impairing the quality of their play (see van Oers 1994a; 1996). Moreover, by comparing three unrelated case studies we could highlight some communalities as to the conditions for the occurrence of meaningful semiotic activity within play. The *functionality* of semiotic activity in the play activity of the children turned out to be one important factor. This functionality can be related to the play itself (and be related to the child's wish to improve the play, or raise the attractivity of the play). Or it could be related to the child's wish to communicate with other people about the play.

Moreover, it turned out that there is another very important condition which is that the structure of the semiotic activity is demonstrated by a participating teacher or more capable peer. Public performance of semiotic activity related to the play not only shows the structure of the actions to be performed (which is a basis for any learning/teaching process), but also gets the children involved in this new activity. The cast of the play activity must include the role of *a participating semiotician*. Recently, research is indeed beginning to actually produce evidence of the importance of negotiation and reflection with the help of an expert on the development of children's drawing (Cox, et al. 1994).

Of course there are more conditions that influence the appearance and optimal development of semiotic activity in young children. In all the cases mentioned above, the teachers recognized the importance of early semiotic activity and were able to discover lots of opportunities to show some of the semiotic actions and get the children involved in meaningful play-related semiotic activity. We expect that teacher ability is another basic condition for the promotion of semiotic activity during play. Further research into the characteristics of teacher's expectations about children, as well as their views on knowledge, ability, schooling, and development with respect to young children will be needed in the near future. Besides this, a further psychological analysis of the concept of semiotic activity is needed, as well as further detailed demonstrations of the dynamical factors that influence the promotion and further development of semiotic activity during play. Especially studies of young children's ability to improve the structure of symbols (diagrams, notations) in order to convey intended meaning are badly needed.

References

Athey, C. (1990). *Extending thought in young children. A parent-teacher partnership.* London: P. Chapman.

Bates, E., Benigni, L., Bretherton, I., Camaioni, L. & Volterra, V. (1979). *The emergence of symbols, cognition and communication in infancy.* New York: Academic Press.

Bruner J.S., Jolly, A. & Sylva, K. (eds.), (1976). *Play. Its role in development and evolution.* Harmondsworth: Penguin.

Carpay, J.A.M. & van Oers, B. (1993). Didakticheskie modeli i problema obuchajushchej diskussii. [Models for learning and the problem of classroom discourse.] *Voprosy Psichologii* 4, 20-26.

Cole, M. & Engeström, Y. (1993). A cultural-historical approach to distributed cognition. In Salomon, G. (ed.), *Distributed cognitions. Psychological and educational considerations.* Cambridge: Cambridge University Press, 1-46.

Cox, M.V., Eames, K. & Cook, G. (1994). The teaching of drawing in the infants school: An evaluation of the 'negotiated drawing' approach. *International Journal of Early Years Education* 2(3), 68-84.

Davydov, V.V. (1995). O ponjatii razvivajuščego obučenija [On the concept of developmental teaching]. *Pedagogika* 1, 29-39.

Elkonin, D.B. (1972). Toward the problem of stages in the mental development of the child. *Soviet Psychology* 10, 225-51.

Elkonin, D.B. (1980). *Psychologie des Spiels* [The psychology of play]. Berlin: Volk und Wissen.

Forman, E.A. (1992). Discourse, intersubjectivity and the development of peer collaboration: A Vygotskian approach. In L.T. Winegar & J. Valsiner (eds.), *Children's development within social contexts: Metatheoretical, theoretical and methodological issues*, vol. 1. Hillsdale, N.J.: Erlbaum, 143-59.

Glotova, G.A. (1990). *Čelovek i znak. Semiotiko-psichologičeskie aspekty ontogeneza čeloveka.* [Man and sign. Semiotic-psychological aspects of human ontogenesis]. Sverdlovsk: University of the Urals Press.

Hakkarainen, P. (1985). Learning motivation and instructional intervention. In E. Bol, J. Haenen & M.A.D. Wolters (eds.), *Education for cognitive development.* Den Haag: SVO.

Holodynski, M. (1992). *Leistungstätigkeit und soziale Interaktion. Ein tätigkeitstheoretisches Modell zur Entstehung der Leistungsmotivation* [Performance activity and social interaction. An activity theoretical model of performance motivation]. Heidelberg: Asanger Verlag.

Lave, J. & Wenger, E. (1991). *Situated learning. Legitimate peripheral participation.* Cambridge: Cambridge University Press.

Leontiev, A.N. (1981). *Problemy razvitija psichiki (4-e izd.)* [Problems of psychological development). Moscow: Moscow University Press.

Lisina, M.I. (1978). The development of interaction in the first seven years of life. In W.W. Hartup, I.M. Ahammer & H.L. Pick (eds.), *Review of child development research*. Chicago: University of Chicago Press, 133-74.

Lisina, M.I. & Kapchelja, G.I. (1987). *Obščenie so vzroslymi i psichologicheskaja podgotovka detej k škole* [Communication with adults and the preparation of children for school]. Kishinev: Stinica.

Munn, P. (1994). The early development of literacy and numeracy skills. *European Early Childhood Education Research Journal* 2(1), 5-18.

van Oers, B. (1994a). Semiotic activity of young children in play: The construction and use of schematic representations. *European Early Childhood Education Journal* 2(1), 19-33.

van Oers, B. (1994b). On the narrative nature of young children's iconic representations: Some evidence and implications. Paper presented at the International Conference of 'L.S. Vygotsky and the Contemporary Human Sciences'. Moscow, September 5-8, 1994.

van Oers, B. (1996). Are you sure? Stimulating mathematical thinking during young children's play. *European Early Childhood Education Journal* 4(1), 71- 88.

van Oers, B. (1999). The appropriation of mathematical symbols. A psycho-semiotic approach to mathematics learning. In P. Cobb, K. Gravemeijer & E. Yackel (eds.), *Symbolizing, mathematizing, communicating*. Mahwah, N.J.: Erlbaum.

van Oers, B., Janssen-Vos, F., Pompert, B. & Schiferli, T. (1996). La pédagogie: une activité conjointe [Pedagogy: A joint activity] In S. Rayna, M. Delau & F. Laevers (eds.), *Quels objectifs pédagogiques pour l'education préscolaire?* Paris: Nathan.

Oerter, R. (1993). *Psychologie des Spiels. Ein handlungstheoretische Ansatz* [The psychology of play. An activity oriented approach]. Munich: Quintessenz.

Parreren, C.F. van (1988). *Ontwikkelend Onderwijs* [Developmental education]. Amersfoort: Acco.

Petrovsky, A.V. (1987). Razvitie lichnosti i problema veduščhej dejatel'nosti. [Personality development and the problem of leading activity.] *Voprosy Psichologii* 1, 15-26.

Piaget, J. (1962). *Play, dreams and imitation in childhood*. New York: Norton.

Poddyakov, N.N. & Michailenko, N. Y. (1987). *Problemy doškol'noj igry: Psicho-logo-pedagogičeskij aspekt* [Problems of pre-school play: psychological-educational aspects]. Moscow: Pedagogika.

Pompert, B. (1995). De Nintendo-crossbaan, de Nintendo hindernisbaan, de lavacrossbaan [The Nintendo racetrack, the Nintendo obstacle course, the Lavaracetrack]. Hogeschool Alkmaar: Internal report.

Rubtsov, V.V., Margolis, A.A. & Guruapov, V.A. (1994). Kul'turno-historicheskij tip školy. [A school on a cultural-historical basis.] *Voprosy Psichologii* 5, 100-10.

Salmina, N.G. (1988). *Znak i simvol v obuchenii* [Sign and symbol in education]. Moscow: Moscow University Press.

Salomon, G. (ed.), (1993). *Distributed cognitions. Psychological and educational considerations*. Cambridge: Cambridge University Press.

Sapogova, E.E. (1993). *Rebënok i znak* [Child and sign]. Tula: Priokskoe Kn. Izdvo.

Selz, O. (1935). Versuche zur Hebung des Intelligenzniveaus. *Zeitschrift für Psychologie* 134, 236-301.

Sinha, Chr. (1989). *Language and representation. A socio-naturalistic approach to human development*. London: Harvester-Wheatsheaf.

Vygotsky, L.S. (1978). *Mind in society*. Cambridge, Mass.: Harvard University Press.

Vygotsky, L.S. (1983). Istorija razvitija vysšich psichicheskich funcij. [History of the development of the higher psychological functions.] *Sobranie Sochinenij* 3. Moscow: Pedagogika.

Werner, H. & Kaplan, B. (1963). *Symbol Formation. An Organismic-Developmental Approach to Language and the Expression of Thought*. New York: Wiley.
Yin, R.K. (1994). *Case study research: design and methods*. London: Sage.

14 Preconditions for Developmental Learning Activity at Pre-School Age

Elena E. Kravtsova

In psychology late pre-school age is known as a transitive and crucial period. Vygotsky wrote about a new intellectual formation that typically arises at the crucial age of seven, 'the generalization of experience' or 'intellectualization of temporary insanity'. A sign of this 'new formation' can be seen in the child's action ability which changes from behaviour caused directly by the perceived situation to actions depending on some social rules and demands. After this formation has occurred, the child displays that he both understands the meaning of the demands, as well as having a generalized positive emotional attitude towards them, and this shows that a new intrinsic affective and motivational determinant of his activity has arisen.

When defining and researching the sources of psychical development, we build on the famous statement by Marx that 'the essence of the person is not abstract, being an inherent quality of a separate individual. In its existence it is the totality of all social relations'. Arsenyev cites this basic statement by Marx, 'from this point of view history can be considered as the development of communication forms'. This means that both the history of psychical development and a person's ontogenetic development can be represented as change in communication forms. The change of basic activities in ontogenesis is thus interpreted and considered as the change of communication forms between the child and his environment.

It must be noted that it was Marxist philosophy that defined the place of communication in the person's psychical development. As our basic conception, which serves as our working hypothesis, we use Marx's conception that 'an individual is a social being', and that 'the development of the individual is caused by the other individuals with whom he/she directly or indirectly communicates'.

In Russian and Soviet psychology the conception that placed communication as the key in the child's psychical development was formulated and worked out by Vygotsky, who stressed that 'the psychological charac-

Investigations of Communication between Child and Adult

Defining the purpose of the given study we base ourselves on the general conception in Soviet psychology concerning the role of communication in a child's development. We suppose that there must arise forms of communication meeting the specific requirements and conditions of a new kind of educational activity, so that children become successful in school.

To find out about the special features inherent in the 'children-adult' form of communication we have observed the behaviour of pre-school children and of junior school children during lessons at school, as well as conducted a series of experiments.

The Forbidden Words Method

This method was based on the well-known Forfeits game, which was quite similar to that used by Leontiev and Vygotsky when they studied free attention. The child had to answer the questions avoiding 'the forbidden words' — 'yes', 'no', 'not', 'white' and 'black'. But the questions were asked in a manner that made it difficult to avoid them (e.g., 'Do you like ice-cream?' or 'What is the colour of the doctor's coat?'). The experiments were aimed at finding out the boundaries within which the child could avoid acting on impulse, but could fulfil the task given by the adult and behave in accordance with the special terms necessary to accomplish the task (not to utter the forbidden words, etc.).

The results of the experiments revealed that by the end of pre-school age a definite number of children developed a new form of relationship with the adults. We called it a context free communication. Children of this age can understand the 'dual' position of adults, the special part they take in the educational, artificially created, experimental situation, and they thus base their actions and answers on the specific terms of the task, but not on the direct meaning of the questions asked.

We think that the difficulties which children unprepared or 'underprepared' for school education often face, and of which psychologists are fully aware, are caused by undeveloped communication skills, i.e., that context free communication with the adults is still not formed.

Who Is Bigger? And The Pencils Method

These methods were worked out by us. 'Who is bigger?' consisted of the following pattern suggested to children:

'A hare is bigger than a wolf. A wolf is bigger than a bear. Who is bigger — a hare or a bear?'

The 'Pencils' method was a modified version of one used by Piaget. Two pencils of different lengths — so that one pencil looked a bit longer — were shown to a child who was asked to say which of the pencils was the longest.

To fulfil the given tasks the child has to acquire the results through communication with adults; reacting not on the directly perceived circumstances but using the mental skills which he/she has already practiced in social relations.

The results of these experiments display the difficulties the child faces, like those he faces when confronting educational problems, where the new form of communication with adults has not yet arisen.

With the data received through using the method of 'The forbidden words', and having compared the data from school teachers and psychologists regarding the extent to which children taking part in the experiment were prepared for school education, we found the following: those children who were not psychically ready to study at school did not form a new, context free type of communication.

Investigations of Communication between Children

We investigated various forms of communication activities including cooperation of children with each other, with the focus on the child's psychic ability to study at school. This led us to conduct another experiment aimed at finding out the most general features and forms of communication and collaboration between children.

The Labyrinth Method

There was a complicated labyrinth, made on a board of 60 x 70 cm. Two garages of different colours were diagonally placed at the corners, with four toy cars inside each garage. The colours of the cars were the same as the colours of the garages. Before the game started, the cars were put into the wrong garages. Two children were asked to 'drive' the cars through the labyrinth so that every car would come to the right coloured garage. The rules of the game were the following: one child could not 'drive' more than one car; the cars could run only along the roads of the labyrinth; no child could touch the cars of the partner with his hands.

It must be noted, that the task could only be fulfilled if the children were able to coordinate their actions with each other, otherwise the actions of one partner would hinder the actions of the other, so the aim would not be achieved.

Results: On the basis of the results received from the experiment we found six levels of collaborations between the children. The first level was the lowest in the social hierarchy.

First: Children do not 'see' the partner, and pay no attention to him or his activity.

Second: The partner is a model whose actions are 'blindly' imitated.

Third: Real collaboration arises at last, but the nature of it is merely situational.

Fourth: Children perceive the situation as part of the common task. This level can be called 'competitive-cooperative', as the children co-ordinated their activity with the partner and at the same time they tried to win in the game.

Fifth: Real collaboration is gained within the framework of the situation of the common task.

Sixth: Children first discuss the following actions with the partner, work out a common plan for their activity and fulfil it.

Conclusion

We studied the development of the above levels of communication skills, taking into consideration the statement by Vygotsky about a new crucial formation at the age of seven, and came to the conclusion that only at the fourth level could we find data similar to the peculiar features of the context free communication form which arises between the child and the adult. Only at the competitive-cooperative level could the ability be found to perceive consciously and bear in mind the task and its demands for the duration of the situation of communication between children.

We concluded, therefore, that the deciding factor as to whether the child is ready to study at school, or not, was the competitive-cooperative form of communication between children, alongside the context free form of communication between the child and the adult.

Preparing Children Psychologically for School Education

The next stage of our study was given to the importance of the competitive-cooperative form of communication in preparing children psychologically for school education. The first step we made in this direction was the research with the 'Labyrinth' method.

The Labyrinth Method

We invited pupils from junior forms and divided them into two groups — a well-prepared group and an unprepared group. The results confirmed our idea, i.e., well-prepared children displayed a high level of communication skills (beginning with the fourth one), and as for the unprepared group, they were at the lowest level of collaboration with other children.

It must be noted, that almost all the children participating in the experiment had attended nursery school and were supposed to have acquired good communication skills. But, as the experiment shows, the presence of other children and even being in their company all day long, was not enough for evoking high level communication skills.

The results of the experiment showed a connection between the competitive-cooperative form of communication and the question of the psychical ability of the child to study at school. But still unknown is the nature of this connection and what the psychological mechanism is of the dependence of communication between children on their preparedness for school education. The works by Menchinskaya (1971), Samokhvalova (1952), Volokitina (1949), as well as research works by Bertsfai (1966) and Venger (1970), despite different approaches to the problem, contain one common result: that children who are having difficulties in school education can rarely find a general way of solving problems.

Thus, we have reasons to suppose that the competitive-cooperative form of communication between children, which arises at the late pre-school age, is an important ability which could form a position that would be closely linked with the ability to perceive and acquire general ways of problem solving.

The idea was confirmed by the following experiment conducted by us with the use of two methods called 'Three Chessmen' and 'Indirect Problems'.

Three Chessmen and Indirect Problems

The child was given a chessboard, a strip of coloured paper and three chessmen. He was asked to place the chessmen on the board in such a way as to make it impossible for the experimenter to place the strip of paper on any three chess squares in a rank and file row, or diagonally.

It must be noted that children could only manage to fulfil the task if, from the very beginning, they took into consideration both their own position and that of the experimenter who checked the correctness of the placed chessmen by putting the coloured paper on the chessboard. Thus, the method aimed at finding out the ability of children to actualize the dual position which would allow them to bear in mind the possible results of their actions, as well as the actions of the partner, and constantly co-ordinate their behaviour with them.

Results: According to the results, the children were divided into three groups. The children of the first group could not cope with the task. Their behaviour displayed their inability to take into account the position of the experimenter who checked the correctness of their actions. The children of the second group also failed to fulfil the task, but they tried to take into account the position of the experimenter. The children of the third group could find the solution very quickly. From the very beginning of the game, they took into consideration the position of the experimenter.

The comparison of the data received from using the 'Labyrinth' and 'Three Chessmen' methods confirmed our idea. Most of the children who successfully fulfilled the chessmen task, and placed by us into group 3, were, according to the 'Labyrinth' method, at least at the fourth level of communication skills development (competitive-cooperative). As for the children who failed to fulfil the task, they displayed the third or lower level of communication skills between children.

Indirect Problems Method

To avoid the artificial nature of the tasks used by us and the vague character of the connection between the way they are to be decided and general ways of solving traditional school problems, we asked the same children to fulfil the tasks called 'Indirect Problems'. The contents of the problems were the following:

1) There were birds sitting on a tree. Two more birds joined them, so there appeared to be 5 birds after that. How many birds were sitting on the tree at first?

2) There were some trees growing in the school yard. When 3 trees were dug up, there were 4 trees left. How many trees were there in the yard at first?

3) A boy had sweets. When he was given three more sweets, he had 6 in all. How many sweets did the boy have at first?

The results: The mistakes the children made solving the problems and the results of the experiment allowed us to divide the children into 3 groups. Children of the first group could not cope with the task. They tried to solve the indirect problems as if they were direct ones. Children of the second group failed to fulfil the task as well (some of them solved one problem). But they understood that the given problems were unusual and should have been solved in some other way. Children of the third group easily solved the problems.

The results received after conducting experiments with 'Indirect Problems' and the results of using the 'Three Chessmen' and the 'Labyrinth' methods, confirmed our idea that a child's ability to acquire the general ways of solving problems was dependent on a competitive-cooperative form of communication between children.

Thus, we confirmed by experiment that the difficulties which children have in solving indirect problems (and of which psychologists are aware), are closely connected with the ability of a child to find a general way of solving a problem, or, in other words, with the occurrence of a new type of activity which depends on the form of communication between children.

Discussion

The new form of communication between children, which arises at the end of the pre-school age, has a double meaning for successful education at school. First, the competitive-cooperative form of communication when arisen, helps the child to acquire communication forms and collaboration skills, necessary for cooperative educational activity at school. Second, the form of communication between children which we researched is a necessary term to acquire general forms of activity by children and is very important psychologically in preparing children for study at school.

We have researched two components necessary to make children ready for school education — communication with adults and with other children. But they do not solve the whole problem. They create, as Vygotsky said, 'a social situation of development', which helps the child to develop and change himself. Changes going on in the sphere of relationships with other people cannot but change the attitude of the child towards himself. So, the next problem we have to solve is to study the change of the child's attitude towards himself which takes place on the boundary of two periods: late pre-school age and junior school age.

Change in the Child's Attitude to Him or Herself

Psychologists, having studied the attitude of pre-school age children towards themselves, noticed that their self appraisal is usually too high. Very few attempts are made by children of late pre-school age to look at themselves in an adequate way so as to forecast an evaluation of their own abilities (before the beginning of some activity) (Sterkina 1977; Tagieva 1983).

The general self appraisal of a pre-school child is usually too high and does not depend on circumstances. (Sterkina 1977; Slutsky 1986; Kucherova 1987).

At late pre-school age many children begin to evaluate themselves in an adequate way with regard to some particular kind of activity. (Tagieva 1983; Slutsky 1986). But, as Basina remarks:

There exist distinctions, which are a matter of principle, between the ability to evaluate themselves in an adequate way, being engaged in some definite form of activity, when exterior circumstances provoke the self-evaluation, and the ability to comprehend themselves on their own, spontaneously, on the whole. (Basina, Elkonin & Venger 1988, 128)

Vygotsky wrote about self appraisal of children at pre-school age:

The child of pre-school age loves himself, but there is no self esteem as a generalized attitude towards himself, which is the same in different situations, and there is, as well, no self esteem and there is no generalized attitude towards his environment and comprehension of self-importance. Thus, by the age of seven there arises a series of complicated formations... . (1983, vol. 4, 380)

But one should not think that the child does not comprehend himself and does not evaluate himself until the crucial age of seven. Self comprehension, though, is of a non-differential, general character: 'I am the strong-est', 'I am the most clever', etc. (Slutsky 1986; Kucherova 1987; Mukhina 1986).

Real self appraisal, i.e., a constant, stable, non-dependent on the situation, attitude towards himself appears, as Vygotsky believes, at the crucial age of seven. But according to the latest data received by conducting experiments, self appraisal of pre-school children does not always depend on circumstances and is constant. Kucherova writes:

Data received when researching law-governed nature of self appraisal develop-ment as the indicator of self-comprehension development at the pre-school age correspond with the fact that the self appraisal of a child at the pre-school age is too high, 'non-objective' and resistible to exterior influence (1987, 115).

The same results were received by other researches. (Lisina 1986; Slutsky 1986).

The above information allows us to propose a series of questions: What goes on with the self appraisal of children at the crucial age of seven? What kind of psychological laws and mechanisms are the changes based on? What are their links with the structure of learning activity? What kind of activity do these psychological mechanisms belong to?

Experimental study of self appraisal between the late pre-school and junior school ages shows that it is the period when the child's qualitative attitude towards himself changes. The self appraisal of a child under school age is integrated, i.e., the child can understand the difference between *his self* as the subject of activity and *the self* as a personality, but the self appraisal of junior school children is more objective, grounded, reflective, differentiated.

Slutsky found that 3-5 year-old children have a 'non-specific' reaction to the estimation given by adults, it means that their self appraisal does not change if they are reproved or if their behaviour is disapproved. The reaction of 6 to 7 year-olds, can be called specific, and this is shown in the fact that success raises their self appraisal, but failure lowers it.

Though we have lots of data based on experiments, some topics are still unknown for us; one of them is the genesis and the dynamics of the changes in the child's attitude towards himself during the pre-school period.

The Method of Self Appraisal

We began the experimental study of the question by using both an authentic and modified indicator constructed by Dembo-Rubinstein. Children attending junior and preparatory forms of nursery school were given pictures of stairs, flying balloons, aeroplanes flying at different heights. On the high-flying balloons and aeroplanes, there were places for the 'cleverest', 'strongest', 'kindest' children. On the low-flying balloons and aeroplanes there were places for the 'most silly', 'weakest', 'most unkind'. It was suggested that the children should place themselves on one of the spots.

Results: Children were divided into three groups. Children of the *first group* placed themselves on the highest 'step' as soon as the adult had time to explain them the task. Children of the *second group* were in doubt and felt shy, but then chose the highest place for themselves. Sometimes they said: 'Well, maybe Vova is stronger than me, he defeated me yesterday... But, all the same, I'm also the strongest.' Children included in the *third group*, thought about it for a long time, murmured something, and wanted to have the opinion of Mum or a nursery-school teacher. In the end they chose quite a high position for themselves, but not the highest one.

Table 14.1 allocates children taking part in the experiment according to the character of the task.

Groups according to the character of the task being fulfilled

Nursery school group	First	Second	Third
Medium form	29	1	0
Late form	22	6	2
Preparatory Form	16	10	4

Table 14.1. Children's self appraisal.

Looking at Table 14.1, we can easily understand that the attitude of the pre-school children to themselves changes when they become older. In order to check which type of communication is necessary for children to be a success at school lessons, we used the same method as we had used to investigate the communication of the child with adults and other children. In the 1st and 2nd forms the teachers selected two groups of children from those who were well-prepared for school and from those children who had difficulties. All were given the same test on self appreciation. When they fulfilled the tasks, Table 14.2. was produced.

Groups according to the character of the given task

	First	Second	Third
Children well-prepared for school	—	4	26
Having no difficulties	24	6	

Table 14.2. Children's self appraisal in relation to preparedness for school.

Thus, we confirmed the idea that the attitude of the child to himself is closely connected with success at school. More objective evaluation appears at about the crucial age of seven and is the third component of psychological preparedness of the child for school education.

It is necessary to note that those children who had difficulties at school did not place themselves on the highest position, i.e., they did not seem to display a pre-school, but a more adult-like self appraisal. But this result can be explained not by an objective attitude of the child towards himself, but rather by peculiar features of his psychological and personal development.

There exists a category of children, still at a pre-school age (pre-crucial children), not with a too high, but, more often, with an unstable appraisal of themselves, with a critical attitude towards themselves, with doubts in their abilities, which are rare for children of this age. And this kind of self-consciousness is an alarming symptom... (Kucherova 1987, 116)

The change in attitude towards 'self' occurs for most children at the crucial age of seven, and correspondingly indicates a psychological readiness to study at school.

To understand the role and importance of the objective attitude of the child towards himself for schooling, we have to look through the school activity structure of junior school children.

Discussion

Speaking of school activity, Davydov notes:

Control and evaluation (marks) play an important part in the acquiring of knowledge by school children... Control and the giving of marks is supposed to attract the attention of children to the contents of their actions; and to show appreciation of their conformity with the results demanded by the task. This appreciation of the grounds for actions, called *reflection*, is an essential term to form and change them correctly. Educational activity and separate parts of it (e.g., control and appreciation) are carried out due to a basic quality in man's consciousness, such as reflection. (1986, 157)

Thus, as the researchers of school activity concluded, the actions of control and evaluation are closely tied with reflexion arising in the child's consciousness, which, as they suppose, is a new formation at the junior school period. This fact allows us to speak about the special role of reflexion premises to be formed in pre-school childhood.

Having based our conclusion on Vygotsky's conception that the development of the child's highest psychical functions takes place through communication with adults and with other children, which results in comprehension by the child of the means of carrying out the activity, we put forward the idea that initial forms of reflectivity arise within the situation of communication. In real communication reflexion is put outside and allocated between partners. The allocation and necessity to coordinate the positions lies in the existence of at least two positions in the joint activity. Further interiorization of activity makes the position of 'the other' one of the possible positions of the subject in activity, and correlation of different positions is the content of reflection. Should the partners take different positions concerning the same object of activity, the child can realize one of three strategies:

1) Adopt the position of the partner, ignoring his own;

2) Realizing his own position and ignoring the partner's;

3) Realizing his own position, as well as taking the position
    of the partner into consideration.

Stages of Elementary Reflective Development at Pre-School Age

According to our data, forming of elementary reflection at the pre-school age goes through three stages.

At the first stage the child distinguishes the position of another person as non-similar to his own. The process was researched by Piaget and called 'decentration'. Unlike Piaget, who connected decentration mostly with development of cognitive structures, we, like Donaldson (1985), study its formation within the context of development of communication between children.

At the second stage the child starts coordinating his and his partner's positions when engaged in joint activity. Here we can speak about the arising of 'the working reflection', as a disagreement between individual actions that brings about the necessity to coordinate between children in a special way, with the coordination being defined by the kind of task.

At the third stage the child goes from 'the working reflexion' to reflection itself, though realizing the existence of a real partner with another position is not necessary. The ability of the child to change his actions in accordance with the partner's position, as well as an ability to explain the necessity of this change, indicates the availability of reflexion.

Hence, it is reasonable to consider that the availability of 'the double position' is an ability to develop control and evaluation of activities. A new attitude to himself arises in the period between going from late pre-school age to junior school age which gives the necessary basis and psychological premises to form these new important parts of educational activity.

Paint the Picture Method

Then the same children were asked to colour a picture according to the model, which revealed an unusual landscape with a red tree, black sky, brown pool and green sun. When children fulfilled the task, they were asked to judge their work and to say whether they did everything properly and whether their pictures were like the model. All the children were divided into four groups.

Results: Children of *the first group* formally fulfilled the task incorrectly. They coloured the picture as they felt it should be. In most cases the colours were natural. When they were asked to compare their pictures with the model, they did not notice the mistakes. Nothing changed even when the adult asked about every detail in the picture: 'Is your tree the same as in my picture?' Children of this group agreed, sometimes even without looking at the pictures being compared.

Children of *the second group* behaved in a similar way. But when the adult asked them to compare details, they saw their mistakes and exclaimed: 'Oh, I should have painted it black!'

Children of *the third group* started their painting using the model colours, but then forgot the task and finished colouring in the traditional way. When they were asked to give an opinion about their work, they answered that trees could not be red, the sun green, and so on. So, we concluded that these children could evaluate the results, but they failed to control the process of their activity.

The representatives of *the fourth group* coped with the task in the way it was demanded. When they asked whether they painted everything correctly, they said that in the model picture the sky was black, and therefore they coloured it black. So they did everything very well.

Discussion of the Picture Method and Children's Evaluation of Themselves

When we compared the results of this task and the task of evaluating themselves, we were surprised by their similarity. Thus, children having placed themselves on the highest position (aeroplane, balloon), failed to paint the picture according to the model and could not evaluate it correctly. Those who expressed doubts about their best qualities, and then put themselves on the highest level, had mistakes in the new task, but noticed them. Children who did not choose the highest position for themselves, managed to fulfil half the task correctly and admitted mistakes.

The behaviour of the children from the third and the fourth groups displayed that they appreciated themselves in different ways according to the method by Dembo-Rubinstein. Where children of the third group felt embarrassed and could not make themselves choose the highest position, i.e., their behaviour showed a conflict as to which choice to make between the different possibilities, children of the fourth group behaved in a more natural and spontaneous way.

We conducted the third part of the experiment to understand what makes the child of 'pre-significant' age have the highest evaluation of himself, while the child of junior school age could be quite objective towards himself.

The aim of the next experiment was to study psychological mechanisms which make the child change his attitude towards himself. Our working hypothesis was that it is easy to find out these mechanisms when the child feels that he has difficulties or fails to fulfil something. Indeed, books on psychology and pedagogic contain data about different attitudes of children to their own failures when fulfilling tasks; some of them stop carrying it out, others try to finish the task. Some ask adults to help them, others sink into themselves and develop negative attitude to both the task and to the adult who gave it to him. Where lies the reason — in the specific features of the character or in the age?

We have watched lots of children of pre-school and junior school age, and based on some preliminary data we concluded that the reason lies, first of all, in the special features of the age. We then researched how we can understand the psychological changes at the crucial age of seven.

Stress Situations Method

To conduct the experiment we used typical situations, which are familiar to each child, but we did not want to create stress situations and offered the children to look at the pictures instead of doing real work.

Children of late pre-school age, as well as junior school children, were shown four pictures. In the first picture there was a girl who wanted to water flowers in the garden, but could not lift the watering-can. The second picture displayed a boy jumping over a bench, but it was clear that he caught his foot in the bench and was falling down. The girl in the third picture was going to swing herself, but could not get onto the swing. In the fourth picture there was a boy on a hillside holding a broken ski. The tested children were told the stories about what had happened to the children in the pictures, and then were asked how these things could have happened, and what to do to avoid such happenings. Before the experiment the adult conducting it found out whether the children had experienced similar situations or not, and then they were divided into the groups of 'pre-significant' and 'post-significant' children. Besides, characteristics of the school children were given by their teachers.

According to the nature of the tasks, we divided children into three groups. Children of the first group answered that the reasons for the failures were 'the watering-can', 'the bench', 'swing', etc., i.e., the objects. So, it was not the fault of the children; hence, to avoid such unpleasant situations, one should simply not choose a big watering-can, a high hill, etc. These children will probably never struggle for success, they will just stop doing what they had started.

Children from the second group explained that the reason was to be found in the subject — the boy was too small; the girls were weak, a boy would do it better, etc. Answering the question what to do to avoid the failure, they advised training, growing-up, asking adults for help.

Children of the third group saw the reason both in the subject and the object — the girl was too little, but the watering-can was too big; the boy could not ski, and the hill was too high, etc.

The answers of children from the second and third groups are natural for children of 'post-crucial' age, as they can evaluate themselves and control their activity. Answers of children from the first group are typical for pre-school children and are explained by a too high self appraisal, and the absence of an ability to control themselves.

Discussion

The results reveal the following: Inability to evaluate himself lies in the fact that the child perceives events from only one point of view, taking only one subjective position. The phenomenon was described by Piaget in detail and called children's 'egocentrism'. The behaviour of children from the second group is also based on a single viewpoint, but the position of the evaluating subject seems to be brought outside, and the evaluation is based on more objective grounds. Children from the third group are able to look at events from several points of view combining different positions and viewpoints. Hence, their ability to evaluate themselves correctly is tied with an ability to 'decentrate oneself', i.e., to look at oneself and the situation from different points of view, forgetting all about unimportant things.

Vygotsky's theory is confirmed by the result of our research, i.e., that generalized self-appreciation is not typical for a child of pre-school age, it is a quality of junior school children. Thus, the qualitative change of the child's attitude to himself, when the crucial period is left behind, lies in the adequate and generalized self appraisal, in its change from an emotional to a rational one, in the ability to take another position into account, in the ability to combine different points of view.

Conclusion

Our research into the change of the child's attitude to his self at the boundary between the late pre-school and junior school age periods allows us to conclude that this change lies at the crucial age of seven. The new attitude to himself, which arises at this age, lies in the ability to generalize, to be more objective towards himself, to take the position or role in which several positions or roles are combined, to see himself and his behaviour 'from outside'. These abilities create the basis for skills of activity control and evaluation to arise, and this directs the child 'to search for a new general way to focus on an educational problem instead of looking for the result of the problem' (Davydov 1986, 186). This new type of attitude which the child has to himself, as well as the communication with adults and other children of the same age, is the most important indication of general psychic and personal development and a fundamental component of psychological readiness for school education.

Thus, we have studied the three most important aspects of psychical preparedness of the child for school education — communication between the child and adults — communication of children with each other — and the attitude of the child to himself. Despite the different nature of these forms of communication and cooperation, we can conclude that they become context free and become the premises of educational activity at the period of pre-school age.

References

Arsenyev, A.S. (1971). Nauka i chelovek. Filosofski spekt [Science and man. Philosophical aspect]. *Nauka i nravstvennost*. Moscow, 114-59.

Basina, E.Z., Elkonin, D.B. & Venger, A.L. (1988). *Osobennosti psikhicheskogo razvitiia detei 6 - 7 - letnego vozrasta* [Characteristics of the psychological development of children from ages 6 - 7]. Moscow: Pedagogika.

Bertsfai, L.S. (1966). Formirovanie umenia v situacii reshenia konkretnykh prakticheskickh i uchebnykh zadach [Skill formation in the situation of solving concrete practical and learning tasks]. *Voprosy psikhologii* 6, 141-53.

Davydov, V.V. (1972). *Vidy obobshchenia v obuchenii* [Kinds of generalization in instruction]. Moscow: Pedagogika.

Davydov, V.V. (1986). *Problemy razvivayushchego obuchenia* [Problems of developmental teaching]. Moscow: Pedagogika.

Donaldson, M. (1985). *Myslitelnaya deyatelnost' detei* [Thinking activity of children]. Moscow: Pedagogika.

Kucherova, E.V. (1987). Problemy razvitia samosoznania v shkolnom vozraste [Problems of the development of self-consciousness in school age]. In *Problemy obuchenia i vospitania detei doshkolnogo vozrasta*. Moscow, 112-17.

Leontiev, A.N. (1948). Aktualnye problemy razvitia psikhiki [Present-day problems of the development of psyche]. *Izvestia Akademii Pedagogicheskikh Nauk RSFSR* 14, 3-11.

Lisina, M.I. (1976). O mekhanizmakh smeny vedushchikh deyatelnostei u detei v pervye sem' let zhizni [On mechanisms of change of children's leading activities in the first seven years of life]. In *Problemy periodizacii psikhiki v ontogeneze*. Moscow, 5-8.

Menchinskaya, N.A. (1957). *Razvitie psikhiki rebenka. Dnevnik materi* [Development of a child's psyche. A mother's diary]. Moscow: Academy of Pedagogical Sciences of the RSFSR.

Menchinskaya. N.A. (1971). Kratki obzor sostoyania problemy neuspevaemosti shkolnikov [A short review concerning the status of the problem of students' underachievement]. In *Psikhologicheskie problemy neuspevayushchikh shkolnikov*. Moscow, 8-31; 253-65.

Mikhailov, F.T. (1967). *Zagadka cheloveskogo ya* [The mystery of the human I]. Moscow: Politizdat.

Mukhina, V.S. (1986). *Shestiletni rebenok v shkole* [Six-year-old children in school]. Moscow: Pedagogika.

Samokhvalova, V.I. (1952). Individualnye razlichia v uchebnoy rabote shkolnikov pervogo klassa [Individual differences in learning in first graders]. PhD thesis. Moscow: Academy of Pedagogical Sciences of the RSFSR.

Slutsky, V.M. (1986): Vlianie ocenki vzroslogo na formitovanie otnoshenia k sebe u detei [The influence of adult's appraisal on the formation of children's attitude to themselves]. Ph.D. thesis. Moscow: Academy of Pedagogical Sciences of the RSFSR.

Smirnova, E.O. (1980): Vlianie formy obshchenia so vzroslymi na effektivnost obuchenia doshkolnikov [The influence of the form of communication with adults on the efficiency of teaching preschoolers]. *Voprosy psikhologii* 5, 105-12.

Sterkina, R.B. (1977). Rol deyatelnosti v formirovanii samoocenki u detei doshkolnogo vozrasta [The role of activity in the formation of self appraisal in children of pre-school age]. Ph.D. thesis. Moscow: Academy of Pedagogical Sciences of the RSFSR.

Tagieva, G.B. (1983). Stanovlenie samoocenki starshikh doshkolnikov kak faktora samoocenki gotovnosti k shkolnomu obucheniu [The development of self appraisal in older pre-schoolers as a factor of self appraisal of readiness for school]. Ph.D. thesis. Moscow: Academy of Pedagogical Sciences of the RSFSR.

Venger, A.L. (1970). Psikhologicheskie voprosy podgotovki detei k obucheniu v shkole. [Psychological questions of preparing children for learning in school]. *Doshkolnoe vospitanie* 4, 36-41.

Volokitina, M.N. (1949). *Ocherki psikhologii shkolnikov pervogo klassa* [Studies of the psychology of first graders]. Moscow: Academy of Pedagogical Sciences of the RSFSR.

Vygotsky, L.S. (1956). *Izbrannye psikhologicheskie issledovania: Myslenie i rech. Problemy psikhologicheskogo razvitia rebenka* [Selected psychological investigations: Thinking and speech. Problems of psychological development of the child]. Moscow: Academy of Pedagogical Sciences of the RSFSR.

Vygotsky, L.S. (1983). *Sobranie sochinenii v shesti tomakh*, 3 [Collected works in 6 volumes, vol. 3]. Moscow: Pedagogika.

15 The Education of Pre-School Children

Gennady C. Kravtsov and
Elena L. Berezlizhkovskaya

Introduction

The child learns from the moment he is born. One can say, the younger the child is, the more intensive the process of his learning. The scope of skills and knowledge acquired by a baby during the first years of life bears no comparison with the results of education at any other age. From the age of one to the age of two the child transcends a much greater distance in learning new skills than throughout the entire period of primary school.

At the same time, the younger the child is, the less purposive the efforts of the adults to teach him. Of course, parents are constantly teaching their baby, but it is not so perceptible in everyday life.

Parents raising a baby cannot avoid the feeling that they merely observe the child revealing his hidden abilities. And to a certain extent this is right, but in the course of a specific child's unique personal development only those qualities and abilities are disclosed which are closely connected to the life of this specific child and his family. Children easily acquire ways of acting and habits from people forming their environment, as well as words and ways to respond to an event; children acquire both good and bad habits, they are constantly absorbing something. The most typical features of the family become reflected in the child.

Spontaneous Teaching

In everyday life a child learns to do lots of things and acquire knowledge without which his further development would be impossible: to use his body, gracile motility of the hands, motor and speaking functions, to take bearings in relations between people, in subjects and their functions within the home, and to acquire first skills of intensive activity in the world, the most simple skills: helping one's self, how to begin games, how to begin productive activity. All of this the child learns 'spontaneously', as Vygotsky points out, 'according to the child's own program', though constantly being accompanied by adults. The ability of children to acquire new skills is very great. For different reasons, though, children will normally have difficulties, but as soon as the reasons are eliminated, the difficulties disappear as well. When the adult gives the child the task of acquiring a skill or learning a way to do something, it takes place as purpose-orientated teaching and is not accomplished before a fairly late stage, at least not before the child is grown enough to make sense of the task. To be taught to do something, the child has to understand, at least roughly, what the adult wants from him. Until then, the type of teaching which adults use for training babies is the same type as is used for training animals. When a mother says that she has taught her six-months-old baby to use the potty, in reality it means that she has learnt to understand the baby's intonations and can catch the moment she is waiting for. At the same time some elements of training cannot be excluded — like simple behaviours (reflex arch) are conditioned — when some parameters of the situation are repeated even though the mother does not notice this. This is not what we call teaching, instead we will reserve this terminology for the purpose-orientated activity, which takes place in more or less degrees throughout the child's life while he grows up. This activity is not as effective as the child's own spontaneous activity. Everybody knows how difficult it is to teach a baby to do something — to brush his teeth or maybe put on shoes if you do it 'directly'. The child is, as a rule, very conservative towards those things in which he/she is not particularly interested. Often the child is afraid of trying to do something new or feels lazy and forgets about it if this new activity appears to be unpleasant or unattractive. When a child learns to brush his teeth imitating his father, it becomes interesting to him — it is a sort of 'adult' activity, and the child wants to be perfect in this. But in such a case the situation of direct teaching is changed into 'instruction according to the child's program', his 'spontaneous' program. Vygotsky, when defining terms 'guided' and 'spontaneous', wrote that 'resultative teaching of small children can only take place connected to *spontaneous* activity', carried out 'according to the child's program'. Teaching children under school age can be spontaneous — and follow the child's program, and only junior school children can be taught in accordance with the adult program (the reactive way). But the fact that this new way of teaching becomes possible does not mean that the results are going to be very good.

We have observed that the most effective way of teaching children under school age, as well as junior school children, is still to relate to the child's spontaneous activity, and at the same time use the adult program. To follow the child's activity as a spontaneous way of teaching is well-motivated, the child is interested in the activity, the contents of teaching correspond with the age and personal capacities and peculiarities of the child, and the results are included in the child's own creative activity.

But the 'spontaneous teaching', or teaching according to the child's program, has its weak points. First, teaching in relation to the child's spontaneous activities; the adult cannot always give the child the knowledge and skills which he/she needs to acquire in accordance with the plans of the adult for the child's teaching and development. Moreover children often learn spontaneously from each other such things which do not correspond with the plans of adults, and even destroy them. The *demands* of 'spontaneous teaching' are to create a special semantic situation helping to display skills and knowledge which the adult wants the child to acquire because he sees them as actual, attractive and necessary for the child, and without which the adult cannot carry out his own plans and intentions. But it is not that easy, often it requires much time and effort. Besides, the child has to acquire the ability to accept learning tasks, fulfil them within his capacity, evaluate the results of his actions, i.e., to be involved in learning activity to a full extent. This is hardly possible within the spontaneous teaching approach based alone on the child's spontaneous activity. That is why it is absolutely necessary to see 'reactive teaching' as a new method, but not the only one which can be of use to the child himself.

When preparing the child to be taught to accept educational tasks, according to the program of adults, it is important not to lose the positive features intrinsic in 'spontaneous teaching' and, if possible, to overcome the negative features intrinsic in 'reactive teaching'. It is difficult to make children perceive and keep the motivation to be educated and this brings 'estrangement' towards the results. Insufficient motivation to study makes the whole process of education insufficient. Children divert their attention from the topic they study, get bored, fulfil the task superficially and all efforts of the teacher are in vain. The result of the teaching is then lowered, the child's attitude to the lessons and his study activity become negative, and the whole life of the child becomes distorted. He spends too much time doing lessons, has no time to go for a walk, to read books, to play with other children. The relations in the family become dependent on the home-work too and this, in turn, cannot but increase school problems.

Often, even if the educational activity at primary school is purpose-orientated, and carried out according to the program of teaching aimed at development, it becomes clear by the 5th grade that it was all of a limited, situative nature. When other teachers come with new demands, forms of work are changed when compared to what the children became used to at primary school. So, it suddenly appears that the educational activity and especially the system of control, is at a very low level. In fact, it means that all the efforts to form educational activity were ineffective. The reasons probably lie in the fact that the motivation to study, which, at first sight seemed to be quite effective, was actually limited and partial. Skills acquired by children through group work are seen as intended for their work in specific lessons, with certain teachers and material. Children fail to see the connection between these skills and new material.

The knowledge acquired by children through 'spontaneous teaching', can be noticed here to be quite different. As a rule, all skills, (except those obtained by chance, as a result of a special event in life), stay in the child's memory and are used as required, even if the situation in which they are used again is not similar to the one in which they were acquired. Some-times the difference between the situations is great.

The Structure of Spontaneous Teaching

To make teaching effective, expedient and full-blooded, according to the adult program, we will first analyze the process of spontaneous teaching, discover its stages, and the regularities with which it changes from one stage to the next according to certain laws. Then we want to find out whether reactive teaching can be brought to conform to these laws. We have researched different learning activities of the small child's life — like learning to handle the most simple materials and means of productive activity i.e., obtaining skills to use a spoon, a comb, the development of spoken language and writing. Features of spontaneous teaching can be found, when children are engaged in painting, drawing in pastel, in pencil, etc.

We watched children at a nursery-school, which was attended by children from age 3 to 7. The children had good facilities for painting and drawing, colour pencils, water-colours, gouache, charcoal, chalks, and all the necessary kinds of paper and paintbrushes. The children did not have special lessons, they were only helped if they asked to be. At the nursery-school children had a life full of interesting events so the situation provoked them to picture scenes from their life, their experience and feelings. Spontaneous painting was very welcome. The groups included children of different ages, so that younger children could learn something from the older children.

The First Stage — Immersion, Creative Manipulation

It turned out that despite the facilities available in the nursery-school, nearly every child, instead of beginning to paint at once, chose at first not to use the material for painting for its proper purpose. Even the older children of 6-7 gave way to the temptation to use them as if they were objects of self-importance, rather than design instruments. Children whose pictures we observed and found good for their age, started using colours like small children do: making colourful 'marshes' on the paper or in the colour-box, painting cotton-wool and paper strips. They modelled in half-dried gouache, or put it on the paper in abundance, like oil.

Often children invented strange things — e.g., painted or mixed glue with water-colours, dried it and then tried to make something from the new material. Big landscapes could arise on the paper. Landscapes of this kind were born occasionally in the process of original productive manipulation, but not from an initial idea. And this is important for the child's creative activity. It is akin to children's romping in a pool, when they play with a stick, a leaf or sand — anything that comes to hand, or to the constructing of sandcastles, or modelling in wet snow — but without having any initial idea, rather immersing into the material, following its means and resources. The child investigates and tests these means and uses the materials in all possible ways, in accordance with the things which come out of it.

Children of all ages begin to act like this, but not at once. There are lots of older children who start painting in a normal way — as they are used to — because they hesitate to try other ways. Among them are children with different drawing skills. Some of them draw well enough for their age, others feel quite helpless, but the main feature distinguishing them is that their pictures present stereotype patterns, favourites which they repeat from one picture to another. They do it well, they have acquired several means which they use every time. All of them prefer to draw first and then just colour the picture.

These children can be divided into two groups. One group cannot draw or paint well, they do not feel confident about themselves or their abilities, they are suppressed and afraid of using the materials as freely as they want. Their pictures are helpless, often they refuse to draw anything. They say that they cannot draw and do not like to do it. These children prefer other kinds of activities and almost never come to the shelf where paper and colours are kept. If they draw, their pictures are poor in colour (normally the children use dark colours or pencils), they repeatedly draw small circles, straight lines, often parallel or crossed ones at right angles, small rectangles, often the subjects in the picture are concentrated at the foot of the page. All these special features show that a child is tense and worried when drawing, sometimes not feeling confident about himself in everyday life. In some few cases these negative feelings appear when a child is actually engaged in drawing, and can be connected with previous unsuccessful experiences and negative evaluation of his work by adults. But more often such children display the same qualities in life; they are inhibited, shy, or the other way round, too uninhibited, often clashing with other children. These children's drawings show extensive personal problems, the reasons for which must be hidden in family problems or way of upbringing.

Other children, whose pictures are bright in colour and done well, use many means and seem to like to paint. They differ greatly from the first group of children. They know lots of means and use them from one picture to the next. These means can be: a house 'in perspective', animals from cartoons, definite ways of depicting a human face and body, it can be a tree, a flower, etc. How complicated and perfect the picture is depends on the age and individual abilities of the child. Typically children enjoy success, the feeling that they 'can' and the appreciation of adults. However, their enjoyment may still not be exhausted over time and could stop the natural researching activity which is normal for children in a situation where they can freely and easily use new interesting material in the way they want. At first sight, it does not look like a problem in the child's development, but repetition and monotonous depicting of the same objects must put adults on guard. The child who looks quite developed in this field actually does not develop his abilities at all. The content of his/her life is not revised in a creative way — it slides away — because the child's own reproduced stereotypes are, in fact, an activity that prevent him or her from being creative. As a rule, this 'good' painting looks good only at an early age, but later, remaining undeveloped, little by little disappears from the child's life as adults and other children do not admire it any more. This, probably, is the tragedy of an infant prodigy in the field of painting.

In both the above named cases the children do not fit into the group who, in order to obtain non-specific experience of work, have the tendency to use paper and colours as materials to investigate rather than just as a means of painting. But these were the children, whether producing good or bad drawings, for whom this way of giving new content to painting appeared to be suitable.

All of the children gradually became interested in a wide choice of attractive materials and began to use them in a free way according to their interests and abilities. Children who could draw well sometimes left their usual way of painting and turned to manipulation, first using felt-tip pens and then, as they began to enjoy coloured spots and lines, moved to using water-colours. The child who relaxes produces spots on the paper, and following them forgets about everything and does not care about the results. This way of 'painting' is a fine opportunity to get rid of stress, to train concentration. It has an important influence on most children. It becomes a natural means of psycho-correcting, when an uninhibited, excitable or rather suppressed child is involved in painting.

For small children up to 3 or 4 years old, 'painting' like this is quite natural. They have not come far from scribbling or 'messing' paper. In order to analyze the drawings of children from 1 to 3 years old, we normally gave them one pencil, in the best cases — a colour pencil. When we worked with older children we gave them a richer choice of materials. Thus, their 'messing' looked even more impressive.

For those older children who can draw well and for those who have difficulties in the field, this type of 'drawing behaviour' looks free and senseless. It is this fact that makes the most inhibited children and those under stress feel embarrassed at first. Adults are often embarrassed too. They feel concerned about unreasonably spoiled paper, paints and brushes. But soon they see the sense in it. As for the children who have 'sunk' into the anarchy of colours, they seem to go down along the age scale and very quickly take the same way already taken some time ago, without realizing their ability at its different stages.

The Second Stage — Appropriation, Method of Action 'Growing up'

It is important to get rid of the 'scribbling stage' in a natural way so that a child, having learnt to draw lines on paper with a pencil and having obtained a certain value in them, can now recognize something familiar in crossed lines and give a name to his 'drawing'. And as he recognizes and notices the shape of an object in it, he wants to repeat and then vary it.

Something similar happened to the children we studied, both younger and older ones, but the means they used to scribble on paper were more varied, and the children were not very small (even junior ones). That is why recognition and reproduction were also complicated and interesting — equal to the level of development of imagination, fantasy, game play and communication.

The time at which each child needs to realize the stage of immersion into material and end up with finding out a representation of an object that comes out by chance is different in each case and depends on both the age and personal features of the child. There are lively children who try to act quickly and in various ways, and if they see something interesting soon get fed up with the 'picture', turn the sheet of paper over and try again. Other children can make one 'pool' for a long time, enjoying it, bathing fingers in it, tirelessly, without wishing anything new. It is important that every child — big or small, lively or slow-moving — can meet his needs in the free handling of colours and paper, obtain his own experiences and his opinions about these materials and means.

At the moment when the child begins to attach a sense to his work with paper and colours — first through recognition, then through imagination — he is able to hear what people around him speak about and notice things done by other people. Then a question arises in his head: 'What else can I do?' He looks for an answer to the question put by himself. New ideas appear, born out of the properties of material familiar to the child and which, as well as drawing, come into his life. If the child gets too tired to recognize something in the seas and rivers involving colours, it means that these impressions are set aside through the action of painting, thereby finding their way into the picture. So, painting materials used before and seen as self-important objects of activity which made the child forget all other things whilst being used, now turn into real materials — into a means of achieving some result.

At this second stage the child actually acquires specific ways of how to work and assimilates them. And this is a real appropriation, or, to be precise, re-creation in the course of the child's personal development, forming all over again a way which was rooted already in the culture. Some of the ways are unknown in the general culture, they are the personal inventions of a specific child, like painted glue or using the painted glue as a new material in painting, a colour producing a yellowish glossy layer contrasting with a matt gouache paint. It was invented by a six-year-old girl and this new paint was used by all the children in her group.

Quite often the child discovers a well known and widely used means as if it were a new one. It is a real discovery for him. It belongs subjectively to him. But, of course, he can notice that other children or adults do the same things. He begins to compare his and their ways and new variations and certain details arise. Thus, children in a nursery school discovered by themselves a new technique similar to copying prints. The first print was made by chance by two children who were busy with a palette. They liked the print and having washed the palette, started painting on it and printed on sheets of paper. Soon other children joined them, and found several new ways to print and compared them with each other. At last the teacher taught them to use an old method, used by artists — to press the paper to a palette with the aid of a spoon, and because a spoon has a handle, children found this way to be the most comfortable. But a spoon is easily changed into any other tool — children pressed the paper by hand — but this is not the main point because the function of a spoon is clear enough.

At this second stage a real research activity begins, but if at the previous stage the subject of the activity was painting material and its non-specific qualities, now creative properties define the material. Children comprehend creative activity tasks which are fulfilled in this or that way. The ways, the tasks, and the personal comprehension of these, vary from child to child, but children like to share the 'secrets of their experience' with each other. They often ask adults for help or advice. The help can be really effective if it is not imposed upon them, it is just an answer to the child's question.

There is an interesting detail at this stage which could divide it into two parts.

The child can discover for himself a new means, like making spots, well known to everybody. If the child's discovery comes in the process of creative manipulation, he is, as a rule, carried away by these round tidy spots which come out of the brush pressed to the paper.

The child experiments with the spots. He makes a blue coloured spot, and then a lot of them, and says: 'Snow'. Then he makes a double chain of them and says: 'Pawprints of a bear'. The spots are a specific way of working with a brush, paint and paper. They are now an 'object' of research activity. The child looks at what comes out and makes up new names. But, if later the same day the same child paints a spot, he can hardly use the new method if he is interested in the purpose of depiction. For example, if the child wishes to depict a naval engagement, in this case he will choose the method he uses skilfully, so that it can become for him a method to express his idea. Making spots is still an object of research activity, not a method.

It gradually becomes a method when the child gains experience in using it, learning its possible meanings. Teaching according to the program which adults have imposed on the pre-school or school-age child, even if organized very well and the child is interested in it, suffers from the serious defect that the child's activity regresses to the first stage. The method children acquire in this way does not become personal, it is still an object of research activity instead of becoming an individual method of expressing one's self. In this case the use of role play to present new material, and the very active behaviour of children in the lesson does not help. Nevertheless, the method which is still to be acquired does not become a part of the child's individual potentiality, it is not absorbed into the newly-forming individuality as 'belonging' to it. Children can enjoy the lesson as interesting and entertaining, they manage to fulfil the tasks, the teacher praises them; but when the lesson is over, the method they have just learnt will not be used in other situations, it will be forgotten until the next lesson by the same teacher.

These are the difficulties which a teacher is faced with when taking over a class from a colleague who has left the school for some reason. Children who study in a 'concrete-situated' way, acquire knowledge and skills mostly of the same kind. If activities organized by the teacher during the lesson do not appeal to the children, then the method used — even though thoroughly worked out — will not appeal to the children either. The study process looks as if it were self-sustained, it exists for itself, on its own, just to answer a question or to do something. Then a second teacher asks in another way, his questions are different, and the children do not know exactly what he wants. Only after children have learnt from experience what is good and nice for the new teacher, and what is the best way to work with him, both during and after lessons, do they find themselves on firm ground. It shows that children perceive the situation of the lesson as integrated, and they do not know which is the main point in it, the content of the subject or the specific character of the relations with the teacher around the content. Or rather, they do not distinguish between these two things, but for them personally, relations with the teacher are, undoubtedly, more important and it is impossible for them to separate the teacher and the content of instruction. It means that the study activity as it is now is still not formed for them with comprehension of the academic task as an essential part. At the same time, when a spontaneous way of teaching is used outside school activity, children of pre-school age can be orientated toward the content of activity itself (if it is an interesting material, or if the way of working with it is important to children).

The Third Stage — Use of a New Way in a Personal Creative Activity

Spontaneous teaching can only be used in situations where an 'activity' of a child takes place as personal, non-specific manipulative-researching, playful or productive; and best where the specific features of all three of these features are combined. Components of the activity belong to the child himself, they are not estranged, that is why its content is still actual for him.

The ability of a child to form his activity is a most important premise for his study activity in the future, entering into a 'reactive instruction' and educational activity. The inability of pre-school and school age children to form this kind of activity, at least on the basis of the familiar material — is a most serious problem of (not only) modern primary education.

The third, very significant stage of education involves the formation of personal creative activity, in which newly acquired skills and knowledge are to be used. In spontaneous teaching it becomes apparent when a child having discovered and acquired a method of making spots, suddenly begins to use it in a free painting, enjoying not the method, but rather the content of painting.

When such a day arrives, it becomes clear that the method really belongs to the child, it is his own instrument now. The result of his studies becomes a 'brick' in the formation of the child's personality, which is developed from 'bricks' like this — recreated, obtained as his new ways of action, but which has been worked out through time within the cultural layers of mankind. If the 'brick' has not grown from the inside, but rather has been brought in from the 'outside', it becomes a mechanical skill without becoming a part of a growing person, and as soon as the chance is given, it will not be 'used' artistically any more, it will be lost without a trace.

But, to tell the truth, it happens that the knowledge 'brought in' from outside stays in perfect harmony with the formations which are already available in the growing personality, i.e., the child already has something like this, or something opposite, or points of similarity in a sense, a form, a place in his life. This something does not make the new indifferent in relation to the child and his experience, or estranged from him. Let us suppose that this is the learning mechanism which is formed not from 'inside', but from 'outside'; according to the method of 'reactive instruction', it nevertheless gives a real, not a formal result. Experienced teachers take into consideration the personal experiences of a child, and that is why their teaching can be effective.

But teaching children of both school and pre-school age according to the adult program nearly always lacks the last stage — the use of a new skill or knowledge of the child's personal creative activity as a method of his own. Often a new method is used during the lesson, but within the framework of a special academic task, which only has symbolic value to the child, and which does not apply to him directly (except for being success-ful, which can worry him very much, but in this case he is worried whether he will succeed in using a new method, not about the contents of the activity. The method is still important in itself, it does not belong to the field of meanings, that are really significant for the child).

There is another way together with children — to create a new area of actual meanings. It is a common phenomenon for secondary school that children begin to be interested in the sciences. Unfortunately, this pheno-menon becomes more and more rare. The reason is the following: creation of these new actual meanings demands the availability of an 'ideal internal area' which they can 'inhabit' and which can be structured with their help. But to take initial steps in this process, the child must have come to the corresponding stage of his development, which means that he needs to have the 'area of actual meanings' adequate to his age.

Resume of Stages in Spontaneous Teaching and Discussions of the Relation between Spontaneous Learning and Teaching

After having studied the process of 'spontaneous teaching' of pre-school children to paint, which is not determined by the adult program, we have divided this process into three stages.

The first is immersion into a material. Free experiments with a new material take place, though on the surface it looks like non-specific manipulation. This process is deeply creative, and the child acquires his own, unique, personal experience in using the material in every possible way. In the end, he prefers some materials, while others are forgotten because he finds nothing interesting in the materials themselves, nor in their results. Only when the first stage is fully realized can the second be acquired.

At the second stage other ways to use new materials arise. Materials considered suitable are selected, and the way the child acts with them develops in accordance with the common cultural meaning which is characteristic for the specific material. These ways become interesting objects of learning, thereby turning from objects important in themselves into objects important for the methods of the child's activity.

The third stage can come into force only when the second one is fully realized. We must stress the importance of a new method or piece of knowledge to be turned from being part of the child's actual activity to becoming a personal opportunity, ability, or instrument.

At the third stage the child uses the acquired knowledge or skill for his own personal and actual purpose. He makes the new method an instrument of his own creative activity.

The three stages in the above mentioned process of education do not transform into each other mechanically. At the stage of 'immersion', when the child's activity is complicated, versatile, significant and non-estranged, one of its components and parts can be included as fragments of abstractions, without losing the general sense and aim of its activity, in which the part is involved. At the third stage, when the method is worked out, it is used as an appropriated method of full value. To fulfil such a complicated and versatile activity, more and more aspects can arise, going through the stages described above. But every separate method of activity has to go through the three stages to become completely developed, though not all of them can be clearly displayed.

On the whole, the process of entering into new life spheres of activity involved in the development of new ways of working and meeting new methods of creative activity can be characterized as a process of 'individualization' of elements to be found in a specific field of culture. The individualization is recreation in ontogenesis of those things which exist in the area of human culture and are results of phylogenetic development.

Let us have a look at the same principles of spontaneous teaching through other examples, like the way a child of about two years old learns to eat with a spoon.

The spoon is one of the objects which is around the child from the start. It is used several times each day, especially for eating. Nevertheless, the attitude of a one-year-old child towards the spoon, undoubtedly knowing what it is to be used for, is the same as his attitude towards other objects — non-specific, situative. He takes it, bangs it on the table, draws it to the mouth, throws it on the floor and listens to the rattle when it falls down, etc. What he does with a spoon is a non-specific action, but his actions are determined by a specific situation: if the child is sitting in a high chair, it is interesting to throw it down, if he is sitting on the floor — to take it with two hands and suck, if an adult is beside him — to touch him with it or give it to him, etc. When the mother feeds him with a spoon, the child can hold another one, and he can touch the plate with the spoon, but it does not mean that he is going to eat with it, he just imitates the movements of adults.

This is, undoubtedly, the first stage of a spontaneous learning process. A child, playing with a spoon, acquires his own experience. He forms his opinion about it: as a hard cool object which gets warm when he holds it in his hand, puts it into his mouth or to the cheek; which can hurt if he bites it with his toothless gums; which nicely rattles when it falls down; its weight, etc. This is the child's own experience, the variety of qualities and ways to use it, among which those main functions must appear which are known as a general cultural way of using a spoon.

An older baby (sometimes it happens at the age of one, sometimes later), having acquired experience in using, playing, and doing various things with a spoon, begins at last to understand its real function. Of course, he has known this for a long time, but did not relate it to his own way of using a spoon. He could even imitate his mother, but it did not occur to him that a spoon could help him to satisfy his hunger.

At the time when the child discovers this function of a spoon and imitates his mother by merely repeating her movements, this is the first sub-stage of the second stage of instruction. The child at this time will try to take food with a spoon, imitating adults, and can even bring it to his mouth. He normally does not bring much, but the skill is worked out little by little. But if one leaves a hungry child holding a spoon in front of a plate with a meal, he will not eat with the spoon, he will eat with his hands. The spoon has not yet become a method, an instrument; he can manipulate it, but not use it yet.

A spoon first becomes a 'means' for a hungry baby when (if the mother does not feed him) having seen a plate with a meal and a spoon on the table in front of him, he takes the spoon and uses it more actively than usual, loses less food, and eats more attentively. It becomes a 'means' at the time one can see a child playing with a spoon, and also using it as an instrument when eating: taking food with it and putting it back, taking milk from the glass and pouring it onto the plate, or 'feeding' his mother, or the cat, or a doll. The child has acquired a spoon as an instrument, and here the individualization of the object takes place. The skill cannot become estranged any more, or 'get lost' as it often happens to skills which children acquire through purpose-orientated teaching.

Therefore we will conclude, in accordance with Vygotsky's theory, that spontaneous education of the pre-school age child is much more effective, because he is already prepared for spontaneous-reactive learning. Reactive teaching at this age is almost impossible.

Learning in Accordance with the Adult Program

Within the framework of spontaneous teaching and spontaneous learning, the child gradually gets ready to be taught by method of reactive teaching — within the context of his own program, in the contents of his activity. The child asks the adult to show him the way this or that word is to be written and is taught 'directly', thus, his interests and needs coincide with the teaching program. He is taught within the framework of guided teaching, without leaving the boundaries of the spontaneous teaching.

This kind of teaching process is defined by the necessity to create and develop a wide semantic context of the child's life, making the child go forward.

If the education is organized in the form of separate fragments of educational activity that are not related to personal development — to the will and wishes that the child communicates — i.e., to the child's activity in general, the results will therefore be restricted only to the educational situation. The other way round, if we create a wide semantic context within which we involve the child in a varied field of daily life and cultural activities, we create the main field of personal life which, within some time, will be covered with educational activity.

The context, or even the plot, according to which all events in the life of the pre-school child take place, is very important; all the rest depends upon it. That is why in the education of the pre-school child the first stage is undoubtedly necessary — immersion — which means creative manipulation and experimenting (a term invented by Poddyakov) with material that is new to the child. It is impossible to teach a child something before he has gone through this stage. It seems sometimes that learning, without immersion, nevertheless takes place, but it is a mere illusion — either the immersion stage was hidden or beyond the teacher's attention, and his effort of instruction could follow the paved way — or on the other hand his instruction did not become effective. This would be obvious as soon as the situation changes, or after some weeks when the child had forgotten everything.

The third stage of the learning process is also absolutely necessary for the pre-school child, i.e., the use of new skill or knowledge in non-educational activity as a method that belongs to the child himself. Without this, even well acquired educational activity will only be on display during the lesson. Teaching aimed at development does not exist somewhere in a space separated from the child; it will change the child's personality and that is why its' results cannot but become part of the child's activity.

The second, main stage, cannot exist without the first and the third ones, or if those are half passed. The third stage cannot be of full value if it is not a section in the chain of the whole process of learning aimed at development.

Index